THREADS OF MY LIFE

The Story of Hilaria Supa Huamán
A Rural Quechua Woman

Library and Archives Canada Cataloguing in Publication

Huamán, Hilaria Supa
The story of Hilaria Supa Huamán : a rural Quechua woman / Hilaria
Supa Huamán.

Translation of: Hilos de mi vida.
ISBN 978-1-894778-22-0

1. Huamán, Hilaria Supa. 2. Quechua Indians--Peru--Biography.
3. Indian women--Peru--Biography. I. Title.

F2230.2.K4H8213 2007   305.48'898323085092   C2007-903991-X

Translated from the original Spanish by Mauricio Carlos Quintana
Spanish Transcriber by Waltraut Stölben
English Proofreading by Leanne Flett Kruger and Anita Large
Illustrations by Waltraut Stölben
Cover Design by Waltraut Stölben
Cover Photo by Heiko Beyer
English Design and Maps by Suzanne Bates
Pictures by Marco Fiorito, Gaby Franger, CMA, and others
Appendix translated from its original Spanish by Anna Laura Tello
Spanish translations proofed by Anna Laura Tello
Special Kudos to Laverne Booth and Paul Bridge for their efforts in making this
English edition possible.

Theytus would like to acknowledge the support of Circle of Habondia Lending
Society, Box 143, Crescent Valley, BC V0G 2J0

Theytus Books, would like to acknowledge the support of the following:
We acknowledge the financial support of the Government of Canada through
the Book Publishing Industry Development Program (BPIDP) for our publishing activities.

 Patrimoine   Canadian
canadien   Heritage

Hilaria Supa Huamán

THREADS OF MY LIFE

———

The Story of Hilaria Supa Huamán
A Rural Quechua Woman

Translated from its original Spanish by
Mauricio Carlos Quintana

Theytus Books

TABLE OF CONTENTS

PART II

PART III

TRANSLATOR'S INTRODUCTION

I met Hilaria on a cold and wet autumn night in Nelson, BC, Canada. Very far from home for both of us, that little town in the interior of British Columbia is probably the only place in the world where we could have met.

You see, Hilaria and I come from opposing camps. As the son of an upper-middle class Mexican family, I am the typical example of the urban "*mestizo*" she describes in her book. As a child in Mexico, I remember the word "Indian" used as a pejorative and an insult. In school we learned that the bronze-skinned men, women and children of the past were immortal heroes, but their descendants belonged to another world, poor, dirty, and backwards. Although my parents never had a housemaid, I remember visiting many of my friends' homes and seeing those women, quiet and shy, scurrying to and from the kitchen under the watchful and, not infrequently, unkind eyes of their employers.

Hilaria and I met each other outside of that context, and I am thankful for that. Hilaria was an honored guest for a local radio show to discuss Native issues, and I had been asked to serve as her interpreter for the night. When we were introduced, right away we jumped into speaking Spanish, and became instant friends. The brief interview left all those present satisfied with the results, and I was asked to lend my services again for a public talk a few nights after.

It was that second time that I realized the magnitude of Hilaria's work. This unassuming little woman, her hands and feet mangled by arthritis, travelled halfway around the world to places like China and Canada, to deliver a message that the world desperately needs to hear. As I translated her words to a rapt audience, my own voice broke when she spoke of the forced sterilizations of the women in her country. I felt great love and admiration for her, and the first pang of a subtle and hard-to-describe feeling, which has stayed with me throughout the year that it took me to translate her book.

The next time I saw Hilaria was another dark night. This time we were outdoors, and I was almost completely naked and barefooted, standing next to a fire after a sweat lodge. As I shivered and waited for my skin to dry so I could get dressed, Hilaria asked me to translate her book. I will never forget her words: *"only you can capture the meaning of what I've said there, without changing a single word."* Reluctantly I agreed, unable to say no to someone whom I had developed such a strong connection with, and who inspired me so much.

The only way I can describe this process of me rendering Hilaria's story into English is atonement. At times her book was interesting, at times mildly annoying and at some, crucial moments, downright unbearable. I realized that she was speaking to me, to the people I'm descended from. Hilaria's story speaks to those who are too far from or unwilling to listen to the voices of those who are oppressed. In many ways, it is because they are oppressed that our lives are the way they are. We all have helped create the conditions for there to be oppressors and oppressed. It was very hard to read about it. Many occasions, I simply neglected to continue translating, sometimes for weeks at a time. I just didn't want to accept my part of the responsibility for what has been done to Hilaria's people, and to all Indigenous people of the world in some form or other. Goaded by teachers and close friends across two countries, and unable to forget the image of Hilaria, I persisted on my effort, until it became clear to me how important this message was. If I was so moved by Hilaria's tale, maybe others would too, and just like I decided to help out by doing this, someone else could maybe offer some other skill, some other part of the work that is needed to rectify our collective wrongs.

*

The vagaries of translation make it impossible to retain every single word from one language to another; one-to-one equivalents are virtually nonexistent. In my experience, speaking in a different language subtly but surely transforms one's experience and perception of things. Even from Spanish into English, two languages that are relatively close to each other, Hilaria's reality is vastly different from that of the people in Canada who decided to have this book translated into their own tongue. Thus, I have done my best effort to convey the essence of her story in as detailed a manner as possible, availing myself of my life-experience, which is in some ways closer to hers than that of the English-language readers of this book.

Modern Western culture is a relatively young phenomenon. Divorced from tradition and always looking away from history, it is hard for it to encompass the depth and breadth of Indigenous traditions. Even when it desires to embrace them (as is common nowadays amongst many people, who seek a return to a more holistic and spiritually satisfying way of life), the Western mind needs to extrapolate and translate, to abstract something readily usable from the vast millenary substrate, which the Indigenous traditions of the world represent. My position is most peculiar in that I come from a culture where both the Western mind and the Indigenous heart are inextricably mingled, under layer upon layer of history. Maybe it was this reason that Hilaria chose me to be her voice. It is my sincere hope that I have somehow managed to bridge the gap, and bring the life story of an Andean peasant woman to an interested Western audience seeking to understand.

To apply the principles of that life to one's own is a valid approach; however, it is important to retain a sense of respect for the context in which that lifestyle arose. Hilaria talks to us about this, too, when she speaks about the attempts of outsiders to "assist" the people in her community. I think it is valuable to remember that, no matter how well we think we understand someone or something, we are always one step removed. Each person, community, or group of people is best suited to understand and help themselves solve their own problems. This is the way in which we can most truly be helpful: listen attentively and then ask how we may best be of service, how the other wants to be helped.

I decided to write this introduction because some of the message is not lost, but certainly obscured by the translation. For that and any other shortcomings of my work, I apologize in advance. My hope is that this book will bring Hilaria's story to a wider audience, and in so doing send a voice, that her people (and all people) may be free.

Mauricio Quintana
New Westminster, BC, November 5, 2005

FOREWORD

This book is a loom, assembled with threads woven by HILARIA SUPA HUAMÁN, a Quechua woman. For nine years I followed her in her task of weaving threads out of the wool of the Quechua people, uniting the threads of different women, tying together threads broken by ignorance and violence, rescuing lost threads of a repressed culture and, in her tireless search for equilibrium, putting together a loom where to weave the Sun with the Moon and the past with the future.

Hilaria tells us, in her own words, her thoughts and experiences as an Indigenous person, a peasant, a woman and a leader, framed in the drawing of her two long braids. The last page in each chapter contain "questions for reflection," developed to help the reader relate Hilaria's story with their own situation. At the back of the book the appendix contains ideas for deepening or bringing into practice some of the topics discussed in the book. This structure is intended to facilitate the use of this book in schools and training sessions.

The Spanish version of this work was made possible through the economic support from Frauen in der Einen Welt (Germany), as well as the love and practical contribution of Gaby Franger, Flor Canelo, Román Vizcarra, Fielding Wood, Héctor Altamirano, Kike Pinto, Heiko Beyer, and Zadir Milla.

In spite of the harsh reality of her life experience, Hilaria not only gives us testimony of her suffering, but of her success, her hopes, and firm steps taken towards a life with dignity, in harmony with her ancestral culture. If we come to reflect and understand what Hilaria wants to tell us in entrusting us with her story, then our intention will have been fulfilled.

Waltraut Stölben

PROLOGUE

In the beginning, even when everything was dark, the *Ñaupamachus*, the giant men, inhabited the Earth. So powerful were they, that their arrogance angered *Pachakamaq*, who sent the Sun. Blinded by the light, they took refuge in the caves of the mountains, in the lakes and the gorges. They have lived there since.

It was from these *Paqarinas*, or places of origin, that another human-kind emerged. Some came from the lakes, others from the caves, always from the *Ukhu Pacha*, the underworld, where the ferment of life is generated.

Thus they lived, trying to organize themselves, and they made mistakes. Then *Pachakamaq* sent *Wiraqocha*, the Being of Light, who went about sharing and giving equally, teaching and building, rewarding some and punishing others. We learned to live in harmony. Our society was a reflection of the cosmic community. We danced the chaotic beat of order, and thus humbly created a culture that fosters and allows itself to be fostered in eternal reciprocity with *Pachamama*, our beloved Mother Universe.

We enjoyed such precious harmony until one day other people came, who claimed to come in the name of the "One God." We welcomed them as visitors, according to our customs, with respect and love; they in turn assaulted us with betrayal and demanded gold.

Thus we came to know humiliation. A dark, cold night fell upon us. Our children were murdered, their bodies mutilated, their arms and legs sown to their mouths. Like macabre dolls, the murdered children were hung from posts along the roads where these strangers walked. We do not understand why they did not present their most dexterous and honorable fighters to face off against our valiant men. We do not understand why they killed the children and the elderly. Terror shook us. The women rubbed their bodies with excrement to avoid being raped.

But nothing stopped them. Hungry for material power, they became even viler and demanded absolute control of bodies and souls, annihilating every thing sacred. Under a campaign directed by the Vatican called "the extrication of idolatries," they systematically prosecuted our ceremonies, our music, and our traditions, obstructing our ability to find and experience the sacred.

In the "divine" colony, the best lands and valleys, the lands we cultivated for millennia with respect and love, were allotted to them. The feudal-like *hacienda* system has persisted for a very long time. The so-called freedom from the colonial yoke, the famous political independence, was a racist farce. For Indigenous people, it merely perpetuated the abuse, and the so-called patriots took the lands that had been usurped by their Spanish ancestors. Our women and children continued to be abused, and our men were poisoned by alcohol, given to them as payment for their indentured servantship.

However, not all of us were caught and enslaved. Many of our brothers and sisters fled to the high mountains, where they lived in relative autonomy, working even harder in order to survive, but free of the harassment of the *hacienda* landlords. Neither soil conditions nor weather were an obstacle for those who knew the language of love and respect for all of Creation. Thus, they established a measure of order based on ancestral reciprocity, the *Ayni*, living practice and guiding principle of community life to this day.

In the meantime, millions of people, trapped in the nightmare, suffered the whip and even the mutilation of their limbs as punishment well into the nineteen-sixties and -seventies. When Indigenous leaders revolted in the *haciendas*, the landlord would make them eat their own excrement in front of everyone. It is shameful to even remember the details of so many insults to human rights. However, we have come from this: a shameful historical trauma.

In the sixties and seventies, Agrarian Reform was initiated in response to the struggle for reclaiming our land. The large *haciendas* were divided into parcels and returned to those who worked them. New Indigenous peasant communities were created. Thus a new generation came to know apparent freedom. The landlord ceased to possess all the land; but he continued to live in our subconscious mind. The fear also remained: fear of walking, fear of thinking, fear of deciding, fear of living, fear of divine punishment, fear of dreaming, fear of fear itself.

There are two kinds of Indigenous people: the ones who did not serve the landlord and those who did. The former are strong in their tradition, the latter pick up the pieces left of us. Both are hidden by history, marginalized by society, drowned in alcohol, reviled by religion, rejected by globalization.

The communities of Anta province could be placed in the second category, and it was there that Hilaria Supa Huamán was born. After her early years of *Hacienda* life, she was forced to make the long and tortuous journey through the dark roads of dominant society, full of racism and double moral standards. Now returned to the heart of her land and her people, she is one of the many Indigenous women who have suffered, and one of the few who speak about it from her heart, and who has given herself over to the struggle for recovering our ancient culture.

Román Vizcarra

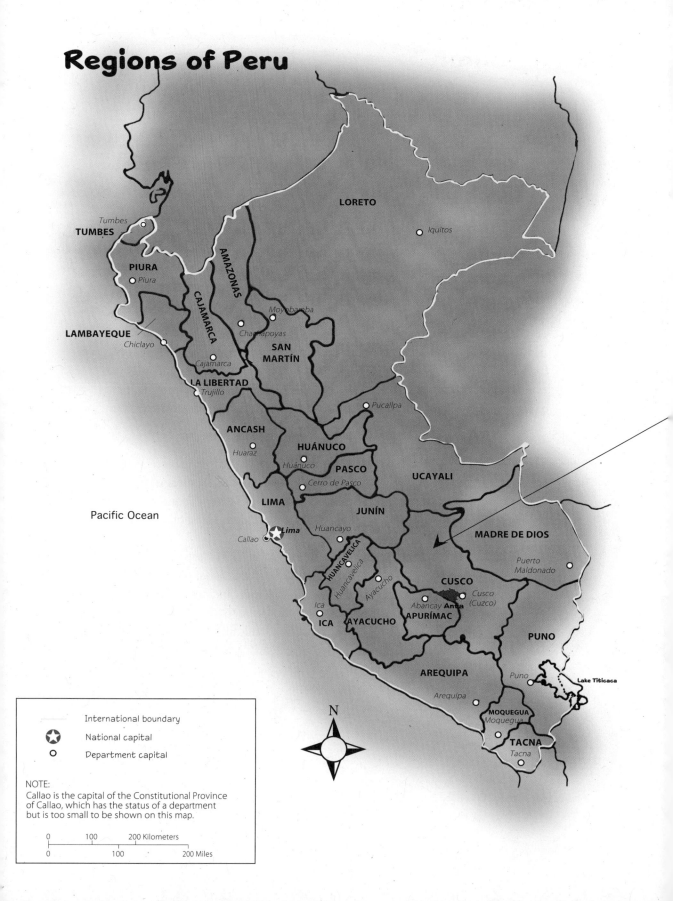

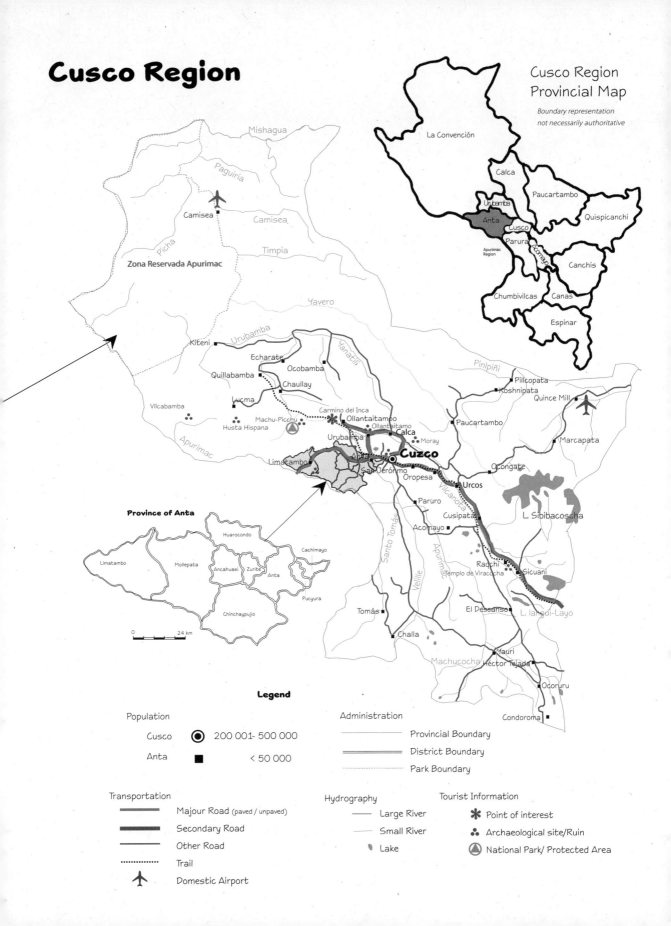

Cusco Region

Cusco Region Provincial Map

Boundary representation
not necessarily authoritative

La Convención

Calca

Paucartambo

Urubamba

Anta

Quispicanchi

Cusco

Parura

Acomayo

Apurimac
Region

Canchis

Chumbivilcas

Canas

Espinar

Mishagua

Paguiria

Camisea

Camisea

Timpia

Yavero

Zona Reservada Apurimac

Picha

Urubamba

Pinlpiñi

Kiteni

Echarate

Ocobamba

Yanatili

Pillcopata

Quillabamba

Chaullay

Koshnipata

Quince Mill

Lucma

Carmino del Inca

Ollantaitampo

Vllcabamba

Machu-Picchu

Ollantaitamo

Paucartambo

Husta Hispana

Urubamba

Calca

Marcapata

Apurimac

Moray

Anta

Cuzco

Ocongate

Limatambo

San Jerónmo

Oropesa

Urcos

Paruro

L. Sibibacoscha

Province of Anta

Cusipata

Acomayo

Huarocondo

Cachimayo

Raqchi

Sicuani

Limatambo

Mollepata

Ancahuasi

Zurite

Anta

Templo de Viracocha

Chinchaypujio

Pucyura

Tomás

El Descanso

L. langui-Layo

0   24 km

Challa

Mauri

Machucocha

Héctor Tejada

Ocoruru

Condoroma

Legend

Population

Cusco ◉ 200 001- 500 000

Anta ■ < 50 000

Administration

—————— Provincial Boundary

══════ District Boundary

·············· Park Boundary

Transportation

━━━━ Majour Road (paved / unpaved)

━━━━ Secondary Road

———— Other Road

·········· Trail

✈ Domestic Airport

Hydrography

—— Large River

—— Small River

▮ Lake

Tourist Information

✳ Point of interest

⁂ Archaeological site/Ruin

▲ National Park/ Protected Area

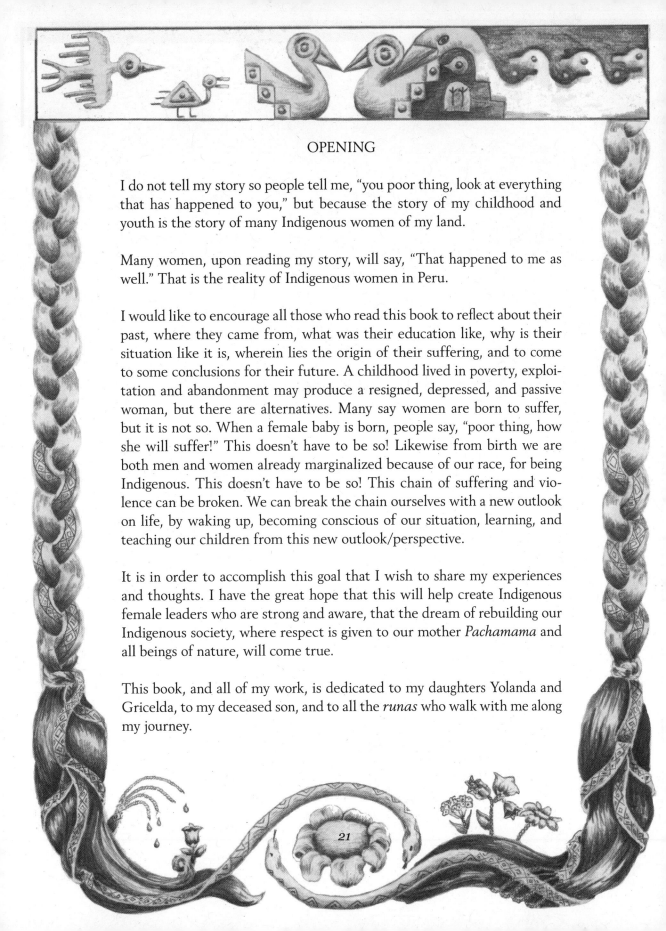

OPENING

I do not tell my story so people tell me, "you poor thing, look at everything that has happened to you," but because the story of my childhood and youth is the story of many Indigenous women of my land.

Many women, upon reading my story, will say, "That happened to me as well." That is the reality of Indigenous women in Peru.

I would like to encourage all those who read this book to reflect about their past, where they came from, what was their education like, why is their situation like it is, wherein lies the origin of their suffering, and to come to some conclusions for their future. A childhood lived in poverty, exploitation and abandonment may produce a resigned, depressed, and passive woman, but there are alternatives. Many say women are born to suffer, but it is not so. When a female baby is born, people say, "poor thing, how she will suffer!" This doesn't have to be so! Likewise from birth we are both men and women already marginalized because of our race, for being Indigenous. This doesn't have to be so! This chain of suffering and violence can be broken. We can break the chain ourselves with a new outlook on life, by waking up, becoming conscious of our situation, learning, and teaching our children from this new outlook/perspective.

It is in order to accomplish this goal that I wish to share my experiences and thoughts. I have the great hope that this will help create Indigenous female leaders who are strong and aware, that the dream of rebuilding our Indigenous society, where respect is given to our mother *Pachamama* and all beings of nature, will come true.

This book, and all of my work, is dedicated to my daughters Yolanda and Gricelda, to my deceased son, and to all the *runas* who walk with me along my journey.

BEGINNING

How are babies born in the country?
The festival of the "Cortapelo"
Shepherding and our toys

Questions for reflection

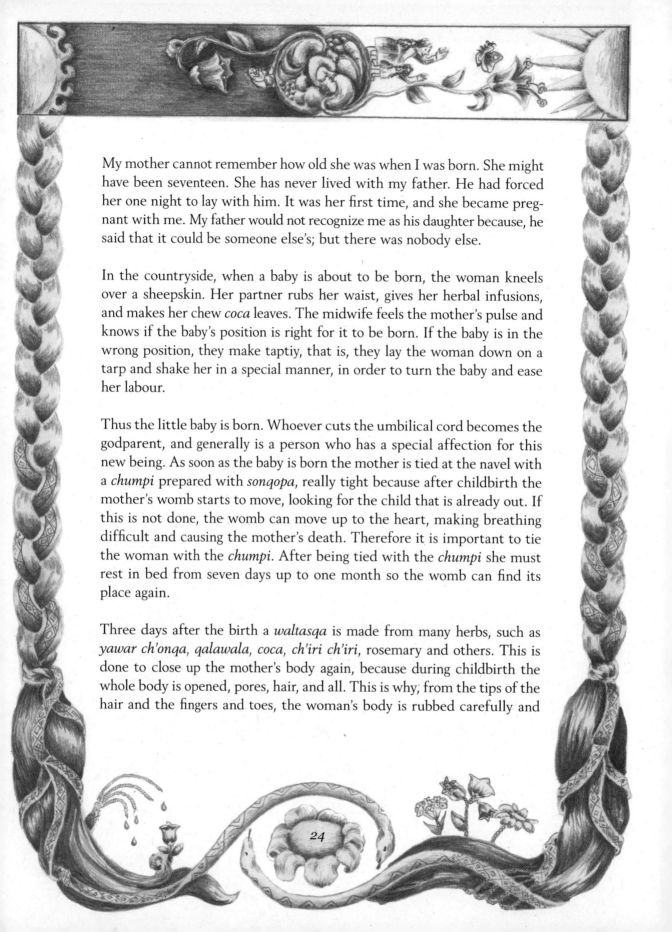

My mother cannot remember how old she was when I was born. She might have been seventeen. She has never lived with my father. He had forced her one night to lay with him. It was her first time, and she became pregnant with me. My father would not recognize me as his daughter because, he said that it could be someone else's; but there was nobody else.

In the countryside, when a baby is about to be born, the woman kneels over a sheepskin. Her partner rubs her waist, gives her herbal infusions, and makes her chew *coca* leaves. The midwife feels the mother's pulse and knows if the baby's position is right for it to be born. If the baby is in the wrong position, they make taptiy, that is, they lay the woman down on a tarp and shake her in a special manner, in order to turn the baby and ease her labour.

Thus the little baby is born. Whoever cuts the umbilical cord becomes the godparent, and generally is a person who has a special affection for this new being. As soon as the baby is born the mother is tied at the navel with a *chumpi* prepared with *sonqopa*, really tight because after childbirth the mother's womb starts to move, looking for the child that is already out. If this is not done, the womb can move up to the heart, making breathing difficult and causing the mother's death. Therefore it is important to tie the woman with the *chumpi*. After being tied with the *chumpi* she must rest in bed from seven days up to one month so the womb can find its place again.

Three days after the birth a *waltasqa* is made from many herbs, such as *yawar ch'onqa*, *qalawala*, *coca*, *ch'iri ch'iri*, rosemary and others. This is done to close up the mother's body again, because during childbirth the whole body is opened, pores, hair, and all. This is why, from the tips of the hair and the fingers and toes, the woman's body is rubbed carefully and

24

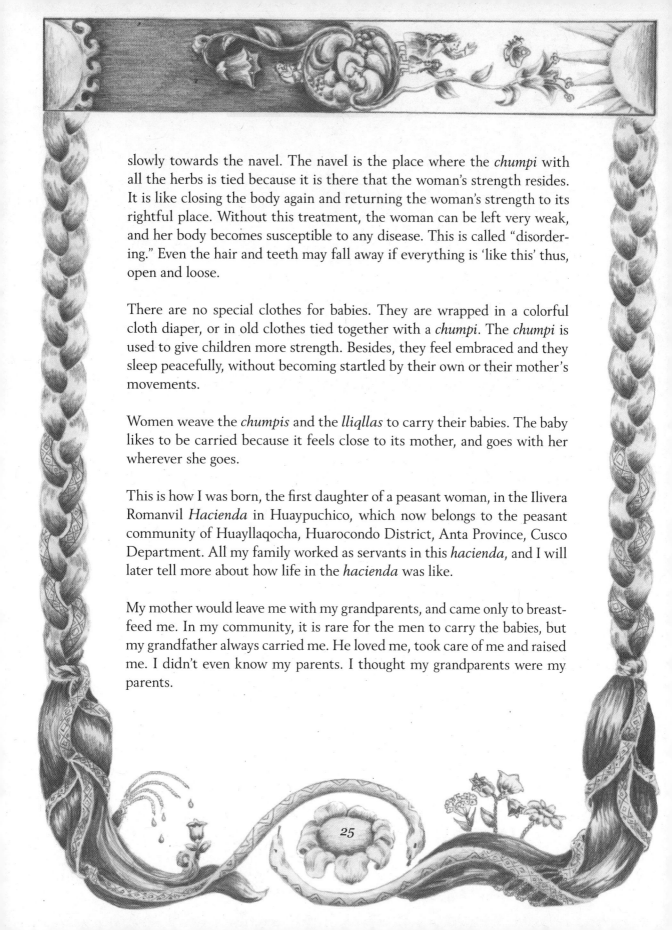

slowly towards the navel. The navel is the place where the *chumpi* with all the herbs is tied because it is there that the woman's strength resides. It is like closing the body again and returning the woman's strength to its rightful place. Without this treatment, the woman can be left very weak, and her body becomes susceptible to any disease. This is called "disordering." Even the hair and teeth may fall away if everything is 'like this' thus, open and loose.

There are no special clothes for babies. They are wrapped in a colorful cloth diaper, or in old clothes tied together with a *chumpi*. The *chumpi* is used to give children more strength. Besides, they feel embraced and they sleep peacefully, without becoming startled by their own or their mother's movements.

Women weave the *chumpis* and the *lliqllas* to carry their babies. The baby likes to be carried because it feels close to its mother, and goes with her wherever she goes.

This is how I was born, the first daughter of a peasant woman, in the Ilivera Romanvil *Hacienda* in Huaypuchico, which now belongs to the peasant community of Huayllaqocha, Huarocondo District, Anta Province, Cusco Department. All my family worked as servants in this *hacienda*, and I will later tell more about how life in the *hacienda* was like.

My mother would leave me with my grandparents, and came only to breast-feed me. In my community, it is rare for the men to carry the babies, but my grandfather always carried me. He loved me, took care of me and raised me. I didn't even know my parents. I thought my grandparents were my parents.

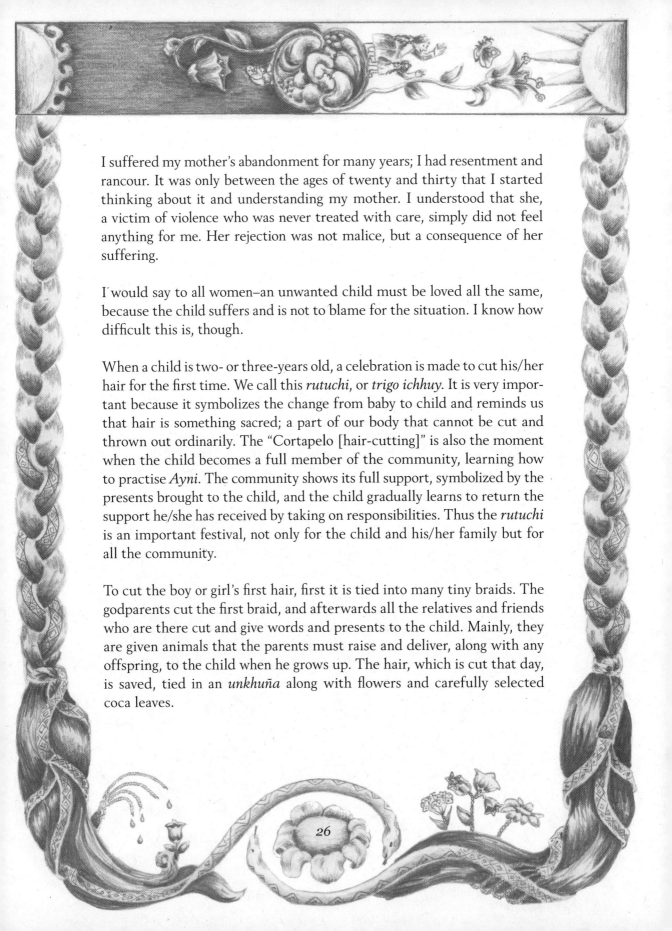

I suffered my mother's abandonment for many years; I had resentment and rancour. It was only between the ages of twenty and thirty that I started thinking about it and understanding my mother. I understood that she, a victim of violence who was never treated with care, simply did not feel anything for me. Her rejection was not malice, but a consequence of her suffering.

I would say to all women–an unwanted child must be loved all the same, because the child suffers and is not to blame for the situation. I know how difficult this is, though.

When a child is two- or three-years old, a celebration is made to cut his/her hair for the first time. We call this *rutuchi*, or *trigo ichhuy*. It is very important because it symbolizes the change from baby to child and reminds us that hair is something sacred; a part of our body that cannot be cut and thrown out ordinarily. The "Cortapelo [hair-cutting]" is also the moment when the child becomes a full member of the community, learning how to practise *Ayni*. The community shows its full support, symbolized by the presents brought to the child, and the child gradually learns to return the support he/she has received by taking on responsibilities. Thus the *rutuchi* is an important festival, not only for the child and his/her family but for all the community.

To cut the boy or girl's first hair, first it is tied into many tiny braids. The godparents cut the first braid, and afterwards all the relatives and friends who are there cut and give words and presents to the child. Mainly, they are given animals that the parents must raise and deliver, along with any offspring, to the child when he grows up. The hair, which is cut that day, is saved, tied in an *unkhuña* along with flowers and carefully selected coca leaves.

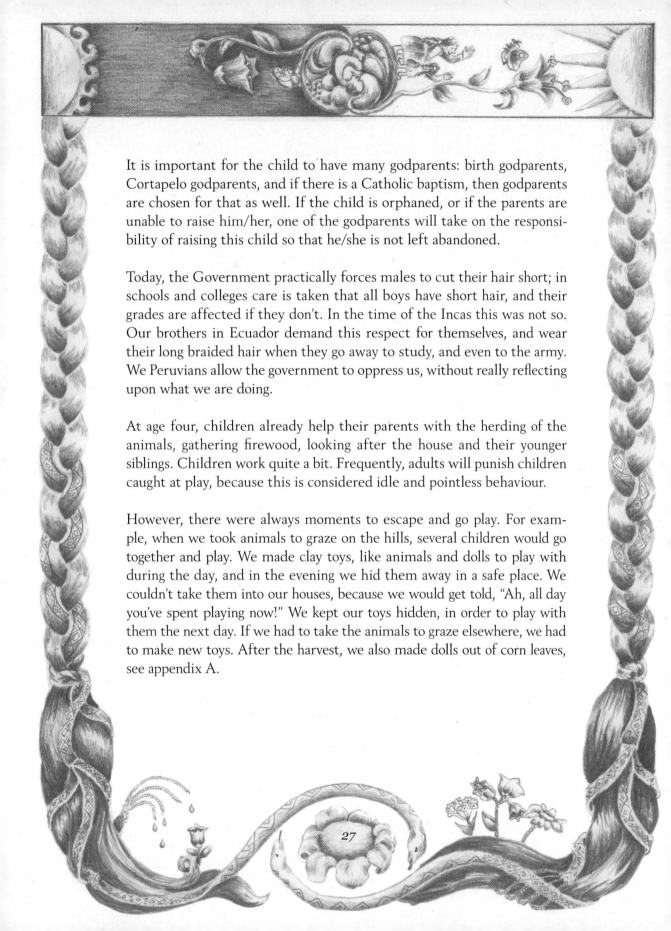

It is important for the child to have many godparents: birth godparents, Cortapelo godparents, and if there is a Catholic baptism, then godparents are chosen for that as well. If the child is orphaned, or if the parents are unable to raise him/her, one of the godparents will take on the responsibility of raising this child so that he/she is not left abandoned.

Today, the Government practically forces males to cut their hair short; in schools and colleges care is taken that all boys have short hair, and their grades are affected if they don't. In the time of the Incas this was not so. Our brothers in Ecuador demand this respect for themselves, and wear their long braided hair when they go away to study, and even to the army. We Peruvians allow the government to oppress us, without really reflecting upon what we are doing.

At age four, children already help their parents with the herding of the animals, gathering firewood, looking after the house and their younger siblings. Children work quite a bit. Frequently, adults will punish children caught at play, because this is considered idle and pointless behaviour.

However, there were always moments to escape and go play. For example, when we took animals to graze on the hills, several children would go together and play. We made clay toys, like animals and dolls to play with during the day, and in the evening we hid them away in a safe place. We couldn't take them into our houses, because we would get told, "Ah, all day you've spent playing now!" We kept our toys hidden, in order to play with them the next day. If we had to take the animals to graze elsewhere, we had to make new toys. After the harvest, we also made dolls out of corn leaves, see appendix A.

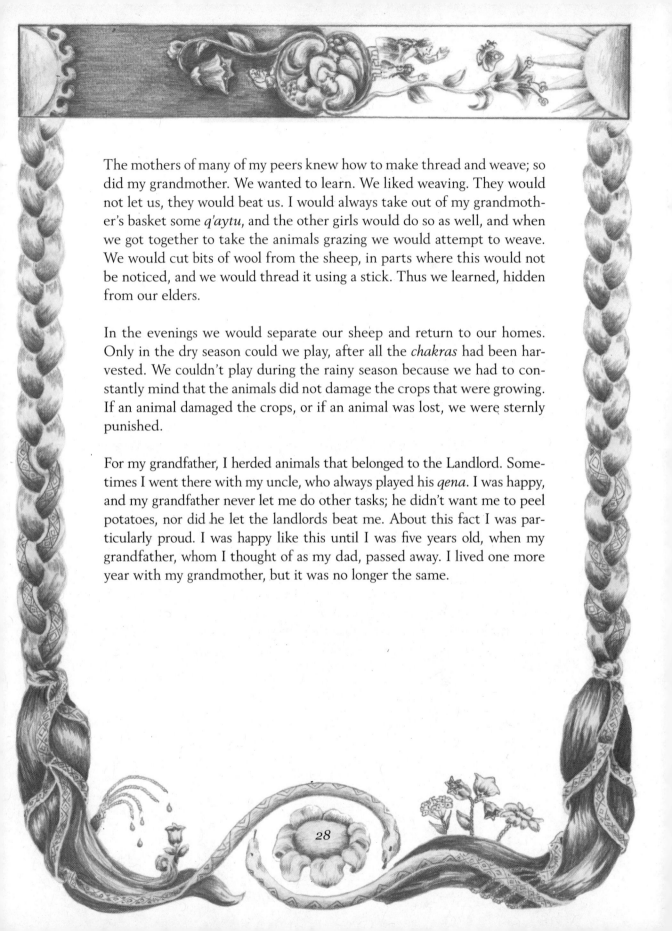

The mothers of many of my peers knew how to make thread and weave; so did my grandmother. We wanted to learn. We liked weaving. They would not let us, they would beat us. I would always take out of my grandmother's basket some *q'aytu*, and the other girls would do so as well, and when we got together to take the animals grazing we would attempt to weave. We would cut bits of wool from the sheep, in parts where this would not be noticed, and we would thread it using a stick. Thus we learned, hidden from our elders.

In the evenings we would separate our sheep and return to our homes. Only in the dry season could we play, after all the *chakras* had been harvested. We couldn't play during the rainy season because we had to constantly mind that the animals did not damage the crops that were growing. If an animal damaged the crops, or if an animal was lost, we were sternly punished.

For my grandfather, I herded animals that belonged to the Landlord. Sometimes I went there with my uncle, who always played his *qena*. I was happy, and my grandfather never let me do other tasks; he didn't want me to peel potatoes, nor did he let the landlords beat me. About this fact I was particularly proud. I was happy like this until I was five years old, when my grandfather, whom I thought of as my dad, passed away. I lived one more year with my grandmother, but it was no longer the same.

QUESTIONS FOR REFLECTION

- How was your children's birth tended?
- Are there recognized midwives in your community?
- Which plants do you know and use during labour?
- Talk about your experiences with hospital births.
- Talk about consequences you've experienced because of lack of postpartum care.
- Have you tied your baby? Why or why not?
- In your opinion, what is the importance of a child's hair-cutting?
- What are the chores that your children must help with in your home?
- Which tasks do you give to the boys and which to the girls?
- Do your children have enough time to play?
- Why do you think play is an important part of a child's development?
- Can you make toys for your children without spending any money?
- What are those toys like?
- Why do you think it is that many parents and grandparents do not want to pass on their knowledge to their children and grandchildren?
- How and when were you punished as a child?
- How do you discipline your children?
- How can a child be punished to make him/her understand what has been done wrong, without causing trauma to the child?

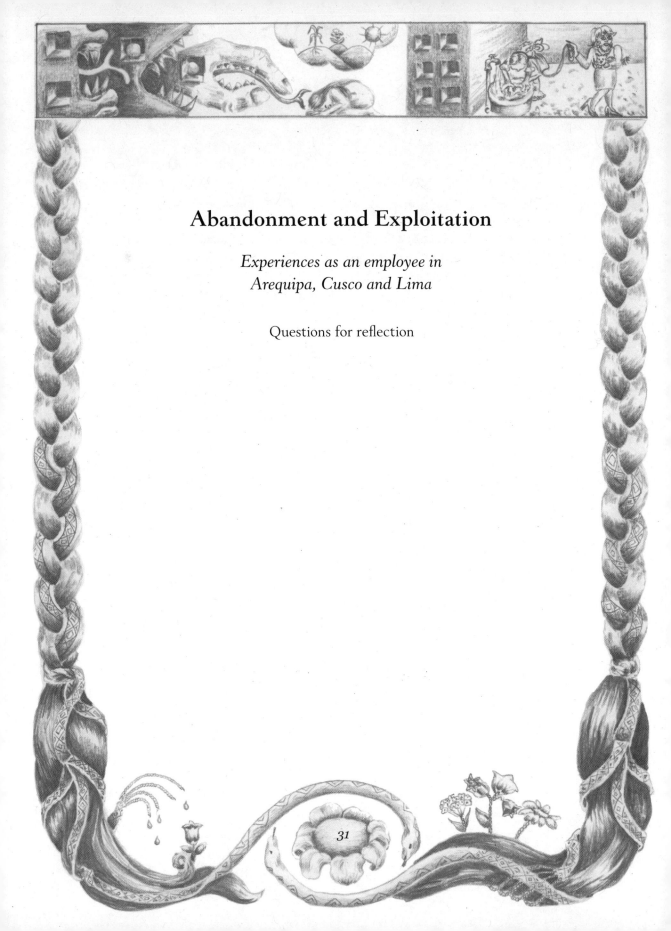

Abandonment and Exploitation

Experiences as an employee in
Arequipa, Cusco and Lima

Questions for reflection

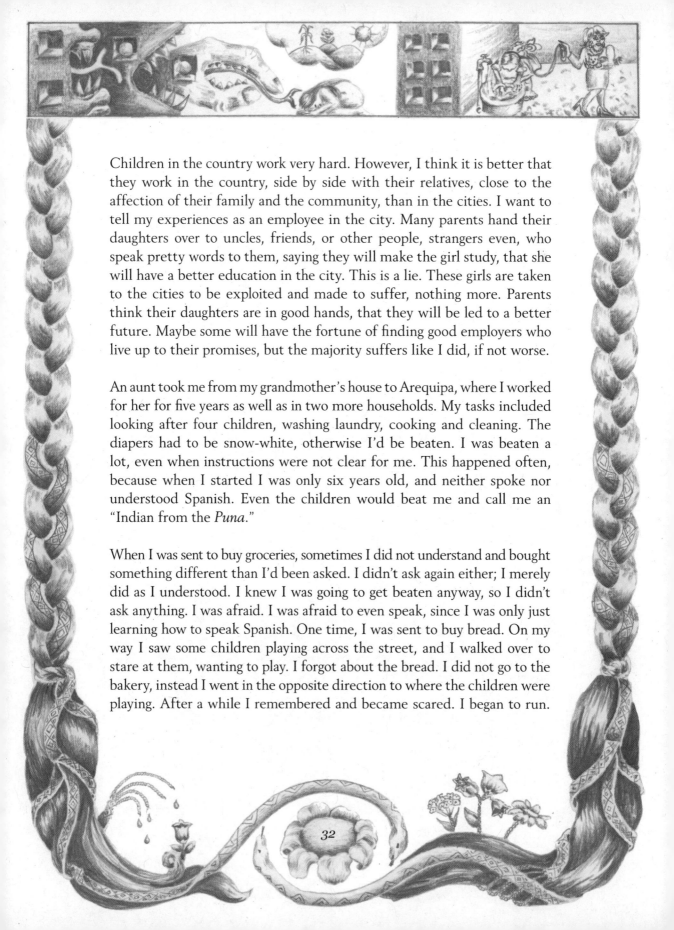

Children in the country work very hard. However, I think it is better that they work in the country, side by side with their relatives, close to the affection of their family and the community, than in the cities. I want to tell my experiences as an employee in the city. Many parents hand their daughters over to uncles, friends, or other people, strangers even, who speak pretty words to them, saying they will make the girl study, that she will have a better education in the city. This is a lie. These girls are taken to the cities to be exploited and made to suffer, nothing more. Parents think their daughters are in good hands, that they will be led to a better future. Maybe some will have the fortune of finding good employers who live up to their promises, but the majority suffers like I did, if not worse.

An aunt took me from my grandmother's house to Arequipa, where I worked for her for five years as well as in two more households. My tasks included looking after four children, washing laundry, cooking and cleaning. The diapers had to be snow-white, otherwise I'd be beaten. I was beaten a lot, even when instructions were not clear for me. This happened often, because when I started I was only six years old, and neither spoke nor understood Spanish. Even the children would beat me and call me an "Indian from the *Puna*."

When I was sent to buy groceries, sometimes I did not understand and bought something different than I'd been asked. I didn't ask again either; I merely did as I understood. I knew I was going to get beaten anyway, so I didn't ask anything. I was afraid. I was afraid to even speak, since I was only just learning how to speak Spanish. One time, I was sent to buy bread. On my way I saw some children playing across the street, and I walked over to stare at them, wanting to play. I forgot about the bread. I did not go to the bakery, instead I went in the opposite direction to where the children were playing. After a while I remembered and became scared. I began to run.

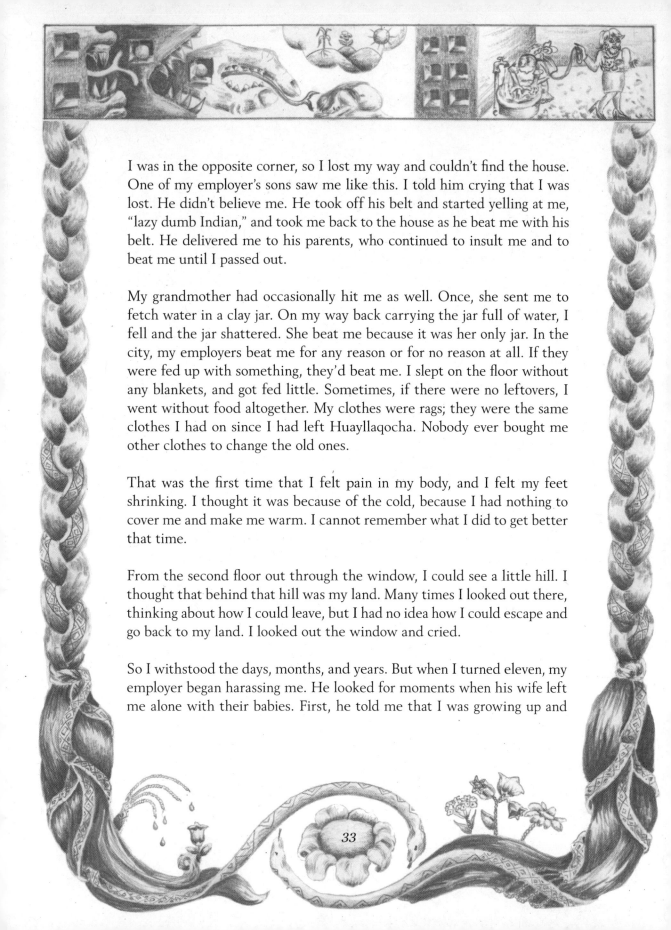

I was in the opposite corner, so I lost my way and couldn't find the house. One of my employer's sons saw me like this. I told him crying that I was lost. He didn't believe me. He took off his belt and started yelling at me, "lazy dumb Indian," and took me back to the house as he beat me with his belt. He delivered me to his parents, who continued to insult me and to beat me until I passed out.

My grandmother had occasionally hit me as well. Once, she sent me to fetch water in a clay jar. On my way back carrying the jar full of water, I fell and the jar shattered. She beat me because it was her only jar. In the city, my employers beat me for any reason or for no reason at all. If they were fed up with something, they'd beat me. I slept on the floor without any blankets, and got fed little. Sometimes, if there were no leftovers, I went without food altogether. My clothes were rags; they were the same clothes I had on since I had left Huayllaqocha. Nobody ever bought me other clothes to change the old ones.

That was the first time that I felt pain in my body, and I felt my feet shrinking. I thought it was because of the cold, because I had nothing to cover me and make me warm. I cannot remember what I did to get better that time.

From the second floor out through the window, I could see a little hill. I thought that behind that hill was my land. Many times I looked out there, thinking about how I could leave, but I had no idea how I could escape and go back to my land. I looked out the window and cried.

So I withstood the days, months, and years. But when I turned eleven, my employer began harassing me. He looked for moments when his wife left me alone with their babies. First, he told me that I was growing up and

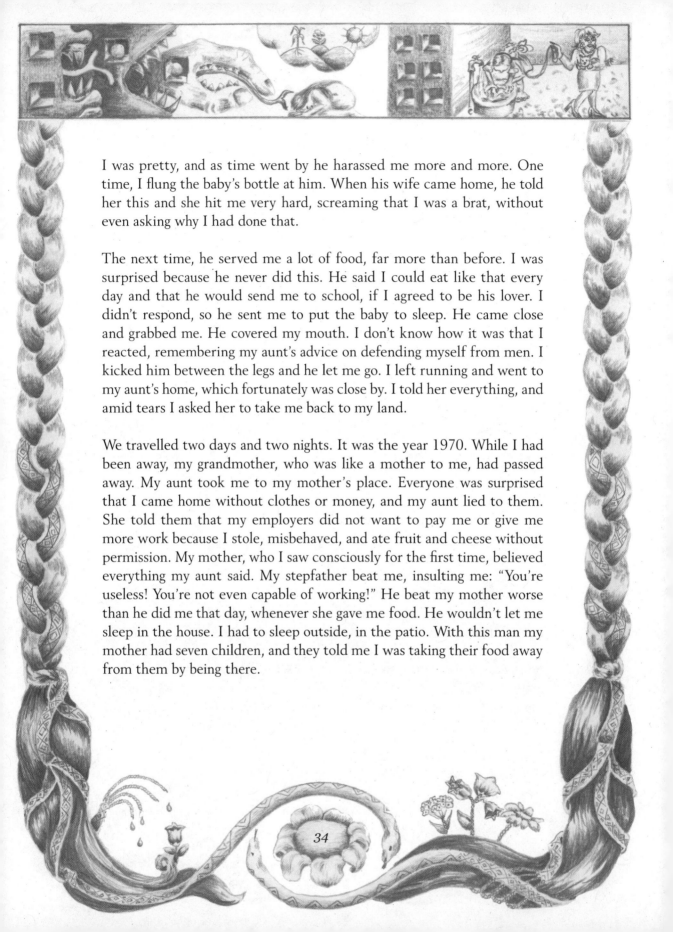

I was pretty, and as time went by he harassed me more and more. One time, I flung the baby's bottle at him. When his wife came home, he told her this and she hit me very hard, screaming that I was a brat, without even asking why I had done that.

The next time, he served me a lot of food, far more than before. I was surprised because he never did this. He said I could eat like that every day and that he would send me to school, if I agreed to be his lover. I didn't respond, so he sent me to put the baby to sleep. He came close and grabbed me. He covered my mouth. I don't know how it was that I reacted, remembering my aunt's advice on defending myself from men. I kicked him between the legs and he let me go. I left running and went to my aunt's home, which fortunately was close by. I told her everything, and amid tears I asked her to take me back to my land.

We travelled two days and two nights. It was the year 1970. While I had been away, my grandmother, who was like a mother to me, had passed away. My aunt took me to my mother's place. Everyone was surprised that I came home without clothes or money, and my aunt lied to them. She told them that my employers did not want to pay me or give me more work because I stole, misbehaved, and ate fruit and cheese without permission. My mother, who I saw consciously for the first time, believed everything my aunt said. My stepfather beat me, insulting me: "You're useless! You're not even capable of working!" He beat my mother worse than he did me that day, whenever she gave me food. He wouldn't let me sleep in the house. I had to sleep outside, in the patio. With this man my mother had seven children, and they told me I was taking their food away from them by being there.

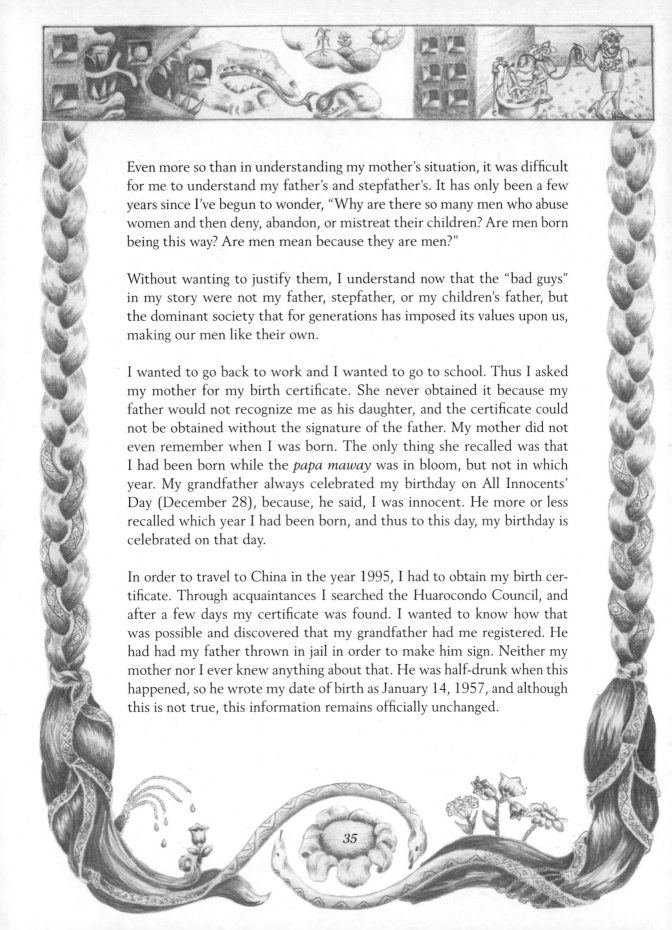

Even more so than in understanding my mother's situation, it was difficult for me to understand my father's and stepfather's. It has only been a few years since I've begun to wonder, "Why are there so many men who abuse women and then deny, abandon, or mistreat their children? Are men born being this way? Are men mean because they are men?"

Without wanting to justify them, I understand now that the "bad guys" in my story were not my father, stepfather, or my children's father, but the dominant society that for generations has imposed its values upon us, making our men like their own.

I wanted to go back to work and I wanted to go to school. Thus I asked my mother for my birth certificate. She never obtained it because my father would not recognize me as his daughter, and the certificate could not be obtained without the signature of the father. My mother did not even remember when I was born. The only thing she recalled was that I had been born while the *papa maway* was in bloom, but not in which year. My grandfather always celebrated my birthday on All Innocents' Day (December 28), because, he said, I was innocent. He more or less recalled which year I had been born, and thus to this day, my birthday is celebrated on that day.

In order to travel to China in the year 1995, I had to obtain my birth certificate. Through acquaintances I searched the Huarocondo Council, and after a few days my certificate was found. I wanted to know how that was possible and discovered that my grandfather had me registered. He had had my father thrown in jail in order to make him sign. Neither my mother nor I ever knew anything about that. He was half-drunk when this happened, so he wrote my date of birth as January 14, 1957, and although this is not true, this information remains officially unchanged.

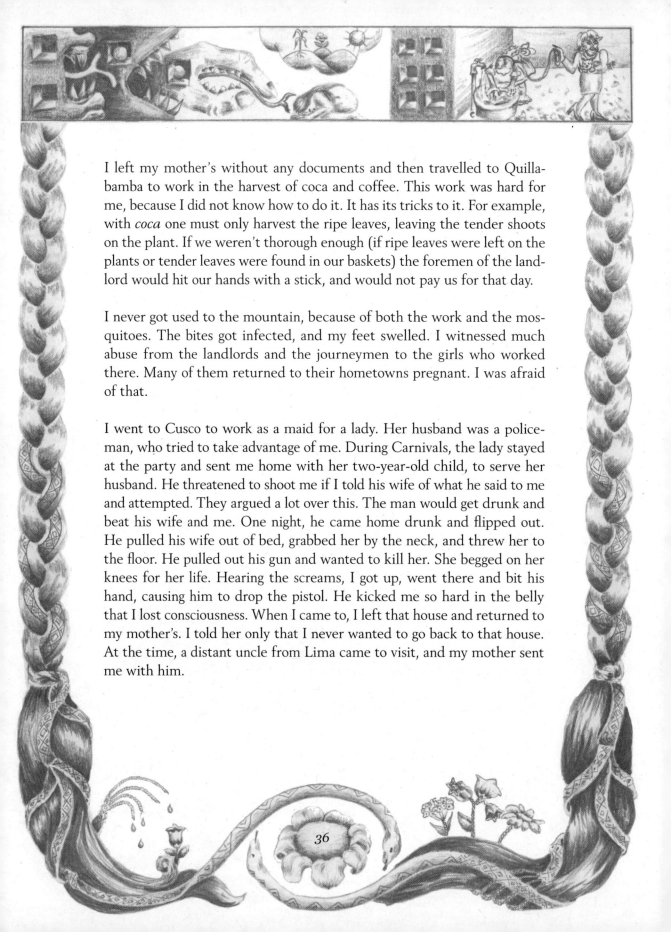

I left my mother's without any documents and then travelled to Quillabamba to work in the harvest of coca and coffee. This work was hard for
me, because I did not know how to do it. It has its tricks to it. For example,
with *coca* one must only harvest the ripe leaves, leaving the tender shoots
on the plant. If we weren't thorough enough (if ripe leaves were left on the
plants or tender leaves were found in our baskets) the foremen of the landlord would hit our hands with a stick, and would not pay us for that day.

I never got used to the mountain, because of both the work and the mos-
quitoes. The bites got infected, and my feet swelled. I witnessed much
abuse from the landlords and the journeymen to the girls who worked
there. Many of them returned to their hometowns pregnant. I was afraid
of that.

I went to Cusco to work as a maid for a lady. Her husband was a policeman, who tried to take advantage of me. During Carnivals, the lady stayed
at the party and sent me home with her two-year-old child, to serve her
husband. He threatened to shoot me if I told his wife of what he said to me
and attempted. They argued a lot over this. The man would get drunk and
beat his wife and me. One night, he came home drunk and flipped out.
He pulled his wife out of bed, grabbed her by the neck, and threw her to
the floor. He pulled out his gun and wanted to kill her. She begged on her
knees for her life. Hearing the screams, I got up, went there and bit his
hand, causing him to drop the pistol. He kicked me so hard in the belly
that I lost consciousness. When I came to, I left that house and returned to
my mother's. I told her only that I never wanted to go back to that house.
At the time, a distant uncle from Lima came to visit, and my mother sent
me with him.

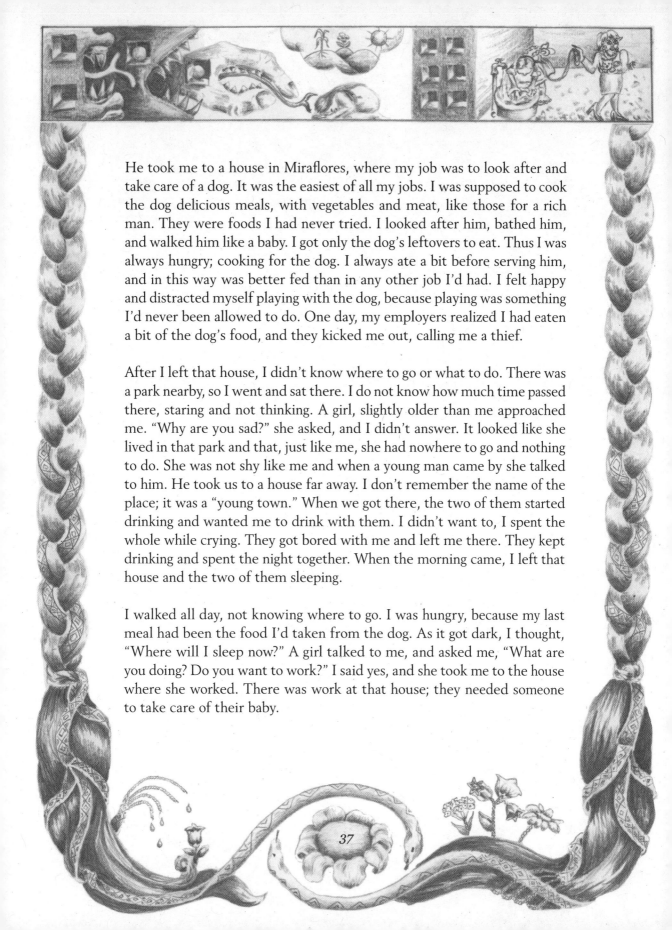

He took me to a house in Miraflores, where my job was to look after and take care of a dog. It was the easiest of all my jobs. I was supposed to cook the dog delicious meals, with vegetables and meat, like those for a rich man. They were foods I had never tried. I looked after him, bathed him, and walked him like a baby. I got only the dog's leftovers to eat. Thus I was always hungry; cooking for the dog. I always ate a bit before serving him, and in this way was better fed than in any other job I'd had. I felt happy and distracted myself playing with the dog, because playing was something I'd never been allowed to do. One day, my employers realized I had eaten a bit of the dog's food, and they kicked me out, calling me a thief.

After I left that house, I didn't know where to go or what to do. There was a park nearby, so I went and sat there. I do not know how much time passed there, staring and not thinking. A girl, slightly older than me approached me. "Why are you sad?" she asked, and I didn't answer. It looked like she lived in that park and that, just like me, she had nowhere to go and nothing to do. She was not shy like me and when a young man came by she talked to him. He took us to a house far away. I don't remember the name of the place; it was a "young town." When we got there, the two of them started drinking and wanted me to drink with them. I didn't want to, I spent the whole while crying. They got bored with me and left me there. They kept drinking and spent the night together. When the morning came, I left that house and the two of them sleeping.

I walked all day, not knowing where to go. I was hungry, because my last meal had been the food I'd taken from the dog. As it got dark, I thought, "Where will I sleep now?" A girl talked to me, and asked me, "What are you doing? Do you want to work?" I said yes, and she took me to the house where she worked. There was work at that house; they needed someone to take care of their baby.

37

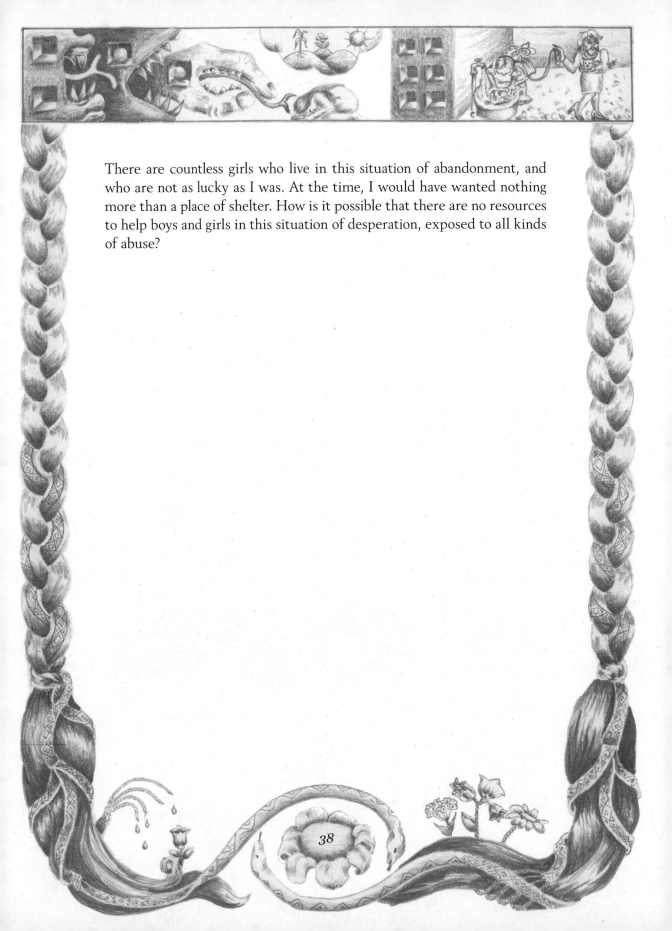

There are countless girls who live in this situation of abandonment, and who are not as lucky as I was. At the time, I would have wanted nothing more than a place of shelter. How is it possible that there are no resources to help boys and girls in this situation of desperation, exposed to all kinds of abuse?

QUESTIONS FOR REFLECTION

- What are your experiences as an employee?
- What are your experiences with work as a child?
- What caused you to suffer the most?
- How did you defend yourself against abuse?
- If you worked as an employee, how would you like to be treated?
- What would you say to a girl going away to work as an employee?
- How could family members help control the working situation where their daughter is?
- Which are the difficulties you currently face with your employer? What solutions can you find?
- Should parents send their children to work at a young age?
- Why don't women household employees who suffer sexual harassment denounce it?

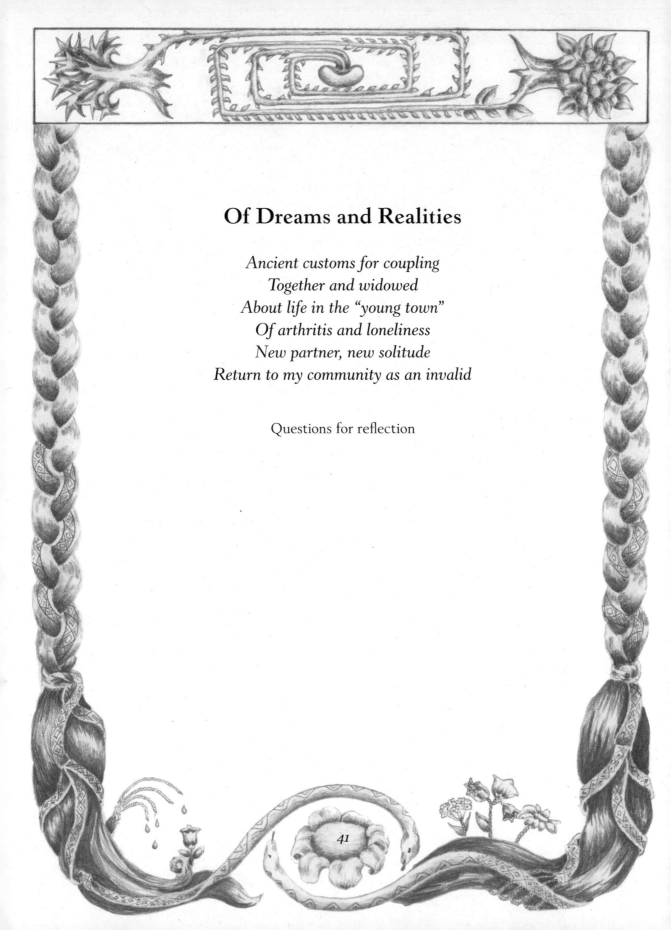

Of Dreams and Realities

Ancient customs for coupling
Together and widowed
About life in the "young town"
Of arthritis and loneliness
New partner, new solitude
Return to my community as an invalid

Questions for reflection

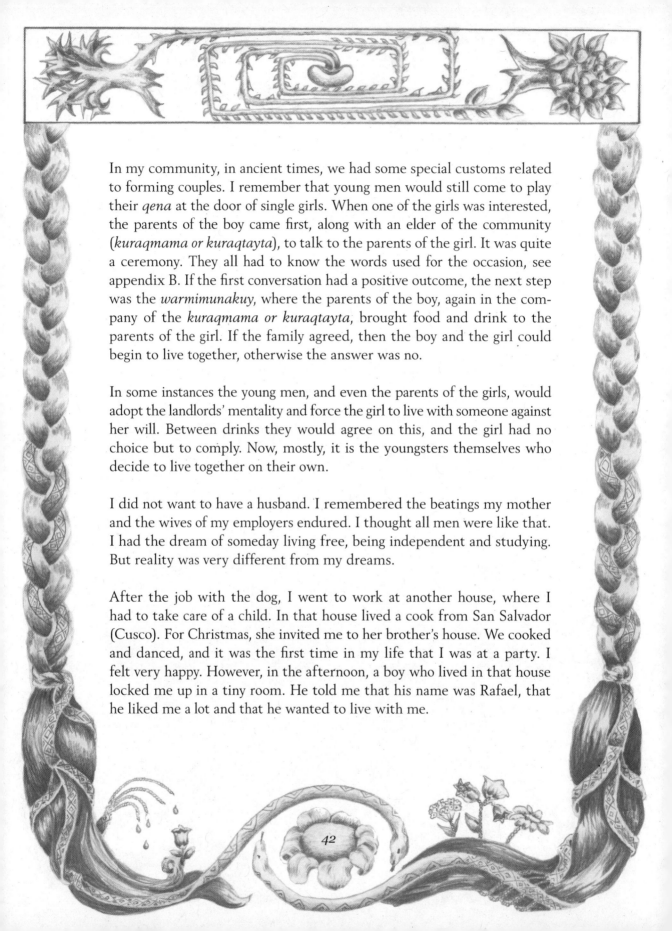

In my community, in ancient times, we had some special customs related to forming couples. I remember that young men would still come to play their *qena* at the door of single girls. When one of the girls was interested, the parents of the boy came first, along with an elder of the community (*kuraqmama or kuraqtayta*), to talk to the parents of the girl. It was quite a ceremony. They all had to know the words used for the occasion, see appendix B. If the first conversation had a positive outcome, the next step was the *warmimunakuy*, where the parents of the boy, again in the company of the *kuraqmama or kuraqtayta*, brought food and drink to the parents of the girl. If the family agreed, then the boy and the girl could begin to live together, otherwise the answer was no.

In some instances the young men, and even the parents of the girls, would adopt the landlords' mentality and force the girl to live with someone against her will. Between drinks they would agree on this, and the girl had no choice but to comply. Now, mostly, it is the youngsters themselves who decide to live together on their own.

I did not want to have a husband. I remembered the beatings my mother and the wives of my employers endured. I thought all men were like that. I had the dream of someday living free, being independent and studying. But reality was very different from my dreams.

After the job with the dog, I went to work at another house, where I had to take care of a child. In that house lived a cook from San Salvador (Cusco). For Christmas, she invited me to her brother's house. We cooked and danced, and it was the first time in my life that I was at a party. I felt very happy. However, in the afternoon, a boy who lived in that house locked me up in a tiny room. He told me that his name was Rafael, that he liked me a lot and that he wanted to live with me.

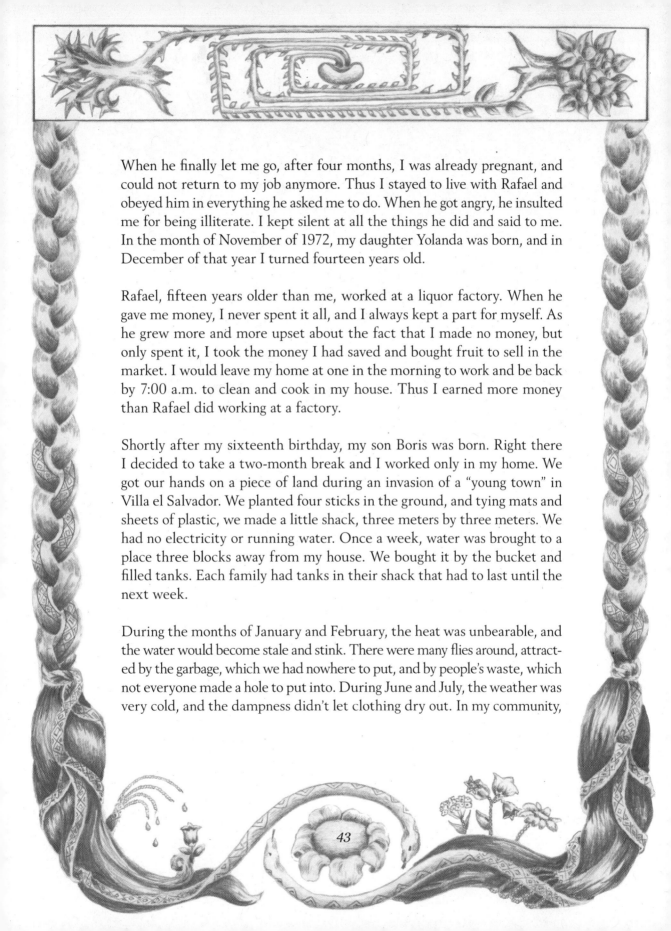

When he finally let me go, after four months, I was already pregnant, and could not return to my job anymore. Thus I stayed to live with Rafael and obeyed him in everything he asked me to do. When he got angry, he insulted me for being illiterate. I kept silent at all the things he did and said to me. In the month of November of 1972, my daughter Yolanda was born, and in December of that year I turned fourteen years old.

Rafael, fifteen years older than me, worked at a liquor factory. When he gave me money, I never spent it all, and I always kept a part for myself. As he grew more and more upset about the fact that I made no money, but only spent it, I took the money I had saved and bought fruit to sell in the market. I would leave my home at one in the morning to work and be back by 7:00 a.m. to clean and cook in my house. Thus I earned more money than Rafael did working at a factory.

Shortly after my sixteenth birthday, my son Boris was born. Right there I decided to take a two-month break and I worked only in my home. We got our hands on a piece of land during an invasion of a "young town" in Villa el Salvador. We planted four sticks in the ground, and tying mats and sheets of plastic, we made a little shack, three meters by three meters. We had no electricity or running water. Once a week, water was brought to a place three blocks away from my house. We bought it by the bucket and filled tanks. Each family had tanks in their shack that had to last until the next week.

During the months of January and February, the heat was unbearable, and the water would become stale and stink. There were many flies around, attracted by the garbage, which we had nowhere to put, and by people's waste, which not everyone made a hole to put into. During June and July, the weather was very cold, and the dampness didn't let clothing dry out. In my community,

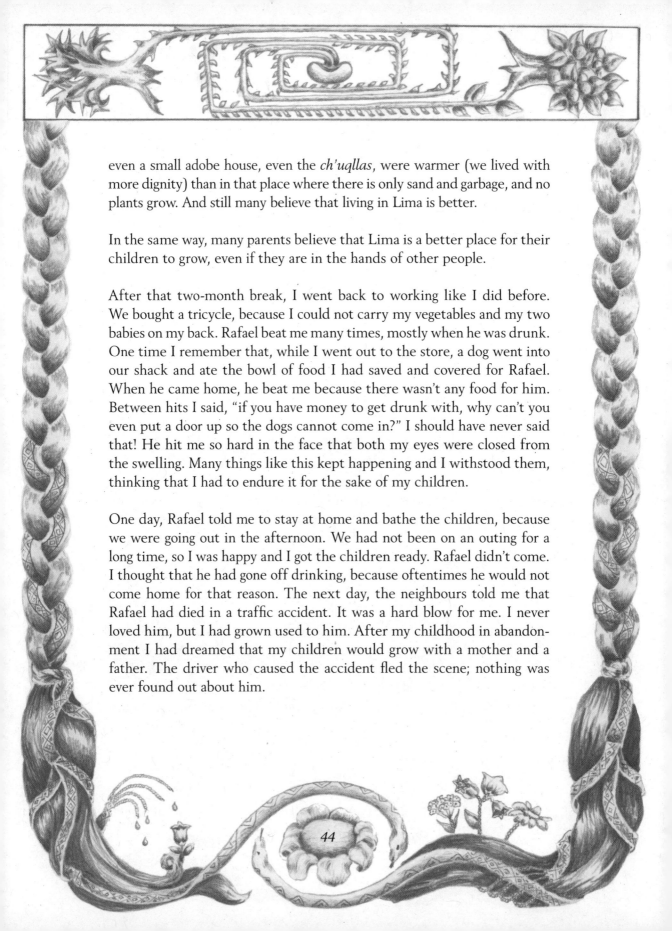

even a small adobe house, even the *ch'uqllas*, were warmer (we lived with more dignity) than in that place where there is only sand and garbage, and no plants grow. And still many believe that living in Lima is better.

In the same way, many parents believe that Lima is a better place for their children to grow, even if they are in the hands of other people.

After that two-month break, I went back to working like I did before. We bought a tricycle, because I could not carry my vegetables and my two babies on my back. Rafael beat me many times, mostly when he was drunk. One time I remember that, while I went out to the store, a dog went into our shack and ate the bowl of food I had saved and covered for Rafael. When he came home, he beat me because there wasn't any food for him. Between hits I said, "if you have money to get drunk with, why can't you even put a door up so the dogs cannot come in?" I should have never said that! He hit me so hard in the face that both my eyes were closed from the swelling. Many things like this kept happening and I withstood them, thinking that I had to endure it for the sake of my children.

One day, Rafael told me to stay at home and bathe the children, because we were going out in the afternoon. We had not been on an outing for a long time, so I was happy and I got the children ready. Rafael didn't come. I thought that he had gone off drinking, because oftentimes he would not come home for that reason. The next day, the neighbours told me that Rafael had died in a traffic accident. It was a hard blow for me. I never loved him, but I had grown used to him. After my childhood in abandonment I had dreamed that my children would grow with a mother and a father. The driver who caused the accident fled the scene; nothing was ever found out about him.

The tricycle had been destroyed, along with all the goods I sold for a living, in the accident, so I was left with nothing. The neighbours pitched in to pay for the burial. I started selling onions in the La Victoria wholesale market, carrying both babies with me all the time. It was an hour journey from my house. It takes guile to survive in that market: otherwise people will steal from, step on, and deceive you; it's a "learn or die" situation. One neighbour from Villa el Salvador also went to this market every day, and he helped me with the babies. His wife was jealous because of this, even though there were never any undue intentions on his part. His was a true help. The loaders also helped me: they allowed me to sit my children on their carts while I got my onions from the trucks. Without these helpers I would have never been able to survive such a cruel and inhuman place.

After Rafael's death I became ill. My hands and knees started hurting me. For the first two years I ignored it. I continued to work in order to support my children, until I could not tolerate the pain anymore. I went to San Salvador (Cusco) to look for my in-laws. I thought maybe they could help me to get better. They wanted me to marry one of Rafael's cousins so that I would stay in the family. I did not want to do this. I did not want my children to have a stepfather. I wanted to go, to try to sell our land in Villa el Salvador, and use the money to pay a doctor to cure me. At the time I did not know that I had arthritis. The pain was unbearable. Every movement hurt, I was desperate. I could not touch water, grasp things, or lift any weight. At times, I could not even walk. Because of my condition and my pain, my mother-in-law persuaded me to leave my children in her care. To this day I suffer with regret that I left them, even though in my conscience I know that there weren't any other options.

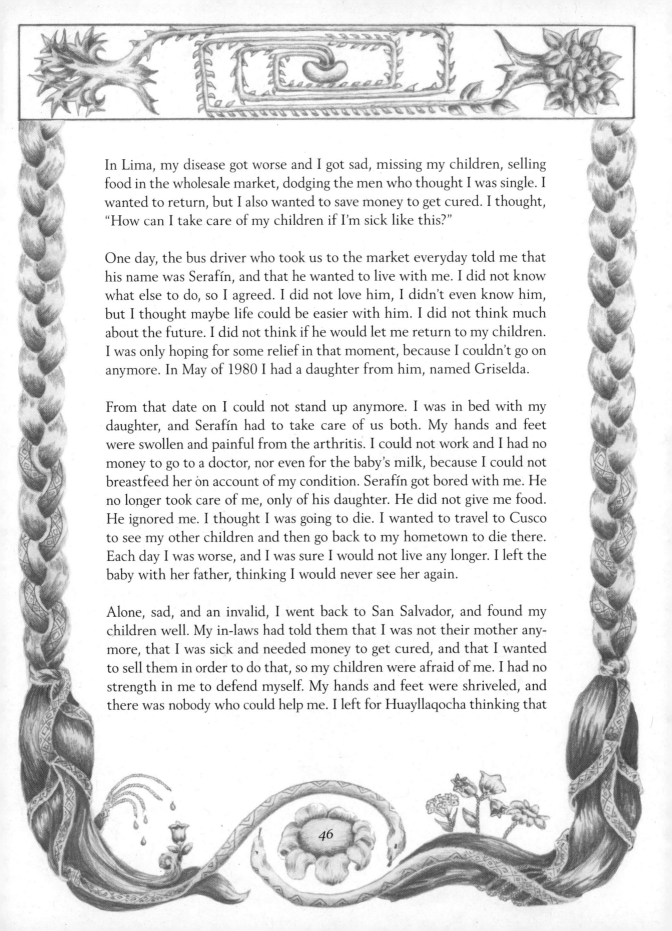

In Lima, my disease got worse and I got sad, missing my children, selling food in the wholesale market, dodging the men who thought I was single. I wanted to return, but I also wanted to save money to get cured. I thought, "How can I take care of my children if I'm sick like this?"

One day, the bus driver who took us to the market everyday told me that his name was Serafín, and that he wanted to live with me. I did not know what else to do, so I agreed. I did not love him, I didn't even know him, but I thought maybe life could be easier with him. I did not think much about the future. I did not think if he would let me return to my children. I was only hoping for some relief in that moment, because I couldn't go on anymore. In May of 1980 I had a daughter from him, named Griselda.

From that date on I could not stand up anymore. I was in bed with my daughter, and Serafín had to take care of us both. My hands and feet were swollen and painful from the arthritis. I could not work and I had no money to go to a doctor, nor even for the baby's milk, because I could not breastfeed her on account of my condition. Serafín got bored with me. He no longer took care of me, only of his daughter. He did not give me food. He ignored me. I thought I was going to die. I wanted to travel to Cusco to see my other children and then go back to my hometown to die there. Each day I was worse, and I was sure I would not live any longer. I left the baby with her father, thinking I would never see her again.

Alone, sad, and an invalid, I went back to San Salvador, and found my children well. My in-laws had told them that I was not their mother anymore, that I was sick and needed money to get cured, and that I wanted to sell them in order to do that, so my children were afraid of me. I had no strength in me to defend myself. My hands and feet were shriveled, and there was nobody who could help me. I left for Huayllaqocha thinking that

maybe my family would help me. Only Catalina, my grandfather's niece, took me to her home and fed me. My stepfather had forbidden my mother to have contact with me, and told her that my condition was contagious, and that she would wind up like me. My mother rejected me completely. Catalina and her husband helped me, but her father kept telling her that surely her husband and I were having an affair, and that's why he helped me. This went on to the point where they told me to leave. I went to a little old house, which was completely empty. I gathered hay from a *chakra* to put on the ground and sleep in. A neighbour, seeing that I didn't have anything to eat, lent me some money to buy alcohol, which is cheapest, to trade for food. My mother, on the other hand, seeing me suffering like this, never lent me a hand.

QUESTIONS FOR REFLECTION

- What customs exist in your community for forming couples?
- What was your experience?
- What were your feelings towards an unwanted child?
- How is your relationship with your children?
- What kind of future would you like for your children?

My Children and I

1976

1975 with my children
Yolanda and Boris

My daughter
Gricelda

My son Boris with his
children

My daughter Yolanda with
my grandsons

49

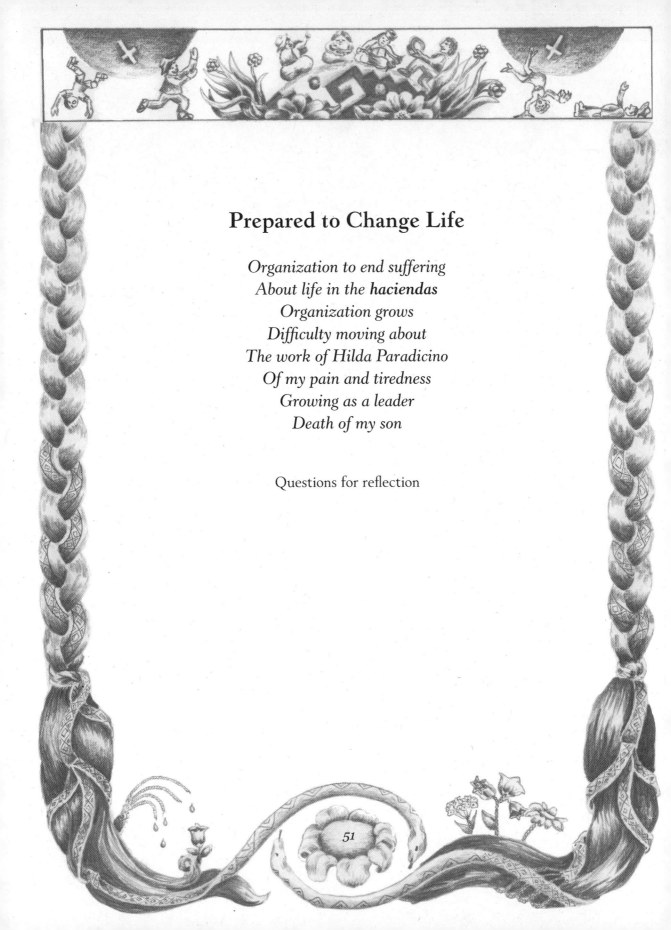

Prepared to Change Life

Organization to end suffering
*About life in the **haciendas***
Organization grows
Difficulty moving about
The work of Hilda Paradicino
Of my pain and tiredness
Growing as a leader
Death of my son

Questions for reflection

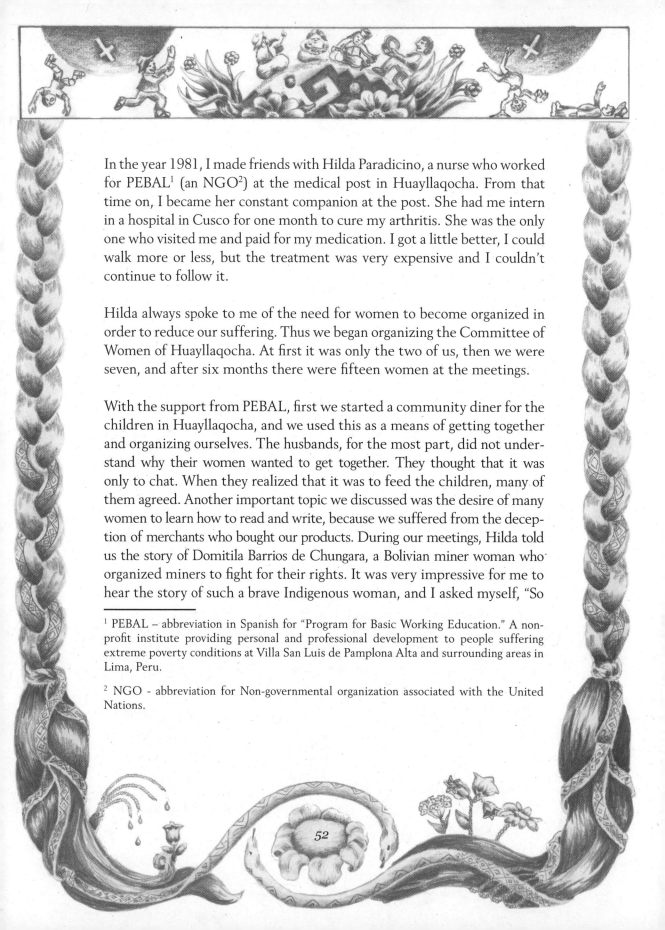

In the year 1981, I made friends with Hilda Paradicino, a nurse who worked for PEBAL[1] (an NGO[2]) at the medical post in Huayllaqocha. From that time on, I became her constant companion at the post. She had me intern in a hospital in Cusco for one month to cure my arthritis. She was the only one who visited me and paid for my medication. I got a little better, I could walk more or less, but the treatment was very expensive and I couldn't continue to follow it.

Hilda always spoke to me of the need for women to become organized in order to reduce our suffering. Thus we began organizing the Committee of Women of Huayllaqocha. At first it was only the two of us, then we were seven, and after six months there were fifteen women at the meetings.

With the support from PEBAL, first we started a community diner for the children in Huayllaqocha, and we used this as a means of getting together and organizing ourselves. The husbands, for the most part, did not understand why their women wanted to get together. They thought that it was only to chat. When they realized that it was to feed the children, many of them agreed. Another important topic we discussed was the desire of many women to learn how to read and write, because we suffered from the deception of merchants who bought our products. During our meetings, Hilda told us the story of Domitila Barrios de Chungara, a Bolivian miner woman who organized miners to fight for their rights. It was very impressive for me to hear the story of such a brave Indigenous woman, and I asked myself, "So

---

[1] PEBAL – abbreviation in Spanish for "Program for Basic Working Education." A non-profit institute providing personal and professional development to people suffering extreme poverty conditions at Villa San Luis de Pamplona Alta and surrounding areas in Lima, Peru.

[2] NGO - abbreviation for Non-governmental organization associated with the United Nations.

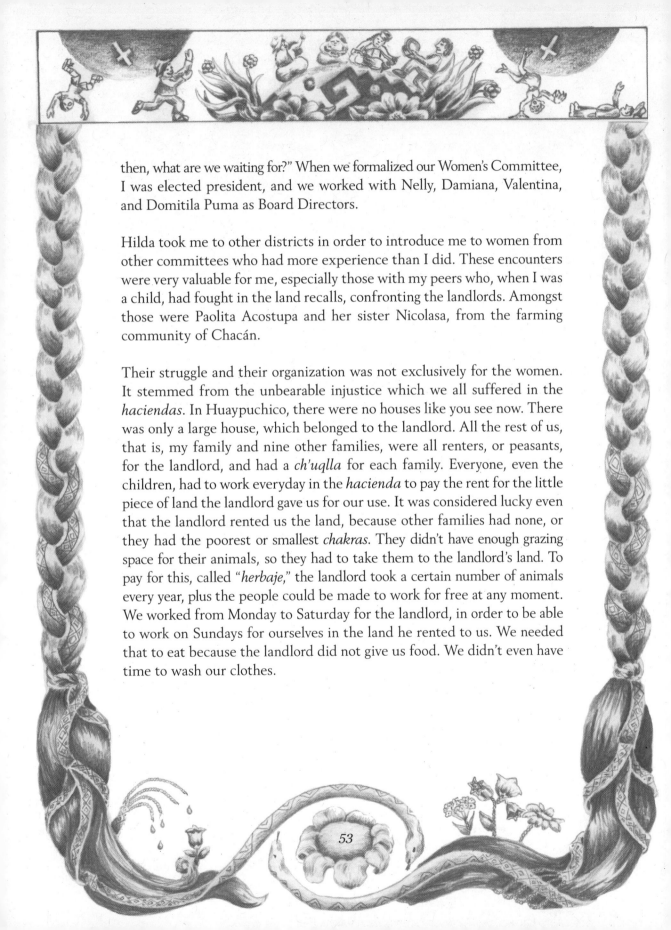

then, what are we waiting for?" When we formalized our Women's Committee, I was elected president, and we worked with Nelly, Damiana, Valentina, and Domitila Puma as Board Directors.

Hilda took me to other districts in order to introduce me to women from other committees who had more experience than I did. These encounters were very valuable for me, especially those with my peers who, when I was a child, had fought in the land recalls, confronting the landlords. Amongst those were Paolita Acostupa and her sister Nicolasa, from the farming community of Chacán.

Their struggle and their organization was not exclusively for the women. It stemmed from the unbearable injustice which we all suffered in the *haciendas*. In Huaypuchico, there were no houses like you see now. There was only a large house, which belonged to the landlord. All the rest of us, that is, my family and nine other families, were all renters, or peasants, for the landlord, and had a *ch'uqlla* for each family. Everyone, even the children, had to work everyday in the *hacienda* to pay the rent for the little piece of land the landlord gave us for our use. It was considered lucky even that the landlord rented us the land, because other families had none, or they had the poorest or smallest *chakras*. They didn't have enough grazing space for their animals, so they had to take them to the landlord's land. To pay for this, called *"herbaje,"* the landlord took a certain number of animals every year, plus the people could be made to work for free at any moment. We worked from Monday to Saturday for the landlord, in order to be able to work on Sundays for ourselves in the land he rented to us. We needed that to eat because the landlord did not give us food. We didn't even have time to wash our clothes.

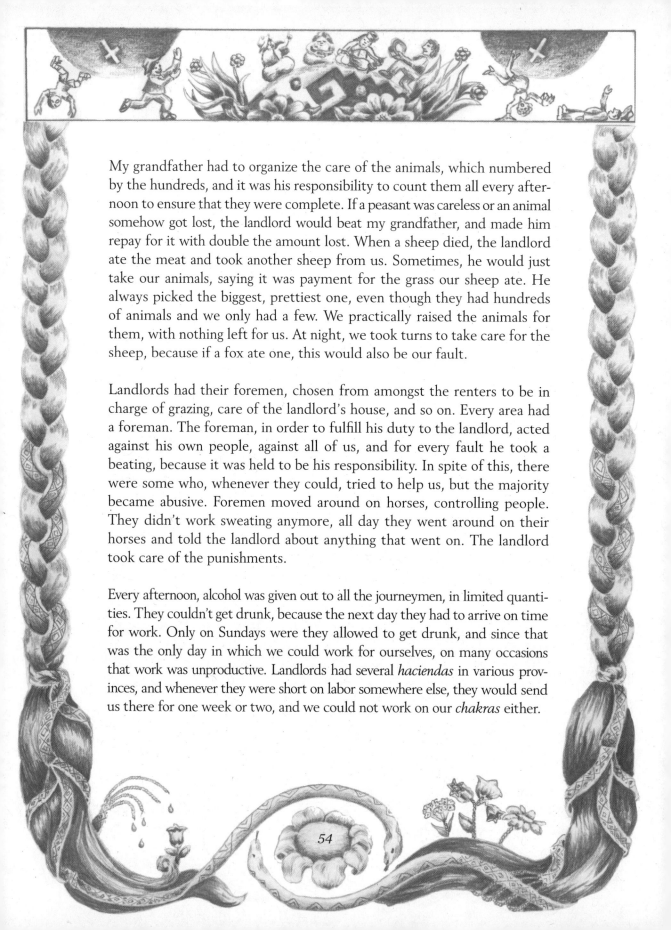

My grandfather had to organize the care of the animals, which numbered by the hundreds, and it was his responsibility to count them all every afternoon to ensure that they were complete. If a peasant was careless or an animal somehow got lost, the landlord would beat my grandfather, and made him repay for it with double the amount lost. When a sheep died, the landlord ate the meat and took another sheep from us. Sometimes, he would just take our animals, saying it was payment for the grass our sheep ate. He always picked the biggest, prettiest one, even though they had hundreds of animals and we only had a few. We practically raised the animals for them, with nothing left for us. At night, we took turns to take care for the sheep, because if a fox ate one, this would also be our fault.

Landlords had their foremen, chosen from amongst the renters to be in charge of grazing, care of the landlord's house, and so on. Every area had a foreman. The foreman, in order to fulfill his duty to the landlord, acted against his own people, against all of us, and for every fault he took a beating, because it was held to be his responsibility. In spite of this, there were some who, whenever they could, tried to help us, but the majority became abusive. Foremen moved around on horses, controlling people. They didn't work sweating anymore, all day they went around on their horses and told the landlord about anything that went on. The landlord took care of the punishments.

Every afternoon, alcohol was given out to all the journeymen, in limited quantities. They couldn't get drunk, because the next day they had to arrive on time for work. Only on Sundays were they allowed to get drunk, and since that was the only day in which we could work for ourselves, on many occasions that work was unproductive. Landlords had several *haciendas* in various provinces, and whenever they were short on labor somewhere else, they would send us there for one week or two, and we could not work on our *chakras* either.

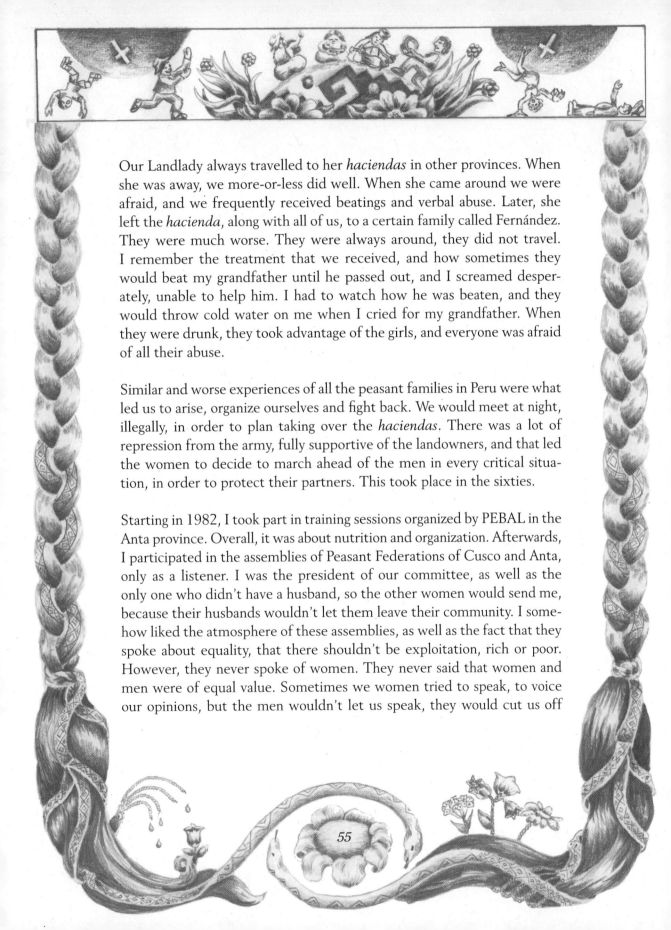

Our Landlady always travelled to her *haciendas* in other provinces. When she was away, we more-or-less did well. When she came around we were afraid, and we frequently received beatings and verbal abuse. Later, she left the *hacienda*, along with all of us, to a certain family called Fernández. They were much worse. They were always around, they did not travel. I remember the treatment that we received, and how sometimes they would beat my grandfather until he passed out, and I screamed desperately, unable to help him. I had to watch how he was beaten, and they would throw cold water on me when I cried for my grandfather. When they were drunk, they took advantage of the girls, and everyone was afraid of all their abuse.

Similar and worse experiences of all the peasant families in Peru were what led us to arise, organize ourselves and fight back. We would meet at night, illegally, in order to plan taking over the *haciendas*. There was a lot of repression from the army, fully supportive of the landowners, and that led the women to decide to march ahead of the men in every critical situation, in order to protect their partners. This took place in the sixties.

Starting in 1982, I took part in training sessions organized by PEBAL in the Anta province. Overall, it was about nutrition and organization. Afterwards, I participated in the assemblies of Peasant Federations of Cusco and Anta, only as a listener. I was the president of our committee, as well as the only one who didn't have a husband, so the other women would send me, because their husbands wouldn't let them leave their community. I somehow liked the atmosphere of these assemblies, as well as the fact that they spoke about equality, that there shouldn't be exploitation, rich or poor. However, they never spoke of women. They never said that women and men were of equal value. Sometimes we women tried to speak, to voice our opinions, but the men wouldn't let us speak, they would cut us off

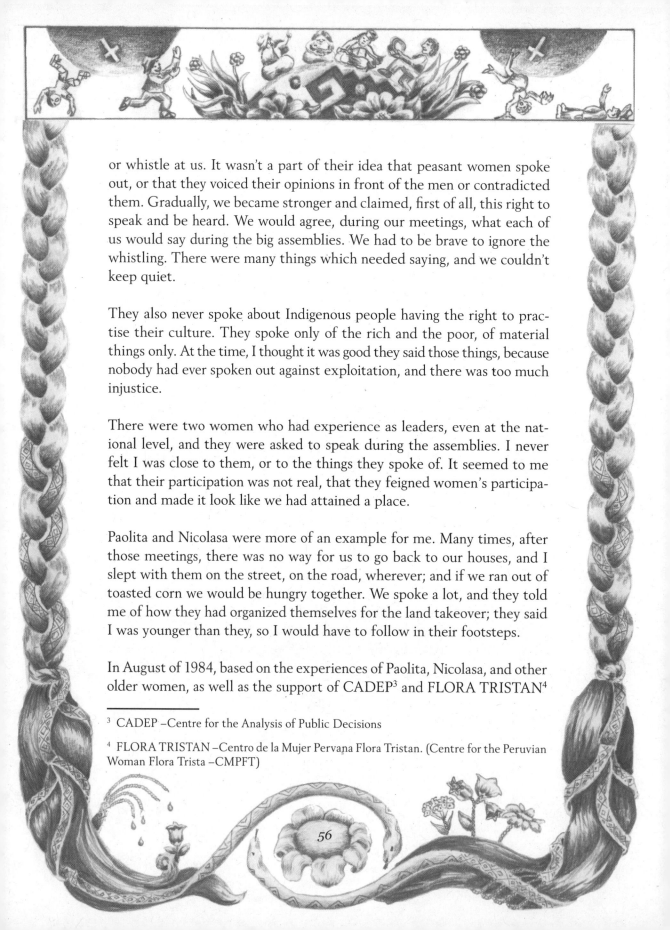

or whistle at us. It wasn't a part of their idea that peasant women spoke out, or that they voiced their opinions in front of the men or contradicted them. Gradually, we became stronger and claimed, first of all, this right to speak and be heard. We would agree, during our meetings, what each of us would say during the big assemblies. We had to be brave to ignore the whistling. There were many things which needed saying, and we couldn't keep quiet.

They also never spoke about Indigenous people having the right to practise their culture. They spoke only of the rich and the poor, of material things only. At the time, I thought it was good they said those things, because nobody had ever spoken out against exploitation, and there was too much injustice.

There were two women who had experience as leaders, even at the national level, and they were asked to speak during the assemblies. I never felt I was close to them, or to the things they spoke of. It seemed to me that their participation was not real, that they feigned women's participation and made it look like we had attained a place.

Paolita and Nicolasa were more of an example for me. Many times, after those meetings, there was no way for us to go back to our houses, and I slept with them on the street, on the road, wherever; and if we ran out of toasted corn we would be hungry together. We spoke a lot, and they told me of how they had organized themselves for the land takeover; they said I was younger than they, so I would have to follow in their footsteps.

In August of 1984, based on the experiences of Paolita, Nicolasa, and other older women, as well as the support of CADEP[3] and FLORA TRISTAN[4]

[3] CADEP –Centre for the Analysis of Public Decisions

[4] FLORA TRISTAN –Centro de la Mujer Pervana Flora Tristan. (Centre for the Peruvian Woman Flora Trista –CMPFT)

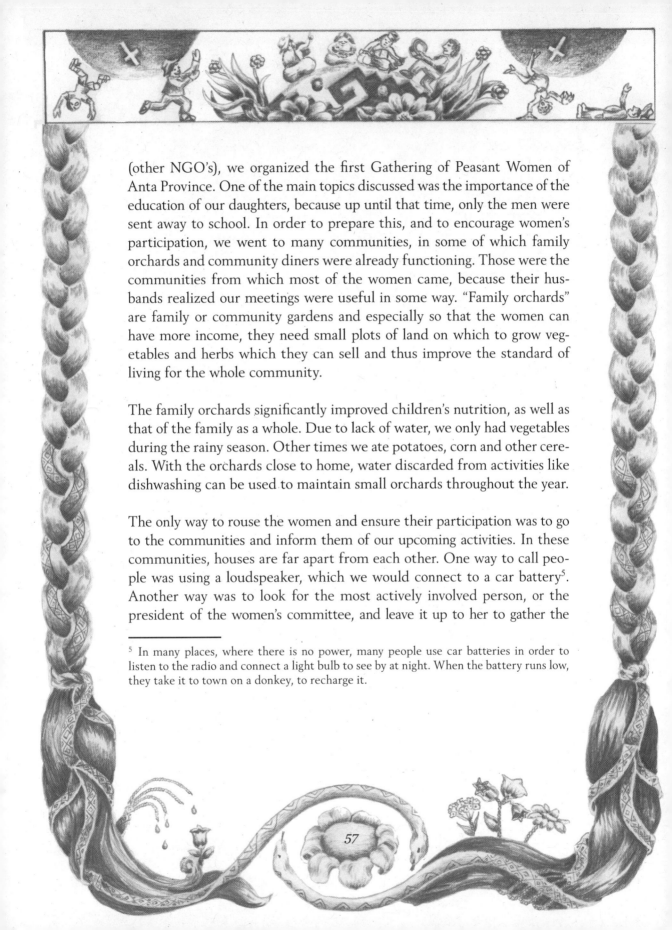

(other NGO's), we organized the first Gathering of Peasant Women of Anta Province. One of the main topics discussed was the importance of the education of our daughters, because up until that time, only the men were sent away to school. In order to prepare this, and to encourage women's participation, we went to many communities, in some of which family orchards and community diners were already functioning. Those were the communities from which most of the women came, because their husbands realized our meetings were useful in some way. "Family orchards" are family or community gardens and especially so that the women can have more income, they need small plots of land on which to grow vegetables and herbs which they can sell and thus improve the standard of living for the whole community.

The family orchards significantly improved children's nutrition, as well as that of the family as a whole. Due to lack of water, we only had vegetables during the rainy season. Other times we ate potatoes, corn and other cereals. With the orchards close to home, water discarded from activities like dishwashing can be used to maintain small orchards throughout the year.

The only way to rouse the women and ensure their participation was to go to the communities and inform them of our upcoming activities. In these communities, houses are far apart from each other. One way to call people was using a loudspeaker, which we would connect to a car battery[5]. Another way was to look for the most actively involved person, or the president of the women's committee, and leave it up to her to gather the

---

[5] In many places, where there is no power, many people use car batteries in order to listen to the radio and connect a light bulb to see by at night. When the battery runs low, they take it to town on a donkey, to recharge it.

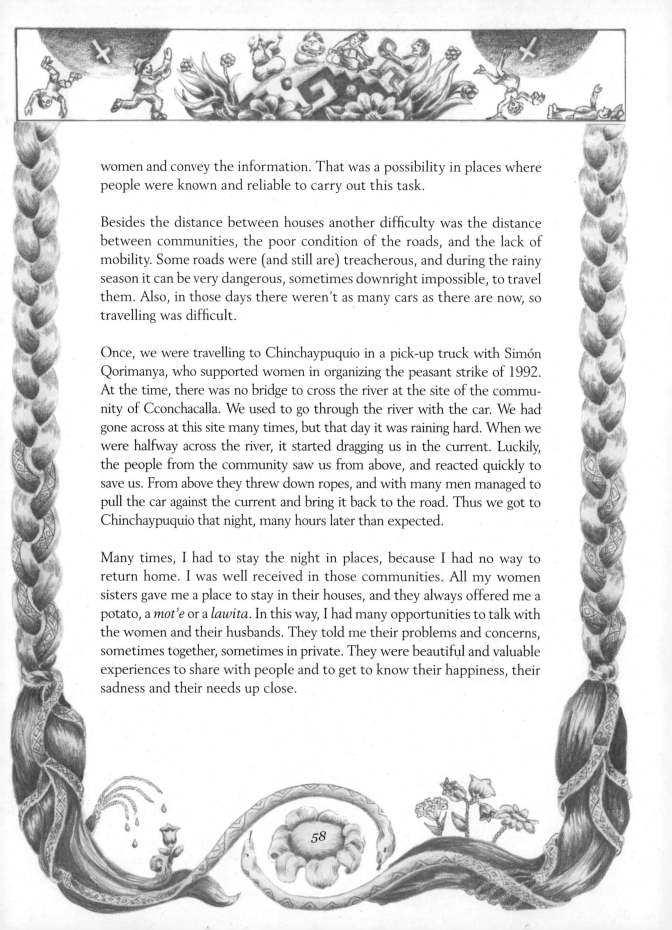

women and convey the information. That was a possibility in places where people were known and reliable to carry out this task.

Besides the distance between houses another difficulty was the distance between communities, the poor condition of the roads, and the lack of mobility. Some roads were (and still are) treacherous, and during the rainy season it can be very dangerous, sometimes downright impossible, to travel them. Also, in those days there weren't as many cars as there are now, so travelling was difficult.

Once, we were travelling to Chinchaypuquio in a pick-up truck with Simón Qorimanya, who supported women in organizing the peasant strike of 1992. At the time, there was no bridge to cross the river at the site of the community of Cconchacalla. We used to go through the river with the car. We had gone across at this site many times, but that day it was raining hard. When we were halfway across the river, it started dragging us in the current. Luckily, the people from the community saw us from above, and reacted quickly to save us. From above they threw down ropes, and with many men managed to pull the car against the current and bring it back to the road. Thus we got to Chinchaypuquio that night, many hours later than expected.

Many times, I had to stay the night in places, because I had no way to return home. I was well received in those communities. All my women sisters gave me a place to stay in their houses, and they always offered me a potato, a *mot'e* or a *lawita*. In this way, I had many opportunities to talk with the women and their husbands. They told me their problems and concerns, sometimes together, sometimes in private. They were beautiful and valuable experiences to share with people and to get to know their happiness, their sadness and their needs up close.

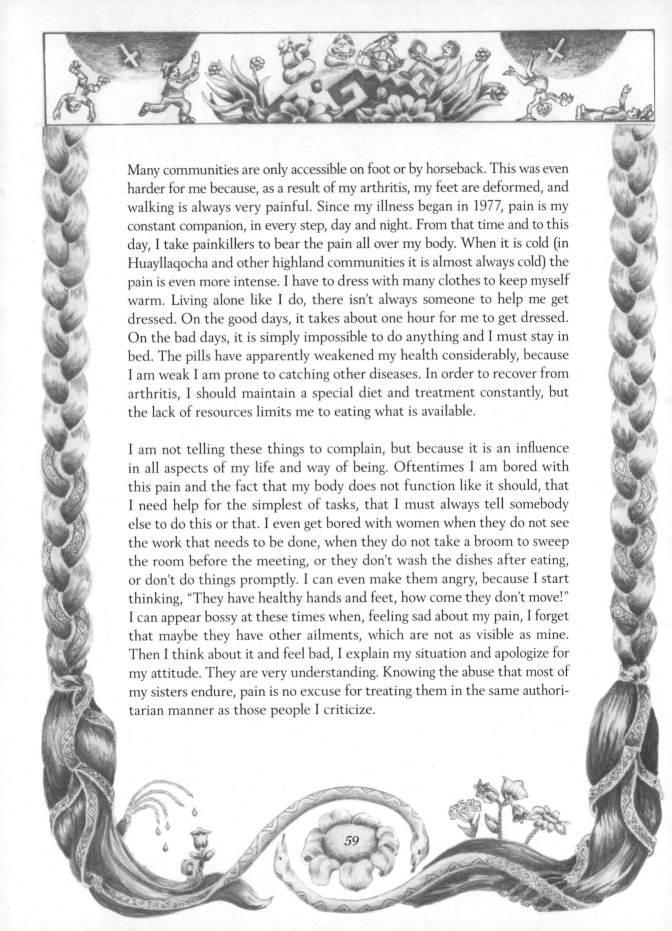

Many communities are only accessible on foot or by horseback. This was even harder for me because, as a result of my arthritis, my feet are deformed, and walking is always very painful. Since my illness began in 1977, pain is my constant companion, in every step, day and night. From that time and to this day, I take painkillers to bear the pain all over my body. When it is cold (in Huayllaqocha and other highland communities it is almost always cold) the pain is even more intense. I have to dress with many clothes to keep myself warm. Living alone like I do, there isn't always someone to help me get dressed. On the good days, it takes about one hour for me to get dressed. On the bad days, it is simply impossible to do anything and I must stay in bed. The pills have apparently weakened my health considerably, because I am weak I am prone to catching other diseases. In order to recover from arthritis, I should maintain a special diet and treatment constantly, but the lack of resources limits me to eating what is available.

I am not telling these things to complain, but because it is an influence in all aspects of my life and way of being. Oftentimes I am bored with this pain and the fact that my body does not function like it should, that I need help for the simplest of tasks, that I must always tell somebody else to do this or that. I even get bored with women when they do not see the work that needs to be done, when they do not take a broom to sweep the room before the meeting, or they don't wash the dishes after eating, or don't do things promptly. I can even make them angry, because I start thinking, "They have healthy hands and feet, how come they don't move!" I can appear bossy at these times when, feeling sad about my pain, I forget that maybe they have other ailments, which are not as visible as mine. Then I think about it and feel bad, I explain my situation and apologize for my attitude. They are very understanding. Knowing the abuse that most of my sisters endure, pain is no excuse for treating them in the same authoritarian manner as those people I criticize.

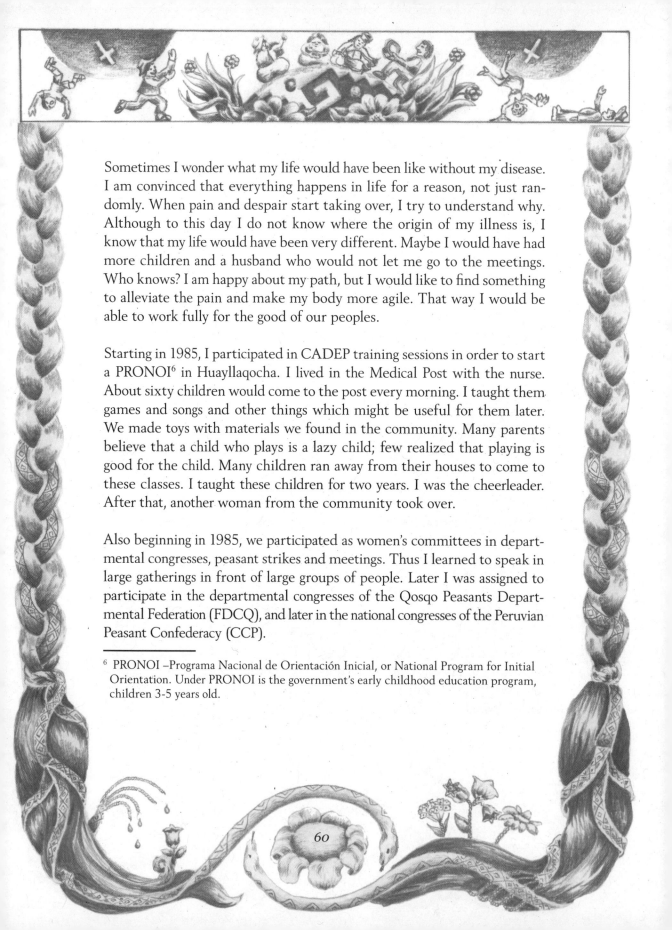

Sometimes I wonder what my life would have been like without my disease. I am convinced that everything happens in life for a reason, not just randomly. When pain and despair start taking over, I try to understand why. Although to this day I do not know where the origin of my illness is, I know that my life would have been very different. Maybe I would have had more children and a husband who would not let me go to the meetings. Who knows? I am happy about my path, but I would like to find something to alleviate the pain and make my body more agile. That way I would be able to work fully for the good of our peoples.

Starting in 1985, I participated in CADEP training sessions in order to start a PRONOI[6] in Huayllaqocha. I lived in the Medical Post with the nurse. About sixty children would come to the post every morning. I taught them games and songs and other things which might be useful for them later. We made toys with materials we found in the community. Many parents believe that a child who plays is a lazy child; few realized that playing is good for the child. Many children ran away from their houses to come to these classes. I taught these children for two years. I was the cheerleader. After that, another woman from the community took over.

Also beginning in 1985, we participated as women's committees in departmental congresses, peasant strikes and meetings. Thus I learned to speak in large gatherings in front of large groups of people. Later I was assigned to participate in the departmental congresses of the Qosqo Peasants Departmental Federation (FDCQ), and later in the national congresses of the Peruvian Peasant Confederacy (CCP).

---

[6] PRONOI –Programa Nacional de Orientación Inicial, or National Program for Initial Orientation. Under PRONOI is the government's early childhood education program, children 3-5 years old.

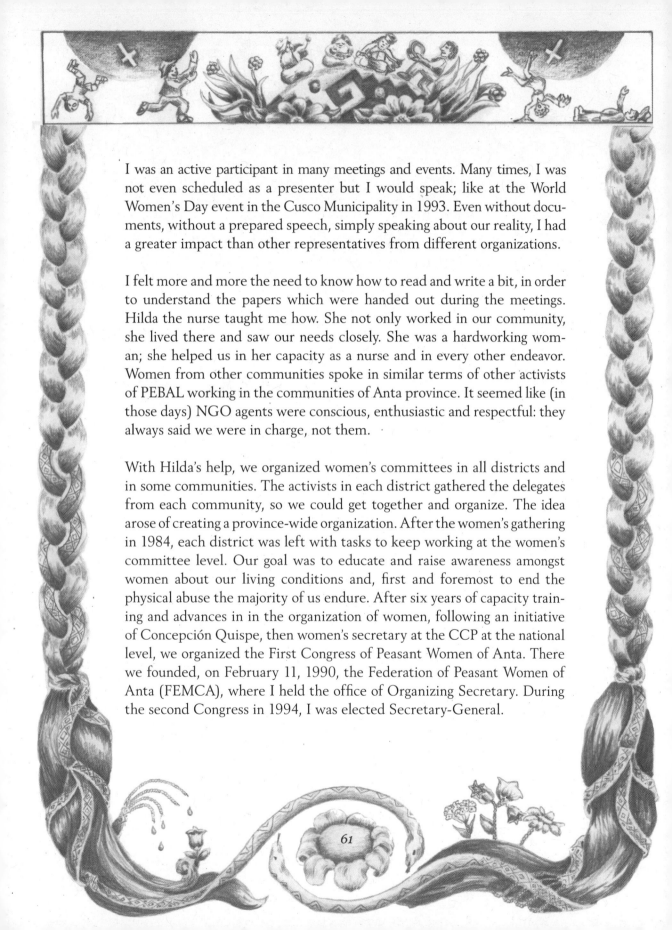

I was an active participant in many meetings and events. Many times, I was not even scheduled as a presenter but I would speak; like at the World Women's Day event in the Cusco Municipality in 1993. Even without documents, without a prepared speech, simply speaking about our reality, I had a greater impact than other representatives from different organizations.

I felt more and more the need to know how to read and write a bit, in order to understand the papers which were handed out during the meetings. Hilda the nurse taught me how. She not only worked in our community, she lived there and saw our needs closely. She was a hardworking woman; she helped us in her capacity as a nurse and in every other endeavor. Women from other communities spoke in similar terms of other activists of PEBAL working in the communities of Anta province. It seemed like (in those days) NGO agents were conscious, enthusiastic and respectful: they always said we were in charge, not them.

With Hilda's help, we organized women's committees in all districts and in some communities. The activists in each district gathered the delegates from each community, so we could get together and organize. The idea arose of creating a province-wide organization. After the women's gathering in 1984, each district was left with tasks to keep working at the women's committee level. Our goal was to educate and raise awareness amongst women about our living conditions and, first and foremost to end the physical abuse the majority of us endure. After six years of capacity training and advances in in the organization of women, following an initiative of Concepción Quispe, then women's secretary at the CCP at the national level, we organized the First Congress of Peasant Women of Anta. There we founded, on February 11, 1990, the Federation of Peasant Women of Anta (FEMCA), where I held the office of Organizing Secretary. During the second Congress in 1994, I was elected Secretary-General.

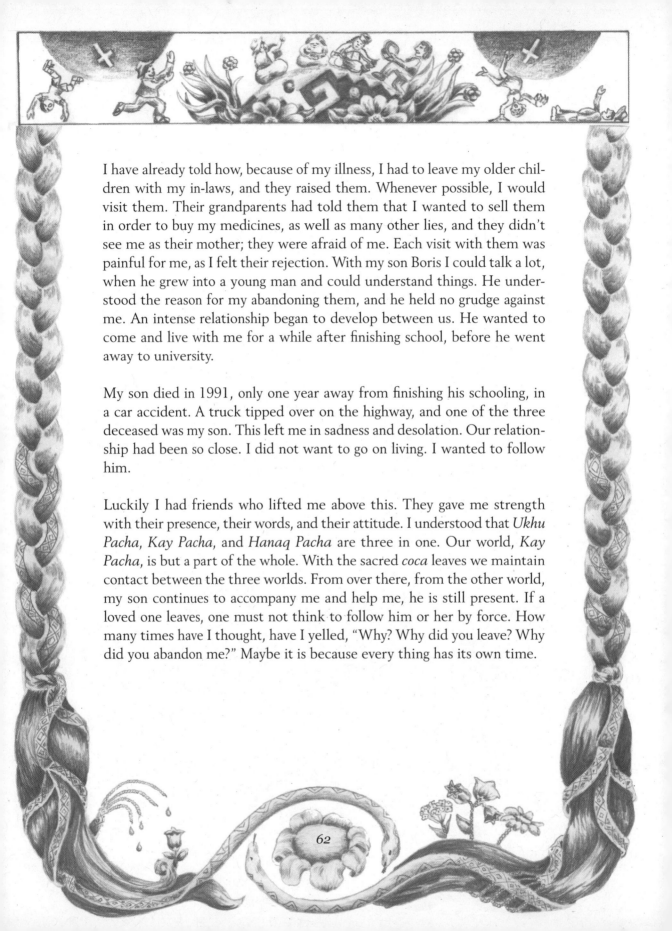

I have already told how, because of my illness, I had to leave my older children with my in-laws, and they raised them. Whenever possible, I would visit them. Their grandparents had told them that I wanted to sell them in order to buy my medicines, as well as many other lies, and they didn't see me as their mother; they were afraid of me. Each visit with them was painful for me, as I felt their rejection. With my son Boris I could talk a lot, when he grew into a young man and could understand things. He understood the reason for my abandoning them, and he held no grudge against me. An intense relationship began to develop between us. He wanted to come and live with me for a while after finishing school, before he went away to university.

My son died in 1991, only one year away from finishing his schooling, in a car accident. A truck tipped over on the highway, and one of the three deceased was my son. This left me in sadness and desolation. Our relationship had been so close. I did not want to go on living. I wanted to follow him.

Luckily I had friends who lifted me above this. They gave me strength with their presence, their words, and their attitude. I understood that *Ukhu Pacha*, *Kay Pacha*, and *Hanaq Pacha* are three in one. Our world, *Kay Pacha*, is but a part of the whole. With the sacred *coca* leaves we maintain contact between the three worlds. From over there, from the other world, my son continues to accompany me and help me, he is still present. If a loved one leaves, one must not think to follow him or her by force. How many times have I thought, have I yelled, "Why? Why did you leave? Why did you abandon me?" Maybe it is because every thing has its own time.

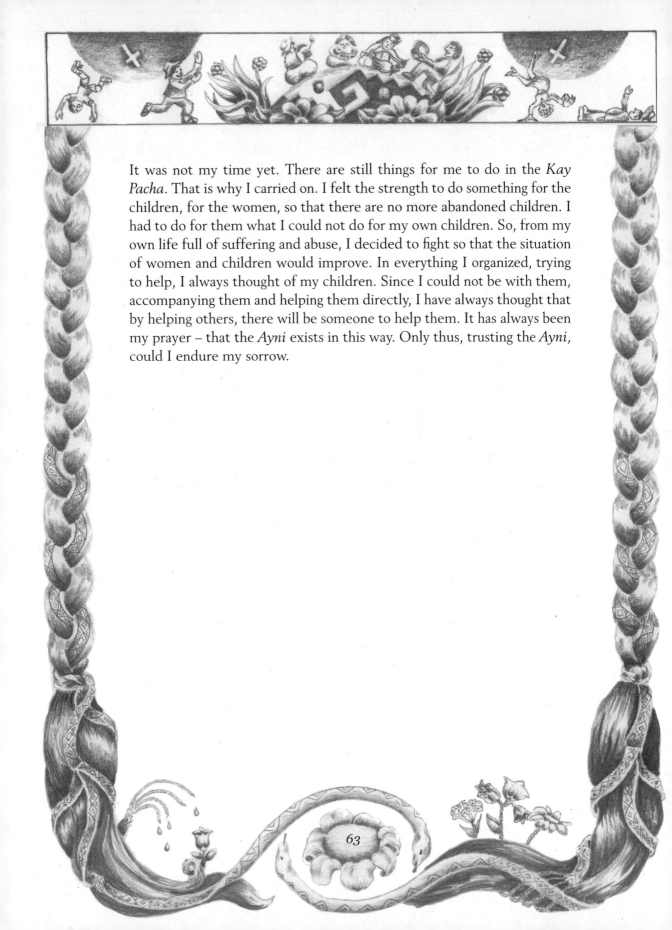

It was not my time yet. There are still things for me to do in the *Kay Pacha*. That is why I carried on. I felt the strength to do something for the children, for the women, so that there are no more abandoned children. I had to do for them what I could not do for my own children. So, from my own life full of suffering and abuse, I decided to fight so that the situation of women and children would improve. In everything I organized, trying to help, I always thought of my children. Since I could not be with them, accompanying them and helping them directly, I have always thought that by helping others, there will be someone to help them. It has always been my prayer – that the *Ayni* exists in this way. Only thus, trusting the *Ayni*, could I endure my sorrow.

QUESTIONS FOR REFLECTION

- In your opinion, is the organization of women necessary?
- How are the women in your community organized?
- Who took the initiative?
- What was the men's first reaction towards women's organization?
- Can you tell of your experiences during the time of the *haciendas* and the land takeovers?
- How did you learn to speak in public?
- Is there recognition for your activities in your community?

"…The family orchards significantly improved children's nutrition…"

Little Plants are Growing

Activities with FEMCA
About ancient authorities
Learning and forgiveness
What is "being modern"?

Questions for reflection

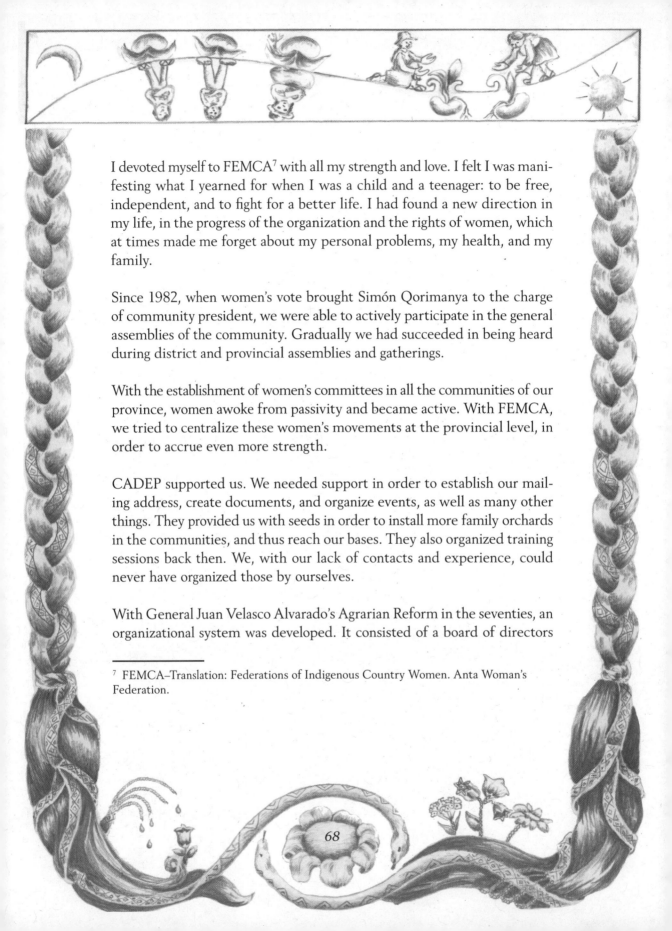

I devoted myself to FEMCA[7] with all my strength and love. I felt I was manifesting what I yearned for when I was a child and a teenager: to be free, independent, and to fight for a better life. I had found a new direction in my life, in the progress of the organization and the rights of women, which at times made me forget about my personal problems, my health, and my family.

Since 1982, when women's vote brought Simón Qorimanya to the charge of community president, we were able to actively participate in the general assemblies of the community. Gradually we had succeeded in being heard during district and provincial assemblies and gatherings.

With the establishment of women's committees in all the communities of our province, women awoke from passivity and became active. With FEMCA, we tried to centralize these women's movements at the provincial level, in order to accrue even more strength.

CADEP supported us. We needed support in order to establish our mailing address, create documents, and organize events, as well as many other things. They provided us with seeds in order to install more family orchards in the communities, and thus reach our bases. They also organized training sessions back then. We, with our lack of contacts and experience, could never have organized those by ourselves.

With General Juan Velasco Alvarado's Agrarian Reform in the seventies, an organizational system was developed. It consisted of a board of directors

---

[7] FEMCA–Translation: Federations of Indigenous Country Women. Anta Woman's Federation.

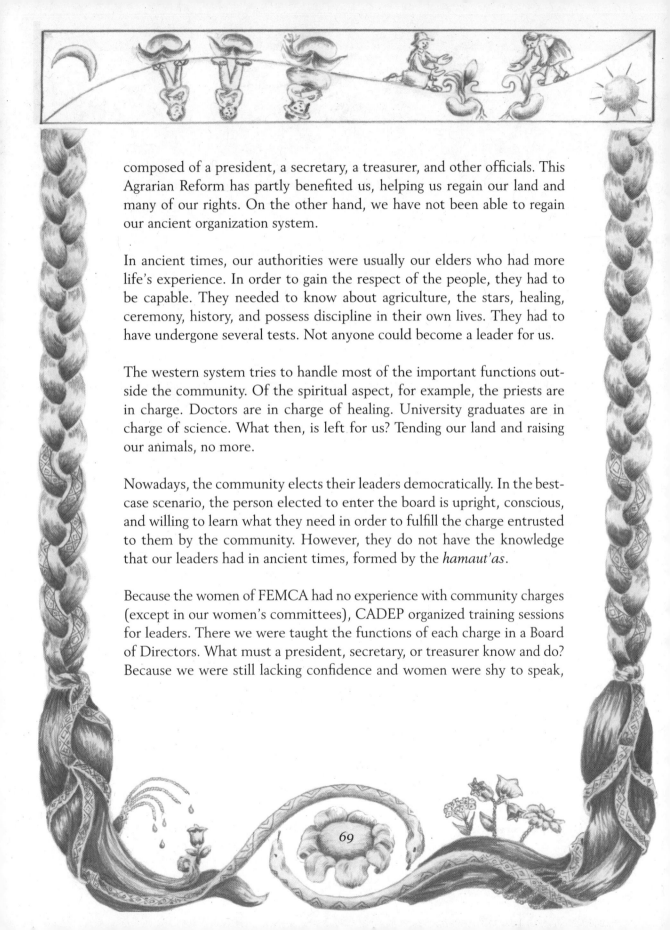

composed of a president, a secretary, a treasurer, and other officials. This Agrarian Reform has partly benefited us, helping us regain our land and many of our rights. On the other hand, we have not been able to regain our ancient organization system.

In ancient times, our authorities were usually our elders who had more life's experience. In order to gain the respect of the people, they had to be capable. They needed to know about agriculture, the stars, healing, ceremony, history, and possess discipline in their own lives. They had to have undergone several tests. Not anyone could become a leader for us.

The western system tries to handle most of the important functions outside the community. Of the spiritual aspect, for example, the priests are in charge. Doctors are in charge of healing. University graduates are in charge of science. What then, is left for us? Tending our land and raising our animals, no more.

Nowadays, the community elects their leaders democratically. In the best-case scenario, the person elected to enter the board is upright, conscious, and willing to learn what they need in order to fulfill the charge entrusted to them by the community. However, they do not have the knowledge that our leaders had in ancient times, formed by the *hamaut'as*.

Because the women of FEMCA had no experience with community charges (except in our women's committees), CADEP organized training sessions for leaders. There we were taught the functions of each charge in a Board of Directors. What must a president, secretary, or treasurer know and do? Because we were still lacking confidence and women were shy to speak,

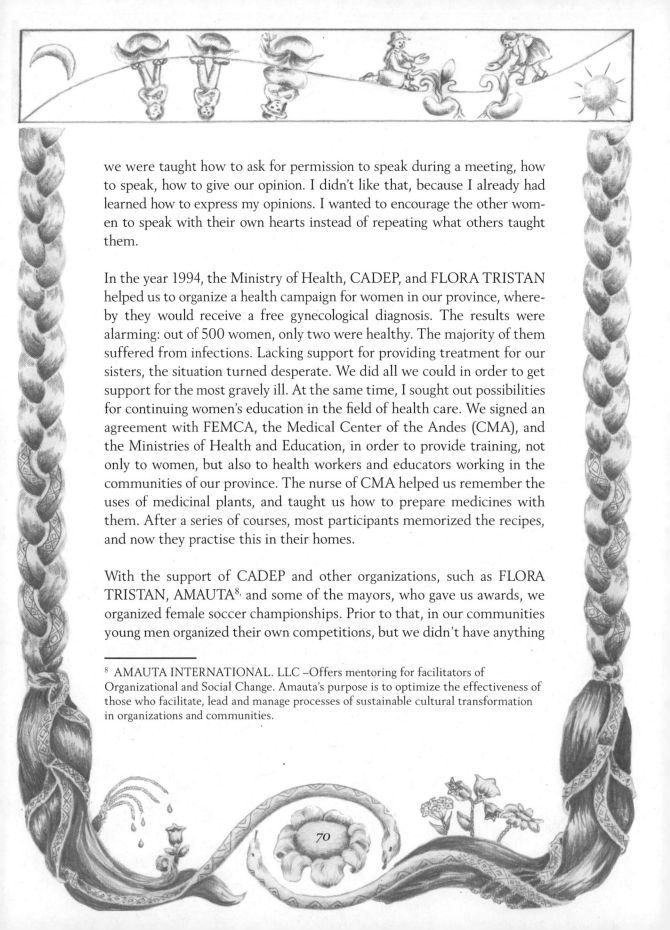

we were taught how to ask for permission to speak during a meeting, how to speak, how to give our opinion. I didn't like that, because I already had learned how to express my opinions. I wanted to encourage the other women to speak with their own hearts instead of repeating what others taught them.

In the year 1994, the Ministry of Health, CADEP, and FLORA TRISTAN helped us to organize a health campaign for women in our province, whereby they would receive a free gynecological diagnosis. The results were alarming: out of 500 women, only two were healthy. The majority of them suffered from infections. Lacking support for providing treatment for our sisters, the situation turned desperate. We did all we could in order to get support for the most gravely ill. At the same time, I sought out possibilities for continuing women's education in the field of health care. We signed an agreement with FEMCA, the Medical Center of the Andes (CMA), and the Ministries of Health and Education, in order to provide training, not only to women, but also to health workers and educators working in the communities of our province. The nurse of CMA helped us remember the uses of medicinal plants, and taught us how to prepare medicines with them. After a series of courses, most participants memorized the recipes, and now they practise this in their homes.

With the support of CADEP and other organizations, such as FLORA TRISTAN, AMAUTA[8,] and some of the mayors, who gave us awards, we organized female soccer championships. Prior to that, in our communities young men organized their own competitions, but we didn't have anything

---

[8] AMAUTA INTERNATIONAL. LLC –Offers mentoring for facilitators of Organizational and Social Change. Amauta's purpose is to optimize the effectiveness of those who facilitate, lead and manage processes of sustainable cultural transformation in organizations and communities.

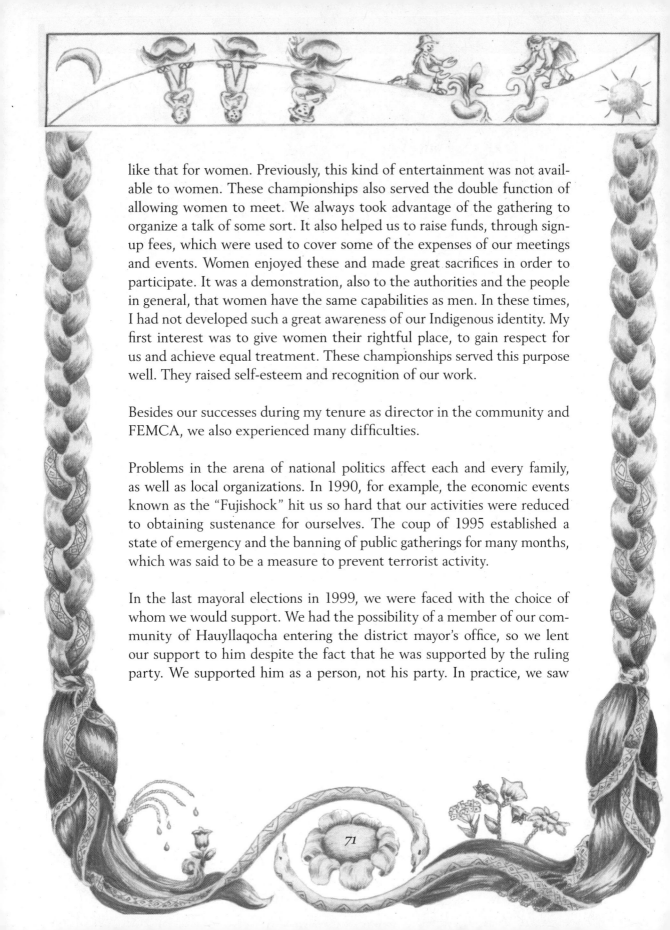

like that for women. Previously, this kind of entertainment was not available to women. These championships also served the double function of allowing women to meet. We always took advantage of the gathering to organize a talk of some sort. It also helped us to raise funds, through sign-up fees, which were used to cover some of the expenses of our meetings and events. Women enjoyed these and made great sacrifices in order to participate. It was a demonstration, also to the authorities and the people in general, that women have the same capabilities as men. In these times, I had not developed such a great awareness of our Indigenous identity. My first interest was to give women their rightful place, to gain respect for us and achieve equal treatment. These championships served this purpose well. They raised self-esteem and recognition of our work.

Besides our successes during my tenure as director in the community and FEMCA, we also experienced many difficulties.

Problems in the arena of national politics affect each and every family, as well as local organizations. In 1990, for example, the economic events known as the "Fujishock" hit us so hard that our activities were reduced to obtaining sustenance for ourselves. The coup of 1995 established a state of emergency and the banning of public gatherings for many months, which was said to be a measure to prevent terrorist activity.

In the last mayoral elections in 1999, we were faced with the choice of whom we would support. We had the possibility of a member of our community of Hauyllaqocha entering the district mayor's office, so we lent our support to him despite the fact that he was supported by the ruling party. We supported him as a person, not his party. In practice, we saw

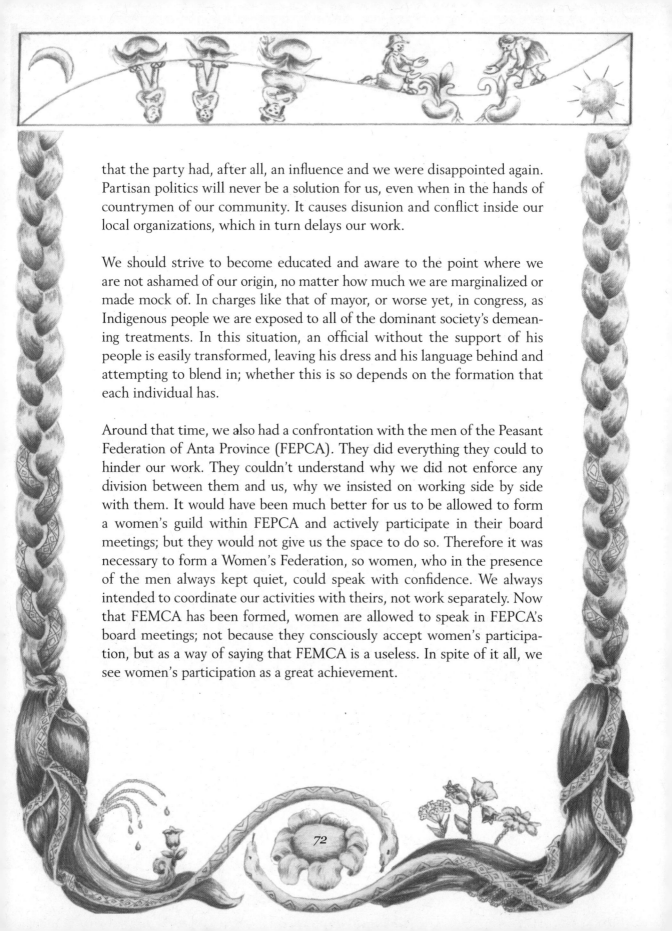

that the party had, after all, an influence and we were disappointed again. Partisan politics will never be a solution for us, even when in the hands of countrymen of our community. It causes disunion and conflict inside our local organizations, which in turn delays our work.

We should strive to become educated and aware to the point where we are not ashamed of our origin, no matter how much we are marginalized or made mock of. In charges like that of mayor, or worse yet, in congress, as Indigenous people we are exposed to all of the dominant society's demeaning treatments. In this situation, an official without the support of his people is easily transformed, leaving his dress and his language behind and attempting to blend in; whether this is so depends on the formation that each individual has.

Around that time, we also had a confrontation with the men of the Peasant Federation of Anta Province (FEPCA). They did everything they could to hinder our work. They couldn't understand why we did not enforce any division between them and us, why we insisted on working side by side with them. It would have been much better for us to be allowed to form a women's guild within FEPCA and actively participate in their board meetings; but they would not give us the space to do so. Therefore it was necessary to form a Women's Federation, so women, who in the presence of the men always kept quiet, could speak with confidence. We always intended to coordinate our activities with theirs, not work separately. Now that FEMCA has been formed, women are allowed to speak in FEPCA's board meetings; not because they consciously accept women's participation, but as a way of saying that FEMCA is a useless. In spite of it all, we see women's participation as a great achievement.

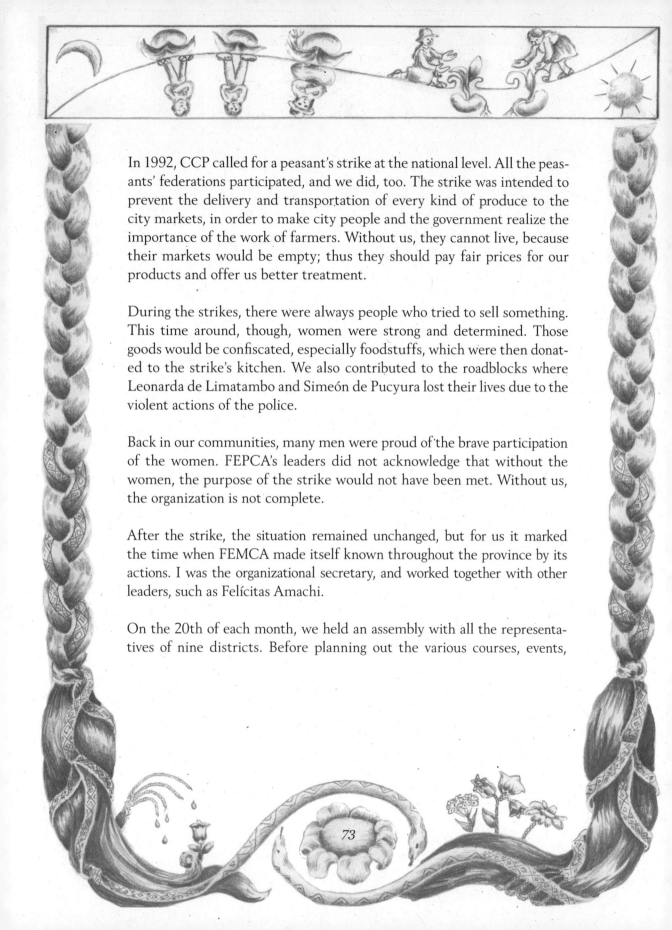

In 1992, CCP called for a peasant's strike at the national level. All the peasants' federations participated, and we did, too. The strike was intended to prevent the delivery and transportation of every kind of produce to the city markets, in order to make city people and the government realize the importance of the work of farmers. Without us, they cannot live, because their markets would be empty; thus they should pay fair prices for our products and offer us better treatment.

During the strikes, there were always people who tried to sell something. This time around, though, women were strong and determined. Those goods would be confiscated, especially foodstuffs, which were then donated to the strike's kitchen. We also contributed to the roadblocks where Leonarda de Limatambo and Simeón de Pucyura lost their lives due to the violent actions of the police.

Back in our communities, many men were proud of the brave participation of the women. FEPCA's leaders did not acknowledge that without the women, the purpose of the strike would not have been met. Without us, the organization is not complete.

After the strike, the situation remained unchanged, but for us it marked the time when FEMCA made itself known throughout the province by its actions. I was the organizational secretary, and worked together with other leaders, such as Felícitas Amachi.

On the 20th of each month, we held an assembly with all the representatives of nine districts. Before planning out the various courses, events,

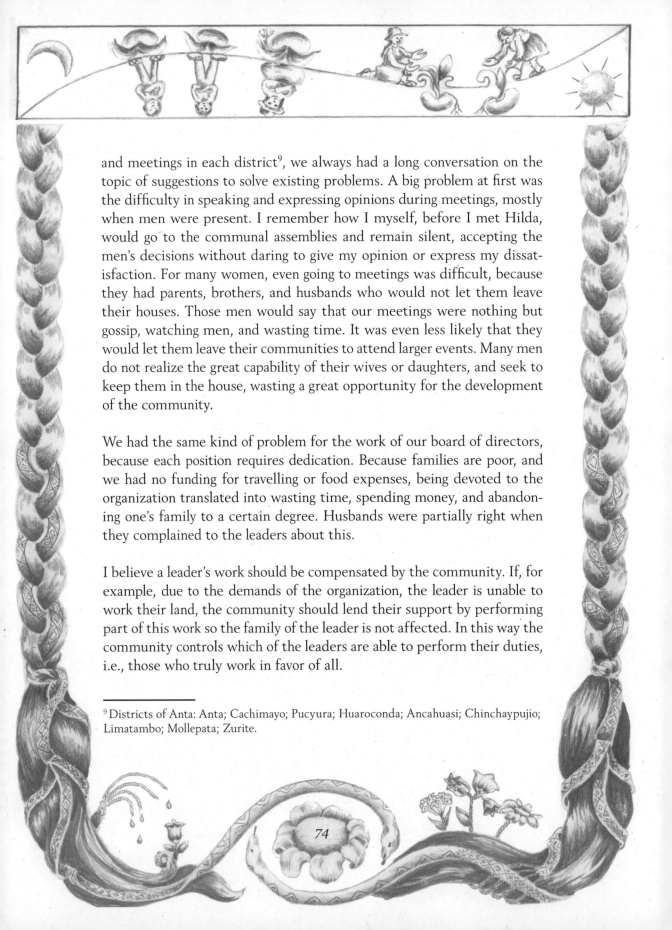

and meetings in each district[9], we always had a long conversation on the topic of suggestions to solve existing problems. A big problem at first was the difficulty in speaking and expressing opinions during meetings, mostly when men were present. I remember how I myself, before I met Hilda, would go to the communal assemblies and remain silent, accepting the men's decisions without daring to give my opinion or express my dissatisfaction. For many women, even going to meetings was difficult, because they had parents, brothers, and husbands who would not let them leave their houses. Those men would say that our meetings were nothing but gossip, watching men, and wasting time. It was even less likely that they would let them leave their communities to attend larger events. Many men do not realize the great capability of their wives or daughters, and seek to keep them in the house, wasting a great opportunity for the development of the community.

We had the same kind of problem for the work of our board of directors, because each position requires dedication. Because families are poor, and we had no funding for travelling or food expenses, being devoted to the organization translated into wasting time, spending money, and abandoning one's family to a certain degree. Husbands were partially right when they complained to the leaders about this.

I believe a leader's work should be compensated by the community. If, for example, due to the demands of the organization, the leader is unable to work their land, the community should lend their support by performing part of this work so the family of the leader is not affected. In this way the community controls which of the leaders are able to perform their duties, i.e., those who truly work in favor of all.

---

[9] Districts of Anta: Anta; Cachimayo; Pucyura; Huaroconda; Ancahuasi; Chinchaypujio; Limatambo; Mollepata; Zurite.

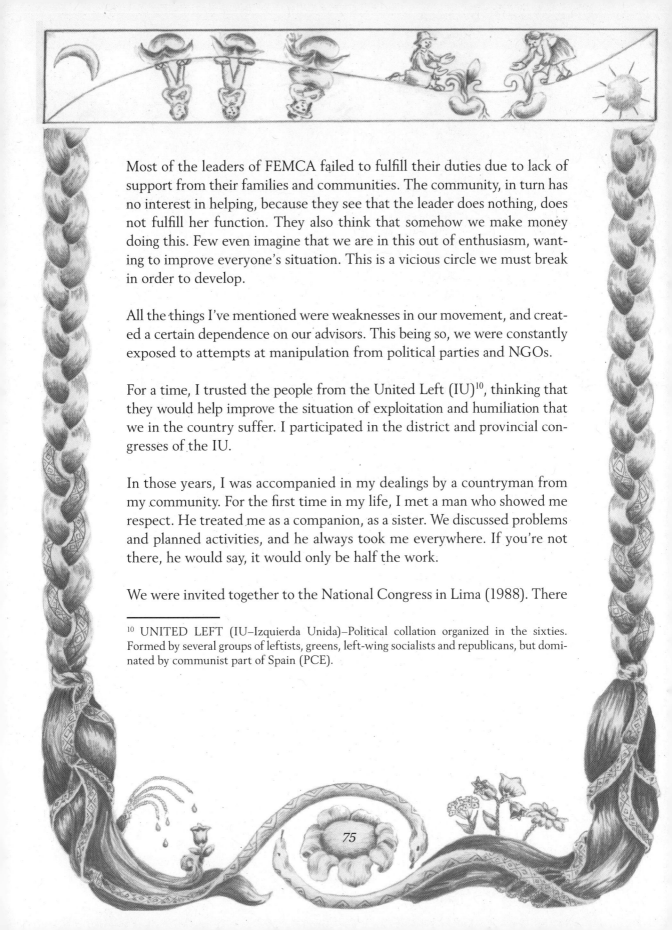

Most of the leaders of FEMCA failed to fulfill their duties due to lack of support from their families and communities. The community, in turn has no interest in helping, because they see that the leader does nothing, does not fulfill her function. They also think that somehow we make money doing this. Few even imagine that we are in this out of enthusiasm, wanting to improve everyone's situation. This is a vicious circle we must break in order to develop.

All the things I've mentioned were weaknesses in our movement, and created a certain dependence on our advisors. This being so, we were constantly exposed to attempts at manipulation from political parties and NGOs.

For a time, I trusted the people from the United Left (IU)[10], thinking that they would help improve the situation of exploitation and humiliation that we in the country suffer. I participated in the district and provincial congresses of the IU.

In those years, I was accompanied in my dealings by a countryman from my community. For the first time in my life, I met a man who showed me respect. He treated me as a companion, as a sister. We discussed problems and planned activities, and he always took me everywhere. If you're not there, he would say, it would only be half the work.

We were invited together to the National Congress in Lima (1988). There

---

[10] UNITED LEFT (IU–Izquierda Unida)–Political collation organized in the sixties. Formed by several groups of leftists, greens, left-wing socialists and republicans, but dominated by communist part of Spain (PCE).

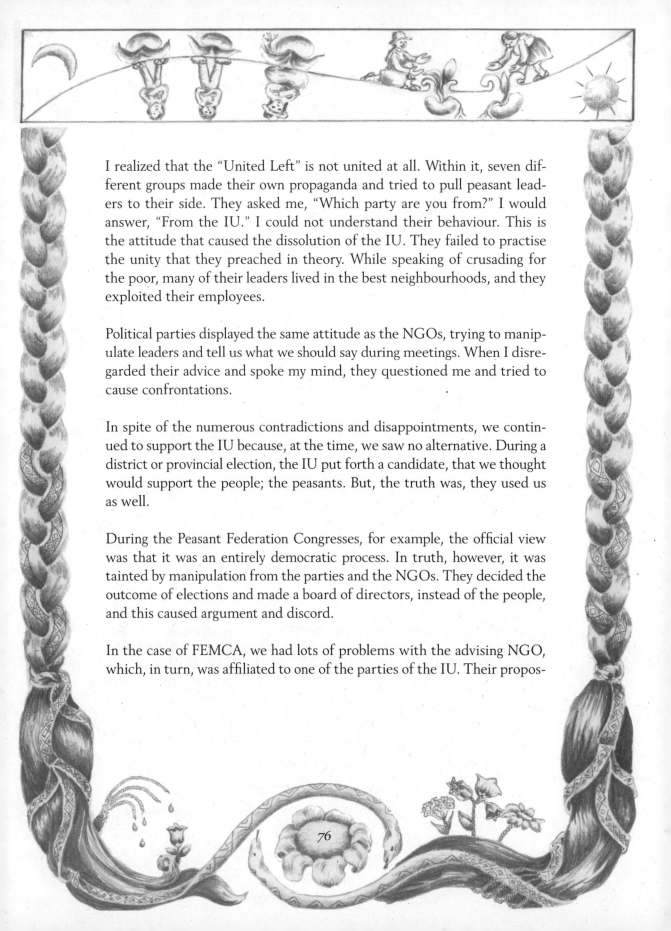

I realized that the "United Left" is not united at all. Within it, seven different groups made their own propaganda and tried to pull peasant leaders to their side. They asked me, "Which party are you from?" I would answer, "From the IU." I could not understand their behaviour. This is the attitude that caused the dissolution of the IU. They failed to practise the unity that they preached in theory. While speaking of crusading for the poor, many of their leaders lived in the best neighbourhoods, and they exploited their employees.

Political parties displayed the same attitude as the NGOs, trying to manipulate leaders and tell us what we should say during meetings. When I disregarded their advice and spoke my mind, they questioned me and tried to cause confrontations.

In spite of the numerous contradictions and disappointments, we continued to support the IU because, at the time, we saw no alternative. During a district or provincial election, the IU put forth a candidate, that we thought would support the people; the peasants. But, the truth was, they used us as well.

During the Peasant Federation Congresses, for example, the official view was that it was an entirely democratic process. In truth, however, it was tainted by manipulation from the parties and the NGOs. They decided the outcome of elections and made a board of directors, instead of the people, and this caused argument and discord.

In the case of FEMCA, we had lots of problems with the advising NGO, which, in turn, was affiliated to one of the parties of the IU. Their propos-

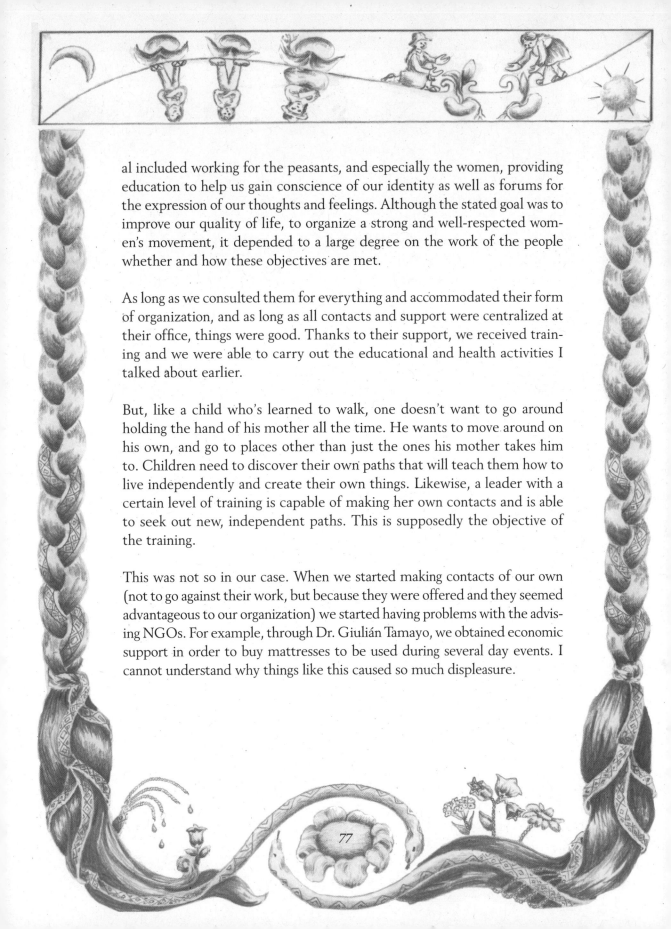

al included working for the peasants, and especially the women, providing education to help us gain conscience of our identity as well as forums for the expression of our thoughts and feelings. Although the stated goal was to improve our quality of life, to organize a strong and well-respected women's movement, it depended to a large degree on the work of the people whether and how these objectives are met.

As long as we consulted them for everything and accommodated their form of organization, and as long as all contacts and support were centralized at their office, things were good. Thanks to their support, we received training and we were able to carry out the educational and health activities I talked about earlier.

But, like a child who's learned to walk, one doesn't want to go around holding the hand of his mother all the time. He wants to move around on his own, and go to places other than just the ones his mother takes him to. Children need to discover their own paths that will teach them how to live independently and create their own things. Likewise, a leader with a certain level of training is capable of making her own contacts and is able to seek out new, independent paths. This is supposedly the objective of the training.

This was not so in our case. When we started making contacts of our own (not to go against their work, but because they were offered and they seemed advantageous to our organization) we started having problems with the advising NGOs. For example, through Dr. Giulián Tamayo, we obtained economic support in order to buy mattresses to be used during several day events. I cannot understand why things like this caused so much displeasure.

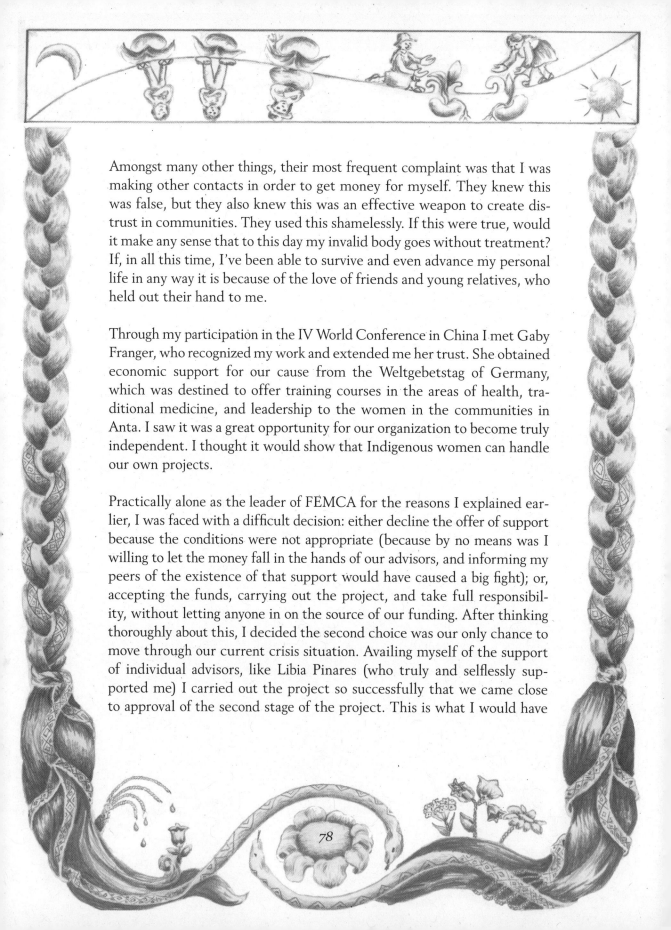

Amongst many other things, their most frequent complaint was that I was making other contacts in order to get money for myself. They knew this was false, but they also knew this was an effective weapon to create distrust in communities. They used this shamelessly. If this were true, would it make any sense that to this day my invalid body goes without treatment? If, in all this time, I've been able to survive and even advance my personal life in any way it is because of the love of friends and young relatives, who held out their hand to me.

Through my participation in the IV World Conference in China I met Gaby Franger, who recognized my work and extended me her trust. She obtained economic support for our cause from the Weltgebetstag of Germany, which was destined to offer training courses in the areas of health, traditional medicine, and leadership to the women in the communities in Anta. I saw it was a great opportunity for our organization to become truly independent. I thought it would show that Indigenous women can handle our own projects.

Practically alone as the leader of FEMCA for the reasons I explained earlier, I was faced with a difficult decision: either decline the offer of support because the conditions were not appropriate (because by no means was I willing to let the money fall in the hands of our advisors, and informing my peers of the existence of that support would have caused a big fight); or, accepting the funds, carrying out the project, and take full responsibility, without letting anyone in on the source of our funding. After thinking thoroughly about this, I decided the second choice was our only chance to move through our current crisis situation. Availing myself of the support of individual advisors, like Libia Pinares (who truly and selflessly supported me) I carried out the project so successfully that we came close to approval of the second stage of the project. This is what I would have

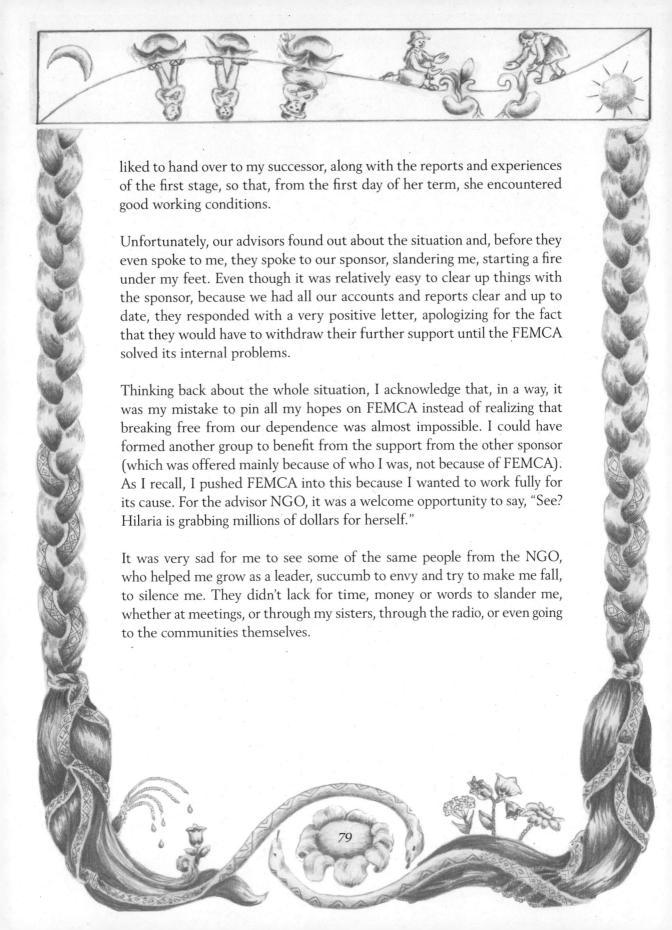

liked to hand over to my successor, along with the reports and experiences of the first stage, so that, from the first day of her term, she encountered good working conditions.

Unfortunately, our advisors found out about the situation and, before they even spoke to me, they spoke to our sponsor, slandering me, starting a fire under my feet. Even though it was relatively easy to clear up things with the sponsor, because we had all our accounts and reports clear and up to date, they responded with a very positive letter, apologizing for the fact that they would have to withdraw their further support until the FEMCA solved its internal problems.

Thinking back about the whole situation, I acknowledge that, in a way, it was my mistake to pin all my hopes on FEMCA instead of realizing that breaking free from our dependence was almost impossible. I could have formed another group to benefit from the support from the other sponsor (which was offered mainly because of who I was, not because of FEMCA). As I recall, I pushed FEMCA into this because I wanted to work fully for its cause. For the advisor NGO, it was a welcome opportunity to say, "See? Hilaria is grabbing millions of dollars for herself."

It was very sad for me to see some of the same people from the NGO, who helped me grow as a leader, succumb to envy and try to make me fall, to silence me. They didn't lack for time, money or words to slander me, whether at meetings, or through my sisters, through the radio, or even going to the communities themselves.

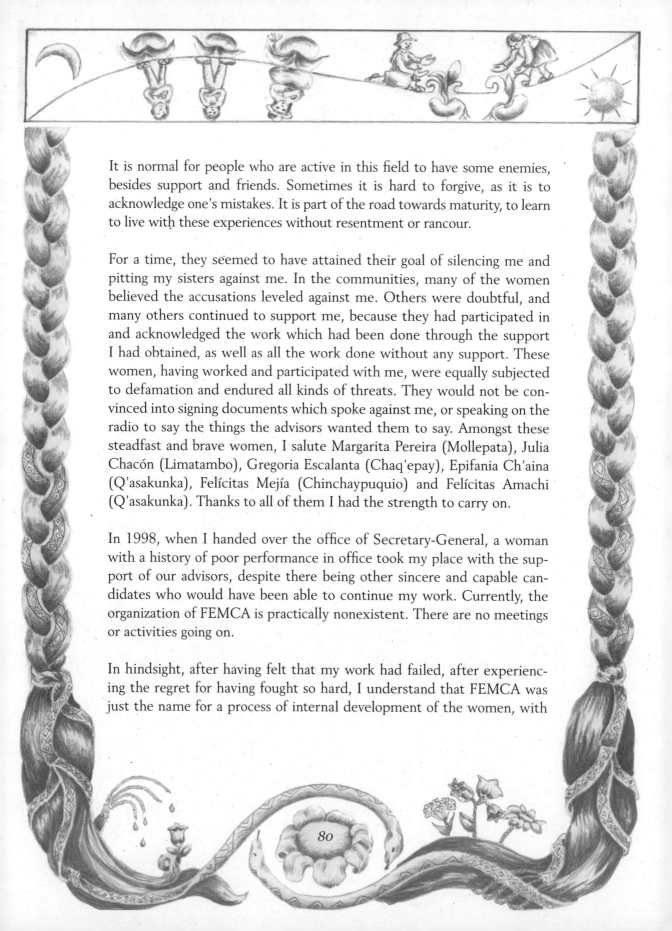

It is normal for people who are active in this field to have some enemies, besides support and friends. Sometimes it is hard to forgive, as it is to acknowledge one's mistakes. It is part of the road towards maturity, to learn to live with these experiences without resentment or rancour.

For a time, they seemed to have attained their goal of silencing me and pitting my sisters against me. In the communities, many of the women believed the accusations leveled against me. Others were doubtful, and many others continued to support me, because they had participated in and acknowledged the work which had been done through the support I had obtained, as well as all the work done without any support. These women, having worked and participated with me, were equally subjected to defamation and endured all kinds of threats. They would not be convinced into signing documents which spoke against me, or speaking on the radio to say the things the advisors wanted them to say. Amongst these steadfast and brave women, I salute Margarita Pereira (Mollepata), Julia Chacón (Limatambo), Gregoria Escalanta (Chaq'epay), Epifania Ch'aina (Q'asakunka), Felícitas Mejía (Chinchaypuquio) and Felícitas Amachi (Q'asakunka). Thanks to all of them I had the strength to carry on.

In 1998, when I handed over the office of Secretary-General, a woman with a history of poor performance in office took my place with the support of our advisors, despite there being other sincere and capable candidates who would have been able to continue my work. Currently, the organization of FEMCA is practically nonexistent. There are no meetings or activities going on.

In hindsight, after having felt that my work had failed, after experiencing the regret for having fought so hard, I understand that FEMCA was just the name for a process of internal development of the women, with

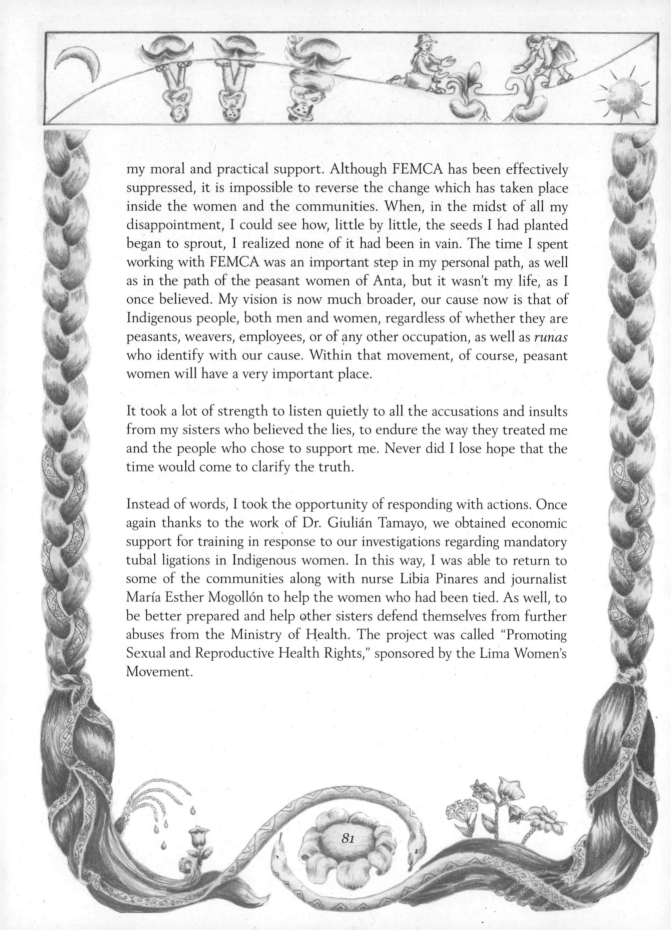

my moral and practical support. Although FEMCA has been effectively suppressed, it is impossible to reverse the change which has taken place inside the women and the communities. When, in the midst of all my disappointment, I could see how, little by little, the seeds I had planted began to sprout, I realized none of it had been in vain. The time I spent working with FEMCA was an important step in my personal path, as well as in the path of the peasant women of Anta, but it wasn't my life, as I once believed. My vision is now much broader, our cause now is that of Indigenous people, both men and women, regardless of whether they are peasants, weavers, employees, or of any other occupation, as well as *runas* who identify with our cause. Within that movement, of course, peasant women will have a very important place.

It took a lot of strength to listen quietly to all the accusations and insults from my sisters who believed the lies, to endure the way they treated me and the people who chose to support me. Never did I lose hope that the time would come to clarify the truth.

Instead of words, I took the opportunity of responding with actions. Once again thanks to the work of Dr. Giulián Tamayo, we obtained economic support for training in response to our investigations regarding mandatory tubal ligations in Indigenous women. In this way, I was able to return to some of the communities along with nurse Libia Pinares and journalist María Esther Mogollón to help the women who had been tied. As well, to be better prepared and help other sisters defend themselves from further abuses from the Ministry of Health. The project was called "Promoting Sexual and Reproductive Health Rights," sponsored by the Lima Women's Movement.

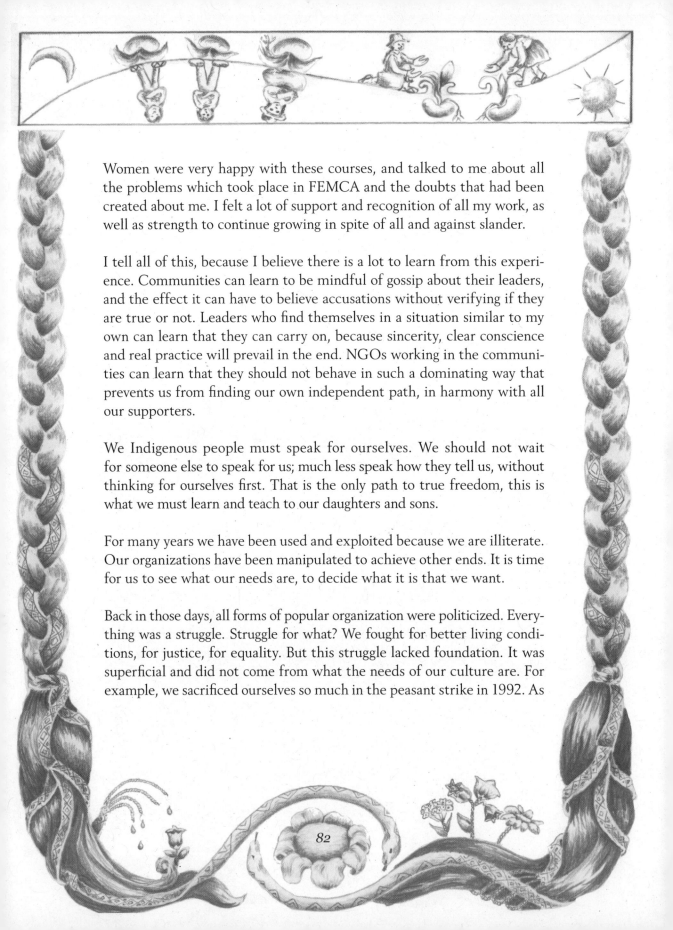

Women were very happy with these courses, and talked to me about all the problems which took place in FEMCA and the doubts that had been created about me. I felt a lot of support and recognition of all my work, as well as strength to continue growing in spite of all and against slander.

I tell all of this, because I believe there is a lot to learn from this experience. Communities can learn to be mindful of gossip about their leaders, and the effect it can have to believe accusations without verifying if they are true or not. Leaders who find themselves in a situation similar to my own can learn that they can carry on, because sincerity, clear conscience and real practice will prevail in the end. NGOs working in the communities can learn that they should not behave in such a dominating way that prevents us from finding our own independent path, in harmony with all our supporters.

We Indigenous people must speak for ourselves. We should not wait for someone else to speak for us; much less speak how they tell us, without thinking for ourselves first. That is the only path to true freedom, this is what we must learn and teach to our daughters and sons.

For many years we have been used and exploited because we are illiterate. Our organizations have been manipulated to achieve other ends. It is time for us to see what our needs are, to decide what it is that we want.

Back in those days, all forms of popular organization were politicized. Everything was a struggle. Struggle for what? We fought for better living conditions, for justice, for equality. But this struggle lacked foundation. It was superficial and did not come from what the needs of our culture are. For example, we sacrificed ourselves so much in the peasant strike in 1992. As

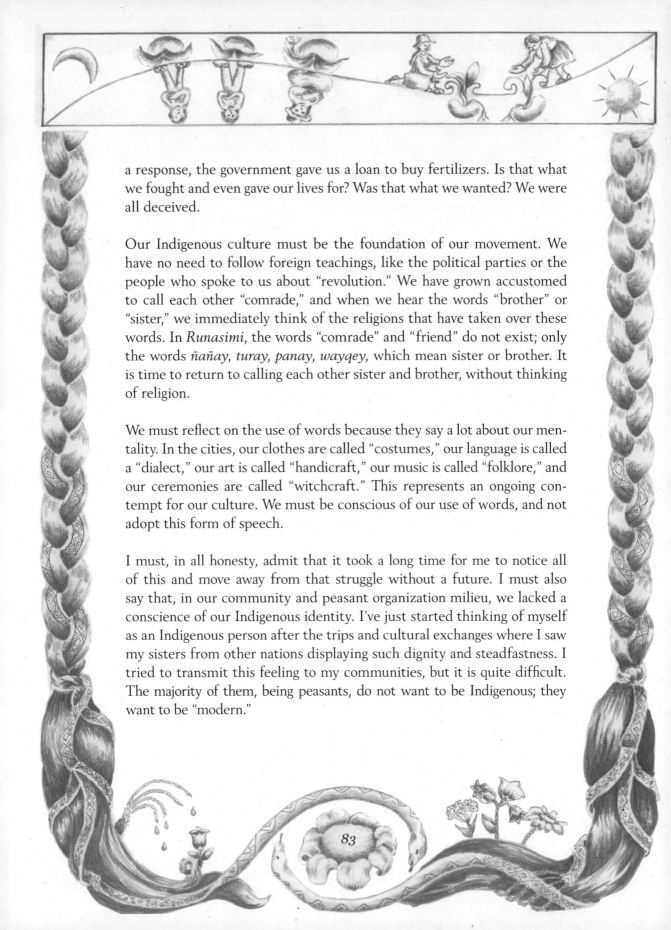

a response, the government gave us a loan to buy fertilizers. Is that what we fought and even gave our lives for? Was that what we wanted? We were all deceived.

Our Indigenous culture must be the foundation of our movement. We have no need to follow foreign teachings, like the political parties or the people who spoke to us about "revolution." We have grown accustomed to call each other "comrade," and when we hear the words "brother" or "sister," we immediately think of the religions that have taken over these words. In *Runasimi*, the words "comrade" and "friend" do not exist; only the words *ñañay*, *turay*, *panay*, *wayqey*, which mean sister or brother. It is time to return to calling each other sister and brother, without thinking of religion.

We must reflect on the use of words because they say a lot about our mentality. In the cities, our clothes are called "costumes," our language is called a "dialect," our art is called "handicraft," our music is called "folklore," and our ceremonies are called "witchcraft." This represents an ongoing contempt for our culture. We must be conscious of our use of words, and not adopt this form of speech.

I must, in all honesty, admit that it took a long time for me to notice all of this and move away from that struggle without a future. I must also say that, in our community and peasant organization milieu, we lacked a conscience of our Indigenous identity. I've just started thinking of myself as an Indigenous person after the trips and cultural exchanges where I saw my sisters from other nations displaying such dignity and steadfastness. I tried to transmit this feeling to my communities, but it is quite difficult. The majority of them, being peasants, do not want to be Indigenous; they want to be "modern."

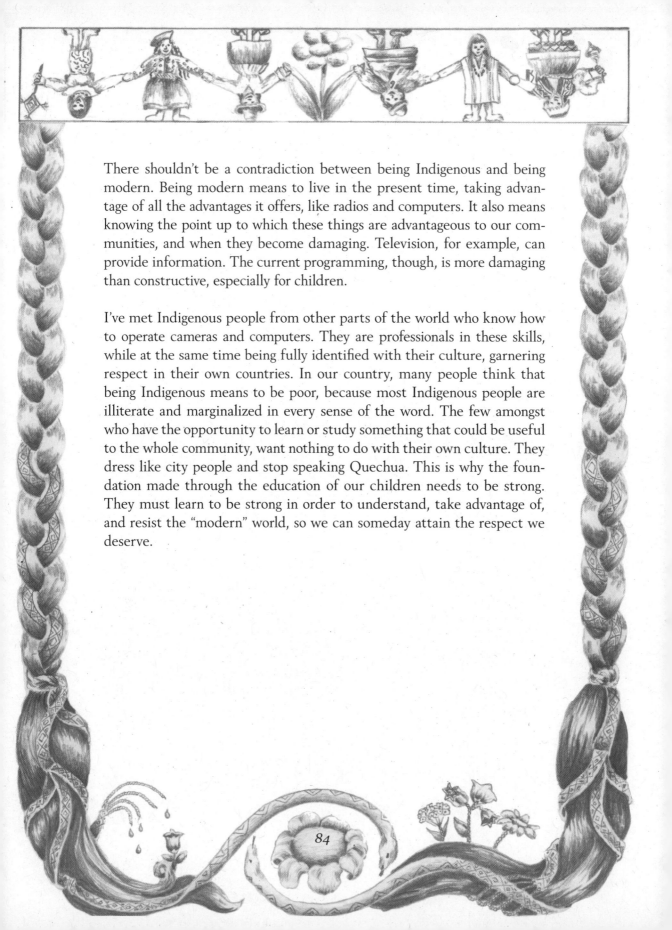

There shouldn't be a contradiction between being Indigenous and being modern. Being modern means to live in the present time, taking advantage of all the advantages it offers, like radios and computers. It also means knowing the point up to which these things are advantageous to our communities, and when they become damaging. Television, for example, can provide information. The current programming, though, is more damaging than constructive, especially for children.

I've met Indigenous people from other parts of the world who know how to operate cameras and computers. They are professionals in these skills, while at the same time being fully identified with their culture, garnering respect in their own countries. In our country, many people think that being Indigenous means to be poor, because most Indigenous people are illiterate and marginalized in every sense of the word. The few amongst who have the opportunity to learn or study something that could be useful to the whole community, want nothing to do with their own culture. They dress like city people and stop speaking Quechua. This is why the foundation made through the education of our children needs to be strong. They must learn to be strong in order to understand, take advantage of, and resist the "modern" world, so we can someday attain the respect we deserve.

QUESTIONS FOR REFLECTION

- Why do women meet in your community?
- Do you participate in the activities of your community's women's organization?
- What have been the accomplishments of your organization?
- What are the difficulties you encounter?
- Has the situation of women improved in recent years?
- Are there NGOs, political parties, or religious groups which influence your community?
- What kind of support do they give, and what problems do they cause?
- Do you think of yourself as being Indigenous?
- In your community and your organization, is there conscience of unifying yourselves as an Indigenous people?
- Which traditional customs are maintained in your community?
- Has your organization found its own independent path?
- What are your needs, those of your family, of your community, specifically of the women?
- What does it mean for you, to be "modern"?

With FEMCA (Federation of Peasant Woman of Anta) we tried to centralize these women's movements in order to accrue even more strength.

Speaking for Indigenous Women

*Participation in the VI Regional Women's Conference
for Latin America and the Caribbean in Argentina*

Participation in the IV World Women's Conference in China

Questions for reflection

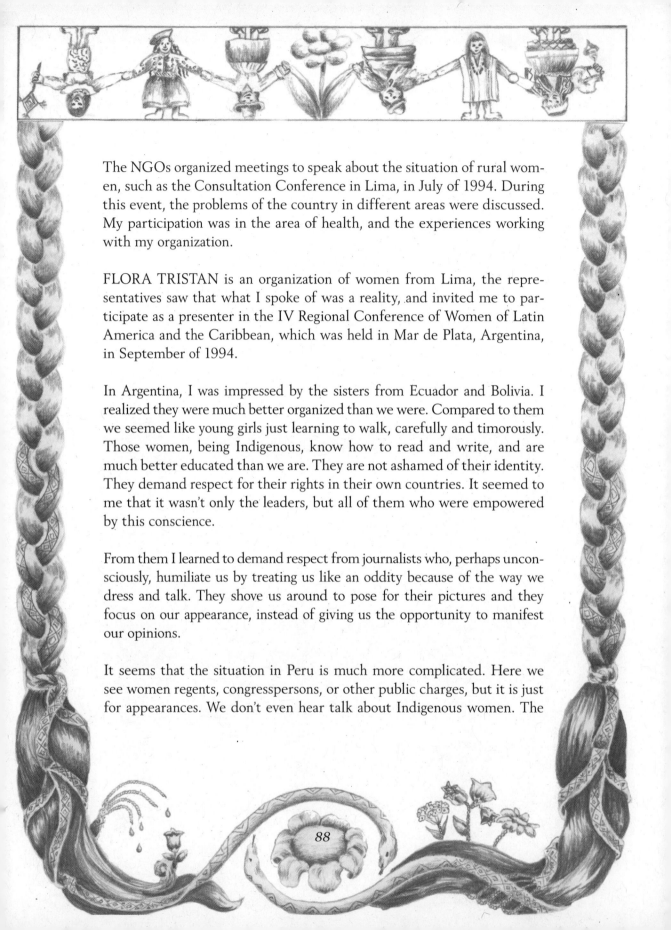

The NGOs organized meetings to speak about the situation of rural women, such as the Consultation Conference in Lima, in July of 1994. During this event, the problems of the country in different areas were discussed. My participation was in the area of health, and the experiences working with my organization.

FLORA TRISTAN is an organization of women from Lima, the representatives saw that what I spoke of was a reality, and invited me to participate as a presenter in the IV Regional Conference of Women of Latin America and the Caribbean, which was held in Mar de Plata, Argentina, in September of 1994.

In Argentina, I was impressed by the sisters from Ecuador and Bolivia. I realized they were much better organized than we were. Compared to them we seemed like young girls just learning to walk, carefully and timorously. Those women, being Indigenous, know how to read and write, and are much better educated than we are. They are not ashamed of their identity. They demand respect for their rights in their own countries. It seemed to me that it wasn't only the leaders, but all of them who were empowered by this conscience.

From them I learned to demand respect from journalists who, perhaps unconsciously, humiliate us by treating us like an oddity because of the way we dress and talk. They shove us around to pose for their pictures and they focus on our appearance, instead of giving us the opportunity to manifest our opinions.

It seems that the situation in Peru is much more complicated. Here we see women regents, congresspersons, or other public charges, but it is just for appearances. We don't even hear talk about Indigenous women. The

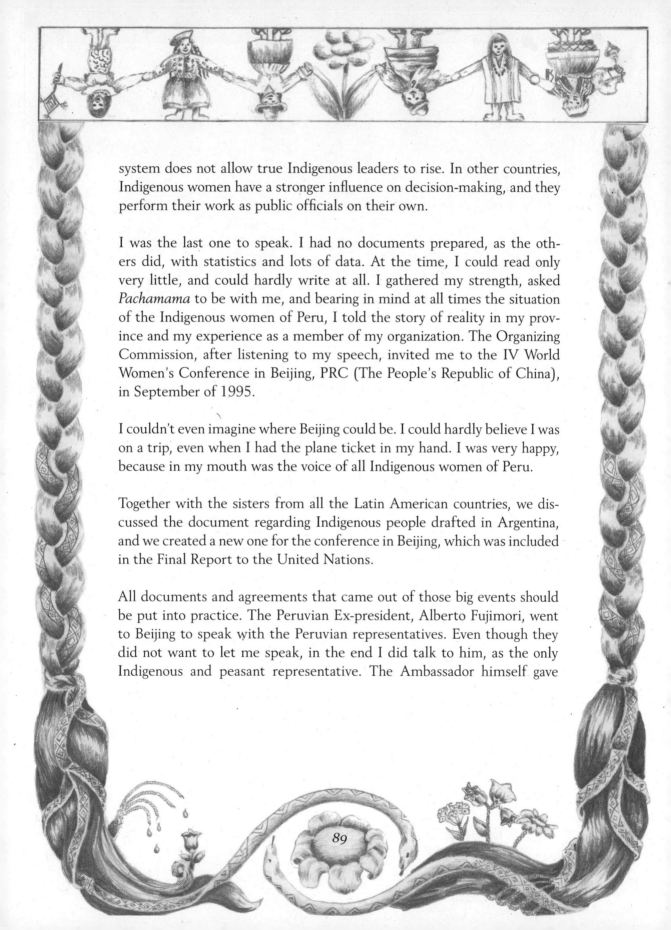

system does not allow true Indigenous leaders to rise. In other countries, Indigenous women have a stronger influence on decision-making, and they perform their work as public officials on their own.

I was the last one to speak. I had no documents prepared, as the others did, with statistics and lots of data. At the time, I could read only very little, and could hardly write at all. I gathered my strength, asked *Pachamama* to be with me, and bearing in mind at all times the situation of the Indigenous women of Peru, I told the story of reality in my province and my experience as a member of my organization. The Organizing Commission, after listening to my speech, invited me to the IV World Women's Conference in Beijing, PRC (The People's Republic of China), in September of 1995.

I couldn't even imagine where Beijing could be. I could hardly believe I was on a trip, even when I had the plane ticket in my hand. I was very happy, because in my mouth was the voice of all Indigenous women of Peru.

Together with the sisters from all the Latin American countries, we discussed the document regarding Indigenous people drafted in Argentina, and we created a new one for the conference in Beijing, which was included in the Final Report to the United Nations.

All documents and agreements that came out of those big events should be put into practice. The Peruvian Ex-president, Alberto Fujimori, went to Beijing to speak with the Peruvian representatives. Even though they did not want to let me speak, in the end I did talk to him, as the only Indigenous and peasant representative. The Ambassador himself gave

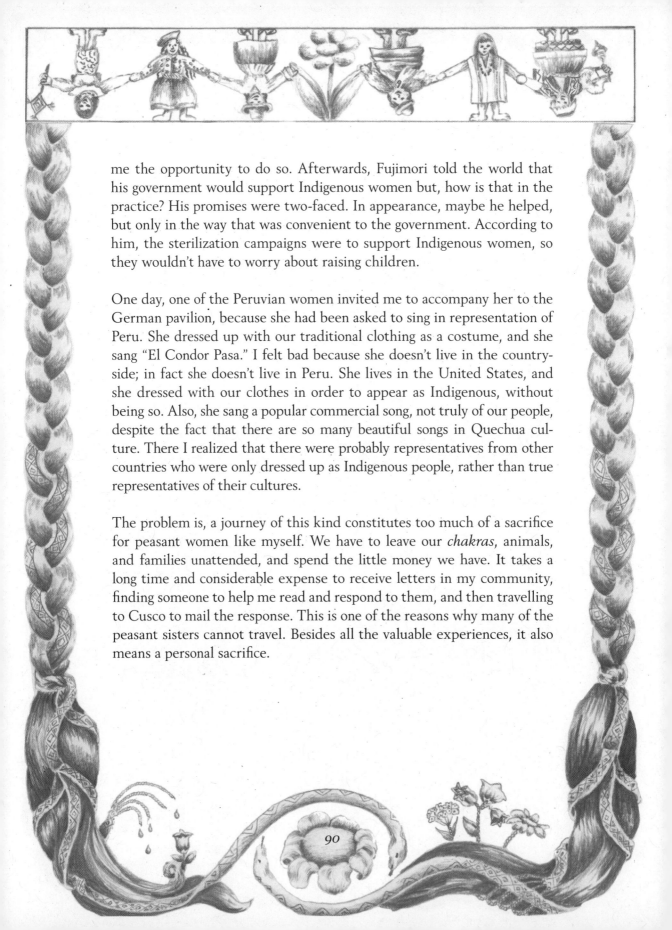

me the opportunity to do so. Afterwards, Fujimori told the world that his government would support Indigenous women but, how is that in the practice? His promises were two-faced. In appearance, maybe he helped, but only in the way that was convenient to the government. According to him, the sterilization campaigns were to support Indigenous women, so they wouldn't have to worry about raising children.

One day, one of the Peruvian women invited me to accompany her to the German pavilion, because she had been asked to sing in representation of Peru. She dressed up with our traditional clothing as a costume, and she sang "El Condor Pasa." I felt bad because she doesn't live in the countryside; in fact she doesn't live in Peru. She lives in the United States, and she dressed with our clothes in order to appear as Indigenous, without being so. Also, she sang a popular commercial song, not truly of our people, despite the fact that there are so many beautiful songs in Quechua culture. There I realized that there were probably representatives from other countries who were only dressed up as Indigenous people, rather than true representatives of their cultures.

The problem is, a journey of this kind constitutes too much of a sacrifice for peasant women like myself. We have to leave our *chakras*, animals, and families unattended, and spend the little money we have. It takes a long time and considerable expense to receive letters in my community, finding someone to help me read and respond to them, and then travelling to Cusco to mail the response. This is one of the reasons why many of the peasant sisters cannot travel. Besides all the valuable experiences, it also means a personal sacrifice.

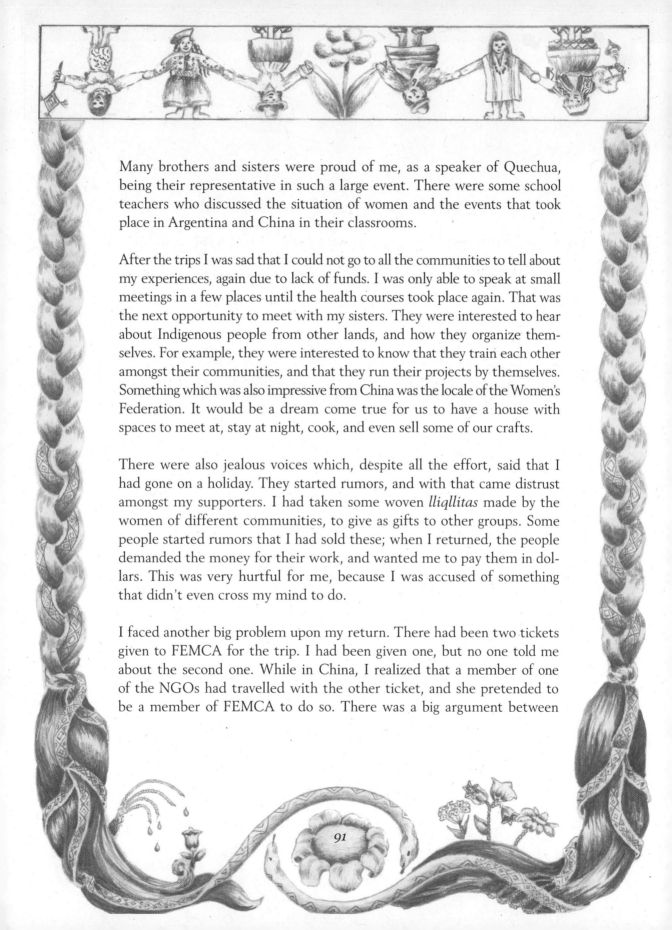

Many brothers and sisters were proud of me, as a speaker of Quechua, being their representative in such a large event. There were some school teachers who discussed the situation of women and the events that took place in Argentina and China in their classrooms.

After the trips I was sad that I could not go to all the communities to tell about my experiences, again due to lack of funds. I was only able to speak at small meetings in a few places until the health courses took place again. That was the next opportunity to meet with my sisters. They were interested to hear about Indigenous people from other lands, and how they organize themselves. For example, they were interested to know that they train each other amongst their communities, and that they run their projects by themselves. Something which was also impressive from China was the locale of the Women's Federation. It would be a dream come true for us to have a house with spaces to meet at, stay at night, cook, and even sell some of our crafts.

There were also jealous voices which, despite all the effort, said that I had gone on a holiday. They started rumors, and with that came distrust amongst my supporters. I had taken some woven *lliqllitas* made by the women of different communities, to give as gifts to other groups. Some people started rumors that I had sold these; when I returned, the people demanded the money for their work, and wanted me to pay them in dollars. This was very hurtful for me, because I was accused of something that didn't even cross my mind to do.

I faced another big problem upon my return. There had been two tickets given to FEMCA for the trip. I had been given one, but no one told me about the second one. While in China, I realized that a member of one of the NGOs had travelled with the other ticket, and she pretended to be a member of FEMCA to do so. There was a big argument between

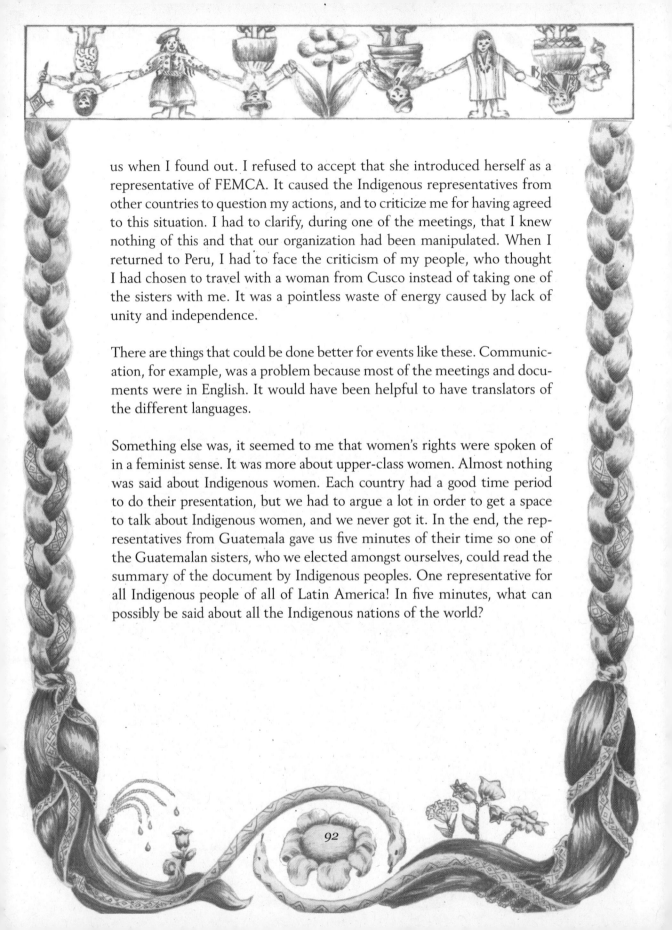

us when I found out. I refused to accept that she introduced herself as a representative of FEMCA. It caused the Indigenous representatives from other countries to question my actions, and to criticize me for having agreed to this situation. I had to clarify, during one of the meetings, that I knew nothing of this and that our organization had been manipulated. When I returned to Peru, I had to face the criticism of my people, who thought I had chosen to travel with a woman from Cusco instead of taking one of the sisters with me. It was a pointless waste of energy caused by lack of unity and independence.

There are things that could be done better for events like these. Communication, for example, was a problem because most of the meetings and documents were in English. It would have been helpful to have translators of the different languages.

Something else was, it seemed to me that women's rights were spoken of in a feminist sense. It was more about upper-class women. Almost nothing was said about Indigenous women. Each country had a good time period to do their presentation, but we had to argue a lot in order to get a space to talk about Indigenous women, and we never got it. In the end, the representatives from Guatemala gave us five minutes of their time so one of the Guatemalan sisters, who we elected amongst ourselves, could read the summary of the document by Indigenous peoples. One representative for all Indigenous people of all of Latin America! In five minutes, what can possibly be said about all the Indigenous nations of the world?

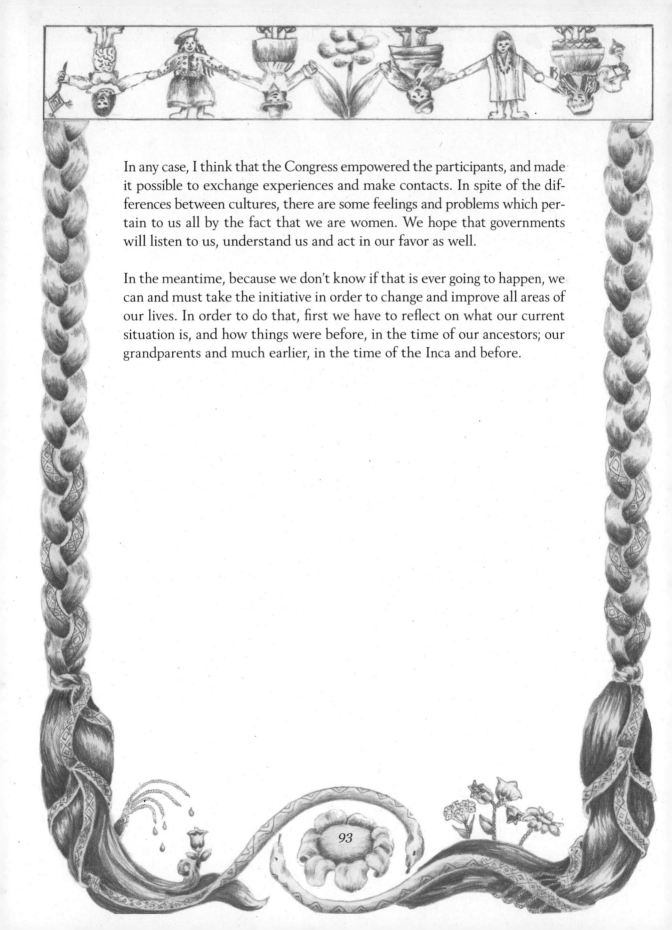

In any case, I think that the Congress empowered the participants, and made it possible to exchange experiences and make contacts. In spite of the differences between cultures, there are some feelings and problems which pertain to us all by the fact that we are women. We hope that governments will listen to us, understand us and act in our favor as well.

In the meantime, because we don't know if that is ever going to happen, we can and must take the initiative in order to change and improve all areas of our lives. In order to do that, first we have to reflect on what our current situation is, and how things were before, in the time of our ancestors; our grandparents and much earlier, in the time of the Inca and before.

QUESTIONS FOR REFLECTION

- What is your experience with meetings and events outside of your community?
- In which way can exchanges amongst leaders enrich and strengthen the people?
- Do you think that the agreements made in the large international events will be put into practice?
- What important points would you propose for the drafting of a document from Indigenous people?
- Why is it, in your opinion, that Indigenous people from other parts of the world receive more respect and better living conditions than in Peru?

1994
Argentina

"…All documents and agreements which come out of those big events should be put to practice…"

1995
China

Our Land, Our Universe

Our view of the universe
The Ayni
The search for equilibrium
About Patron Saint Festivals
Religious sects in our communities
Experiences with ancient ceremonies
from other Indigenous peoples

Questions for reflection

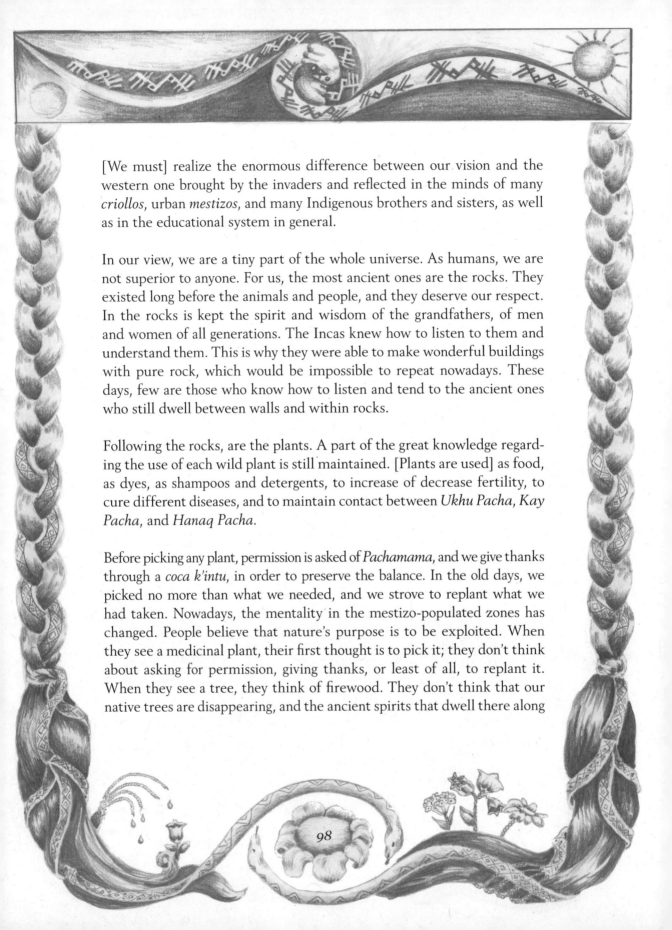

[We must] realize the enormous difference between our vision and the western one brought by the invaders and reflected in the minds of many *criollos*, urban *mestizos*, and many Indigenous brothers and sisters, as well as in the educational system in general.

In our view, we are a tiny part of the whole universe. As humans, we are not superior to anyone. For us, the most ancient ones are the rocks. They existed long before the animals and people, and they deserve our respect. In the rocks is kept the spirit and wisdom of the grandfathers, of men and women of all generations. The Incas knew how to listen to them and understand them. This is why they were able to make wonderful buildings with pure rock, which would be impossible to repeat nowadays. These days, few are those who know how to listen and tend to the ancient ones who still dwell between walls and within rocks.

Following the rocks, are the plants. A part of the great knowledge regarding the use of each wild plant is still maintained. [Plants are used] as food, as dyes, as shampoos and detergents, to increase of decrease fertility, to cure different diseases, and to maintain contact between *Ukhu Pacha*, *Kay Pacha*, and *Hanaq Pacha*.

Before picking any plant, permission is asked of *Pachamama*, and we give thanks through a *coca k'intu*, in order to preserve the balance. In the old days, we picked no more than what we needed, and we strove to replant what we had taken. Nowadays, the mentality in the mestizo-populated zones has changed. People believe that nature's purpose is to be exploited. When they see a medicinal plant, their first thought is to pick it; they don't think about asking for permission, giving thanks, or least of all, to replant it. When they see a tree, they think of firewood. They don't think that our native trees are disappearing, and the ancient spirits that dwell there along

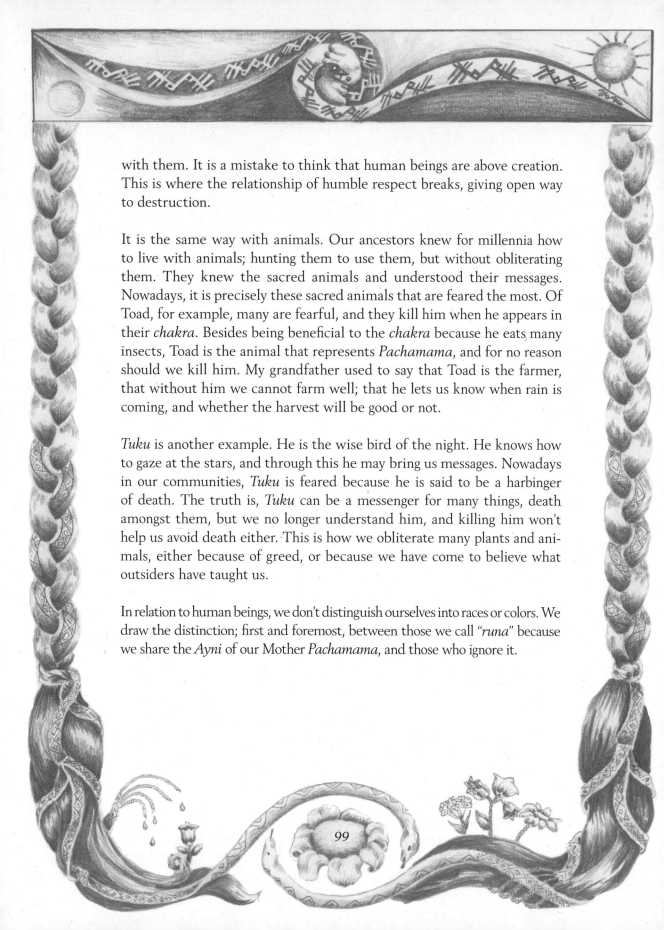

with them. It is a mistake to think that human beings are above creation. This is where the relationship of humble respect breaks, giving open way to destruction.

It is the same way with animals. Our ancestors knew for millennia how to live with animals; hunting them to use them, but without obliterating them. They knew the sacred animals and understood their messages. Nowadays, it is precisely these sacred animals that are feared the most. Of Toad, for example, many are fearful, and they kill him when he appears in their *chakra*. Besides being beneficial to the *chakra* because he eats many insects, Toad is the animal that represents *Pachamama*, and for no reason should we kill him. My grandfather used to say that Toad is the farmer, that without him we cannot farm well; that he lets us know when rain is coming, and whether the harvest will be good or not.

Tuku is another example. He is the wise bird of the night. He knows how to gaze at the stars, and through this he may bring us messages. Nowadays in our communities, *Tuku* is feared because he is said to be a harbinger of death. The truth is, *Tuku* can be a messenger for many things, death amongst them, but we no longer understand him, and killing him won't help us avoid death either. This is how we obliterate many plants and animals, either because of greed, or because we have come to believe what outsiders have taught us.

In relation to human beings, we don't distinguish ourselves into races or colors. We draw the distinction; first and foremost, between those we call "*runa*" because we share the *Ayni* of our Mother *Pachamama*, and those who ignore it.

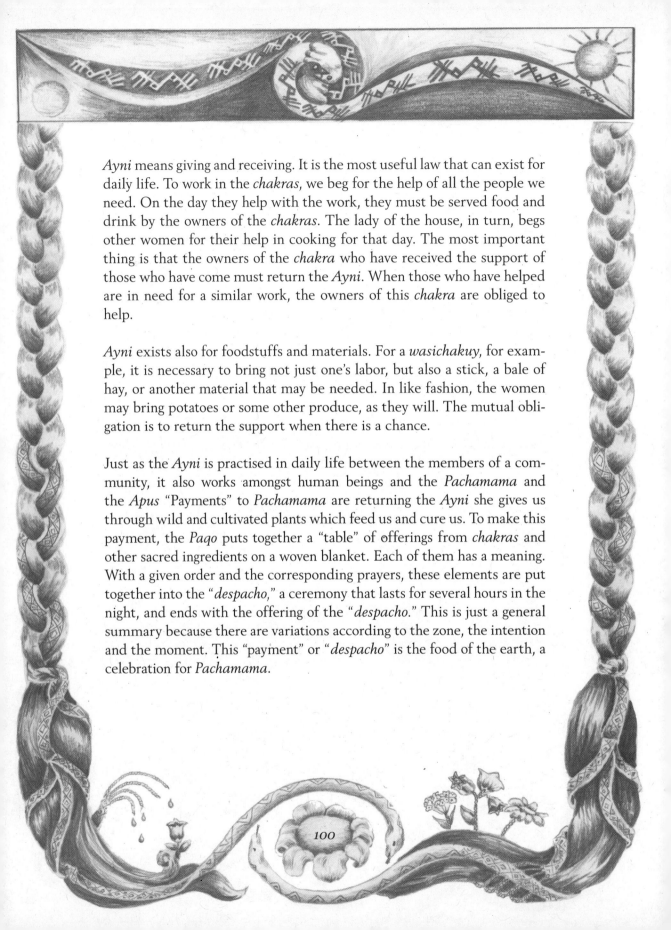

Ayni means giving and receiving. It is the most useful law that can exist for daily life. To work in the *chakras*, we beg for the help of all the people we need. On the day they help with the work, they must be served food and drink by the owners of the *chakras*. The lady of the house, in turn, begs other women for their help in cooking for that day. The most important thing is that the owners of the *chakra* who have received the support of those who have come must return the *Ayni*. When those who have helped are in need for a similar work, the owners of this *chakra* are obliged to help.

Ayni exists also for foodstuffs and materials. For a *wasichakuy*, for example, it is necessary to bring not just one's labor, but also a stick, a bale of hay, or another material that may be needed. In like fashion, the women may bring potatoes or some other produce, as they will. The mutual obligation is to return the support when there is a chance.

Just as the *Ayni* is practised in daily life between the members of a community, it also works amongst human beings and the *Pachamama* and the *Apus* "Payments" to *Pachamama* are returning the *Ayni* she gives us through wild and cultivated plants which feed us and cure us. To make this payment, the *Paqo* puts together a "table" of offerings from *chakras* and other sacred ingredients on a woven blanket. Each of them has a meaning. With a given order and the corresponding prayers, these elements are put together into the "*despacho*," a ceremony that lasts for several hours in the night, and ends with the offering of the "*despacho*." This is just a general summary because there are variations according to the zone, the intention and the moment. This "payment" or "*despacho*" is the food of the earth, a celebration for *Pachamama*.

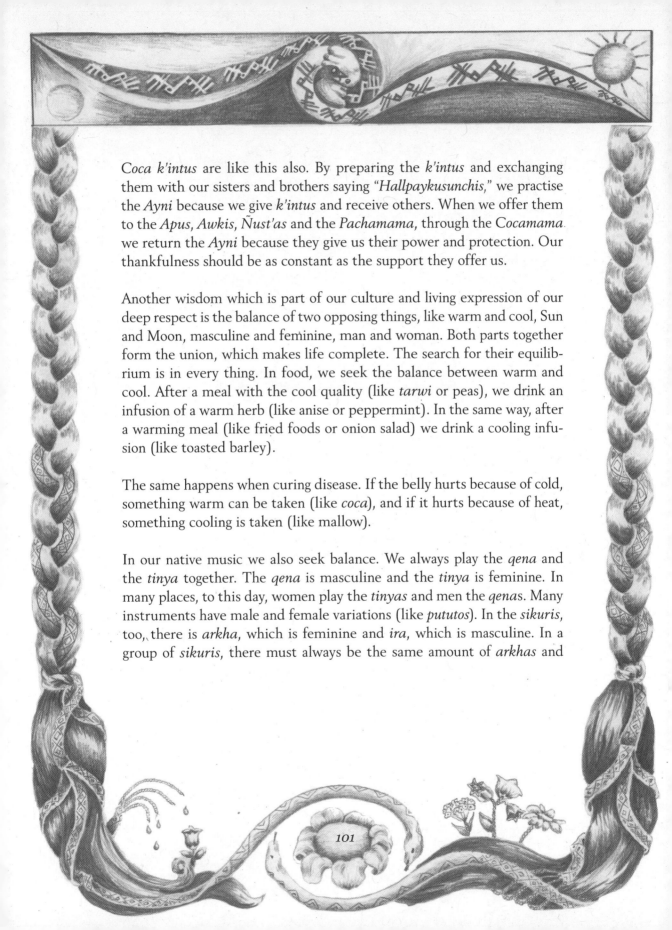

Coca k'intus are like this also. By preparing the *k'intus* and exchanging them with our sisters and brothers saying "*Hallpaykusunchis*," we practise the *Ayni* because we give *k'intus* and receive others. When we offer them to the *Apus*, *Awkis*, *Ñust'as* and the *Pachamama*, through the *Cocamama* we return the *Ayni* because they give us their power and protection. Our thankfulness should be as constant as the support they offer us.

Another wisdom which is part of our culture and living expression of our deep respect is the balance of two opposing things, like warm and cool, Sun and Moon, masculine and feminine, man and woman. Both parts together form the union, which makes life complete. The search for their equilibrium is in every thing. In food, we seek the balance between warm and cool. After a meal with the cool quality (like *tarwi* or peas), we drink an infusion of a warm herb (like anise or peppermint). In the same way, after a warming meal (like fried foods or onion salad) we drink a cooling infusion (like toasted barley).

The same happens when curing disease. If the belly hurts because of cold, something warm can be taken (like *coca*), and if it hurts because of heat, something cooling is taken (like mallow).

In our native music we also seek balance. We always play the *qena* and the *tinya* together. The *qena* is masculine and the *tinya* is feminine. In many places, to this day, women play the *tinyas* and men the *qenas*. Many instruments have male and female variations (like *pututos*). In the *sikuris*, too, there is *arkha*, which is feminine and *ira*, which is masculine. In a group of *sikuris*, there must always be the same amount of *arkhas* and

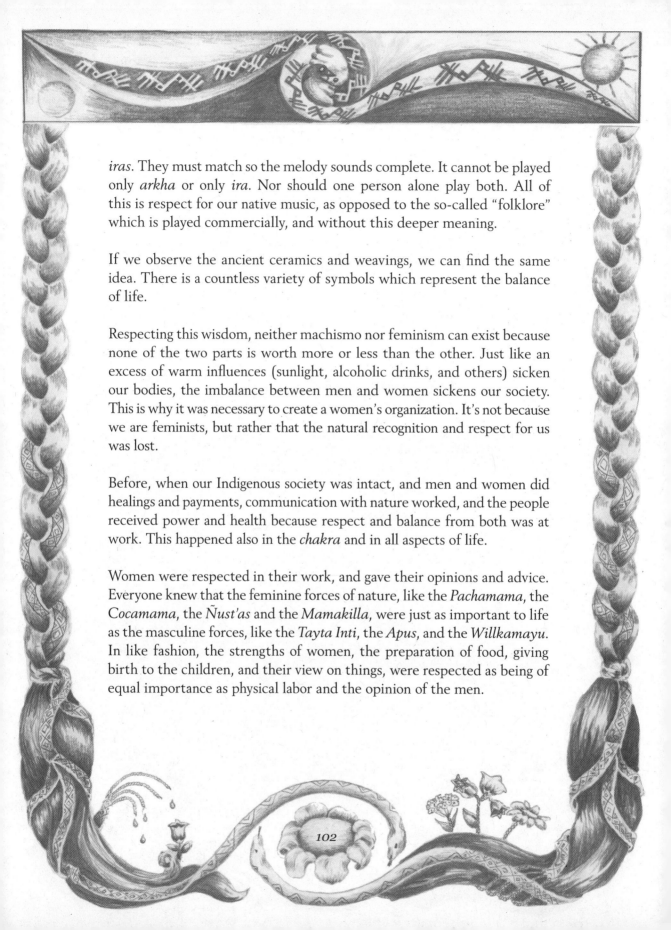

iras. They must match so the melody sounds complete. It cannot be played only *arkha* or only *ira*. Nor should one person alone play both. All of this is respect for our native music, as opposed to the so-called "folklore" which is played commercially, and without this deeper meaning.

If we observe the ancient ceramics and weavings, we can find the same idea. There is a countless variety of symbols which represent the balance of life.

Respecting this wisdom, neither machismo nor feminism can exist because none of the two parts is worth more or less than the other. Just like an excess of warm influences (sunlight, alcoholic drinks, and others) sicken our bodies, the imbalance between men and women sickens our society. This is why it was necessary to create a women's organization. It's not because we are feminists, but rather that the natural recognition and respect for us was lost.

Before, when our Indigenous society was intact, and men and women did healings and payments, communication with nature worked, and the people received power and health because respect and balance from both was at work. This happened also in the *chakra* and in all aspects of life.

Women were respected in their work, and gave their opinions and advice. Everyone knew that the feminine forces of nature, like the *Pachamama*, the *Cocamama*, the *Ñust'as* and the *Mamakilla*, were just as important to life as the masculine forces, like the *Tayta Inti*, the *Apus*, and the *Willkamayu*. In like fashion, the strengths of women, the preparation of food, giving birth to the children, and their view on things, were respected as being of equal importance as physical labor and the opinion of the men.

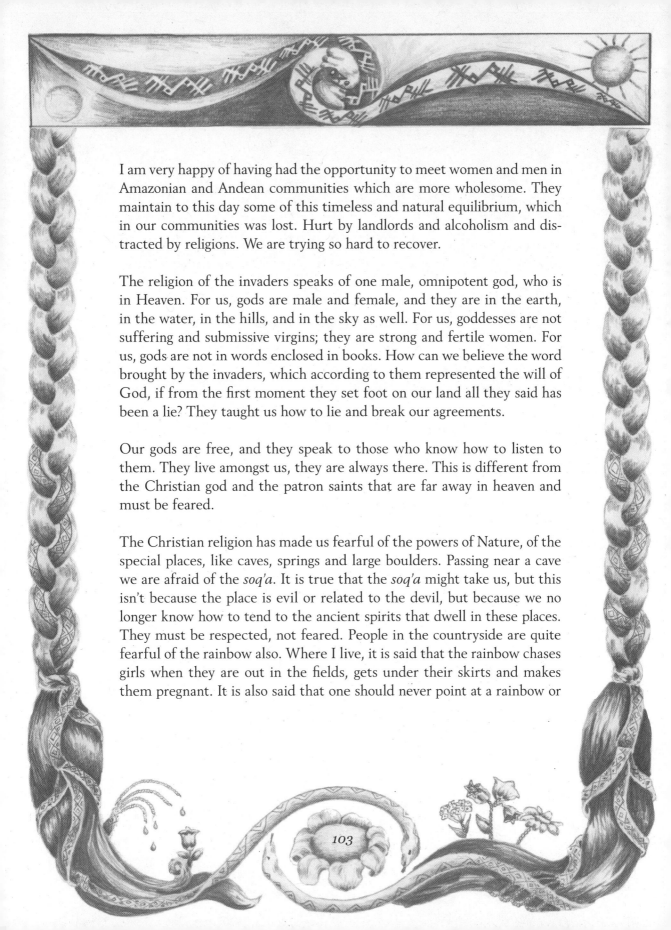

I am very happy of having had the opportunity to meet women and men in Amazonian and Andean communities which are more wholesome. They maintain to this day some of this timeless and natural equilibrium, which in our communities was lost. Hurt by landlords and alcoholism and distracted by religions. We are trying so hard to recover.

The religion of the invaders speaks of one male, omnipotent god, who is in Heaven. For us, gods are male and female, and they are in the earth, in the water, in the hills, and in the sky as well. For us, goddesses are not suffering and submissive virgins; they are strong and fertile women. For us, gods are not in words enclosed in books. How can we believe the word brought by the invaders, which according to them represented the will of God, if from the first moment they set foot on our land all they said has been a lie? They taught us how to lie and break our agreements.

Our gods are free, and they speak to those who know how to listen to them. They live amongst us, they are always there. This is different from the Christian god and the patron saints that are far away in heaven and must be feared.

The Christian religion has made us fearful of the powers of Nature, of the special places, like caves, springs and large boulders. Passing near a cave we are afraid of the *soq'a*. It is true that the *soq'a* might take us, but this isn't because the place is evil or related to the devil, but because we no longer know how to tend to the ancient spirits that dwell in these places. They must be respected, not feared. People in the countryside are quite fearful of the rainbow also. Where I live, it is said that the rainbow chases girls when they are out in the fields, gets under their skirts and makes them pregnant. It is also said that one should never point at a rainbow or

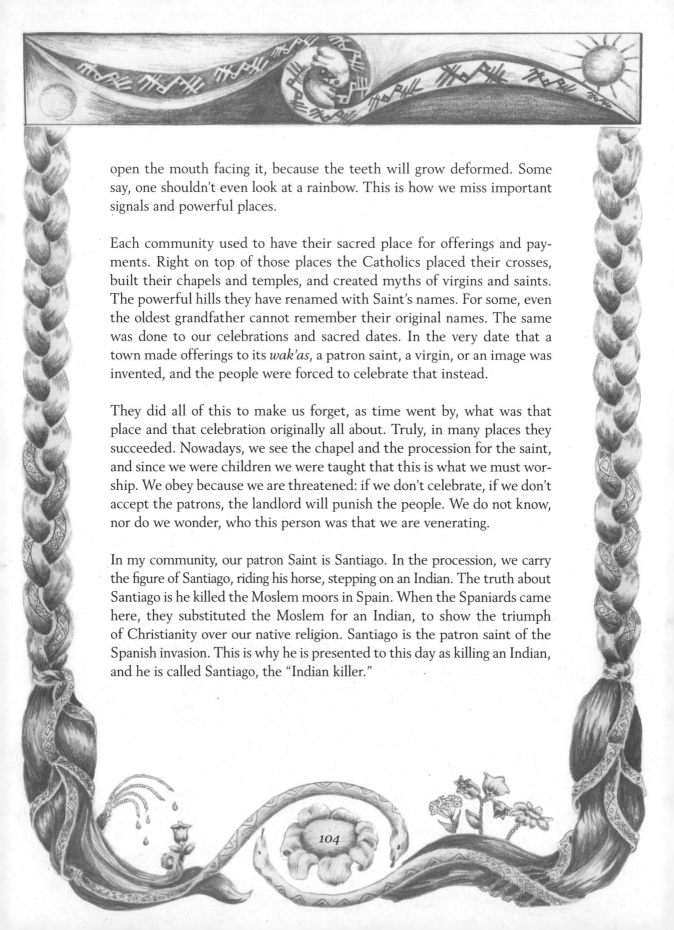

open the mouth facing it, because the teeth will grow deformed. Some say, one shouldn't even look at a rainbow. This is how we miss important signals and powerful places.

Each community used to have their sacred place for offerings and payments. Right on top of those places the Catholics placed their crosses, built their chapels and temples, and created myths of virgins and saints. The powerful hills they have renamed with Saint's names. For some, even the oldest grandfather cannot remember their original names. The same was done to our celebrations and sacred dates. In the very date that a town made offerings to its *wak'as*, a patron saint, a virgin, or an image was invented, and the people were forced to celebrate that instead.

They did all of this to make us forget, as time went by, what was that place and that celebration originally all about. Truly, in many places they succeeded. Nowadays, we see the chapel and the procession for the saint, and since we were children we were taught that this is what we must worship. We obey because we are threatened: if we don't celebrate, if we don't accept the patrons, the landlord will punish the people. We do not know, nor do we wonder, who this person was that we are venerating.

In my community, our patron Saint is Santiago. In the procession, we carry the figure of Santiago, riding his horse, stepping on an Indian. The truth about Santiago is he killed the Moslem moors in Spain. When the Spaniards came here, they substituted the Moslem for an Indian, to show the triumph of Christianity over our native religion. Santiago is the patron saint of the Spanish invasion. This is why he is presented to this day as killing an Indian, and he is called Santiago, the "Indian killer."

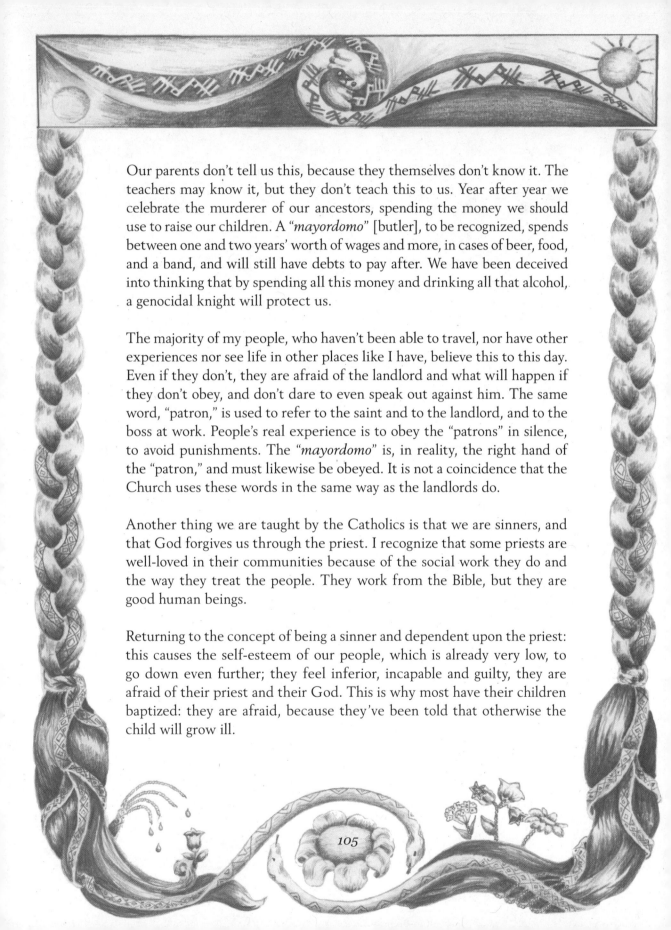

Our parents don't tell us this, because they themselves don't know it. The teachers may know it, but they don't teach this to us. Year after year we celebrate the murderer of our ancestors, spending the money we should use to raise our children. A *"mayordomo"* [butler], to be recognized, spends between one and two years' worth of wages and more, in cases of beer, food, and a band, and will still have debts to pay after. We have been deceived into thinking that by spending all this money and drinking all that alcohol, a genocidal knight will protect us.

The majority of my people, who haven't been able to travel, nor have other experiences nor see life in other places like I have, believe this to this day. Even if they don't, they are afraid of the landlord and what will happen if they don't obey, and don't dare to even speak out against him. The same word, "patron," is used to refer to the saint and to the landlord, and to the boss at work. People's real experience is to obey the "patrons" in silence, to avoid punishments. The *"mayordomo"* is, in reality, the right hand of the "patron," and must likewise be obeyed. It is not a coincidence that the Church uses these words in the same way as the landlords do.

Another thing we are taught by the Catholics is that we are sinners, and that God forgives us through the priest. I recognize that some priests are well-loved in their communities because of the social work they do and the way they treat the people. They work from the Bible, but they are good human beings.

Returning to the concept of being a sinner and dependent upon the priest: this causes the self-esteem of our people, which is already very low, to go down even further; they feel inferior, incapable and guilty, they are afraid of their priest and their God. This is why most have their children baptized: they are afraid, because they've been told that otherwise the child will grow ill.

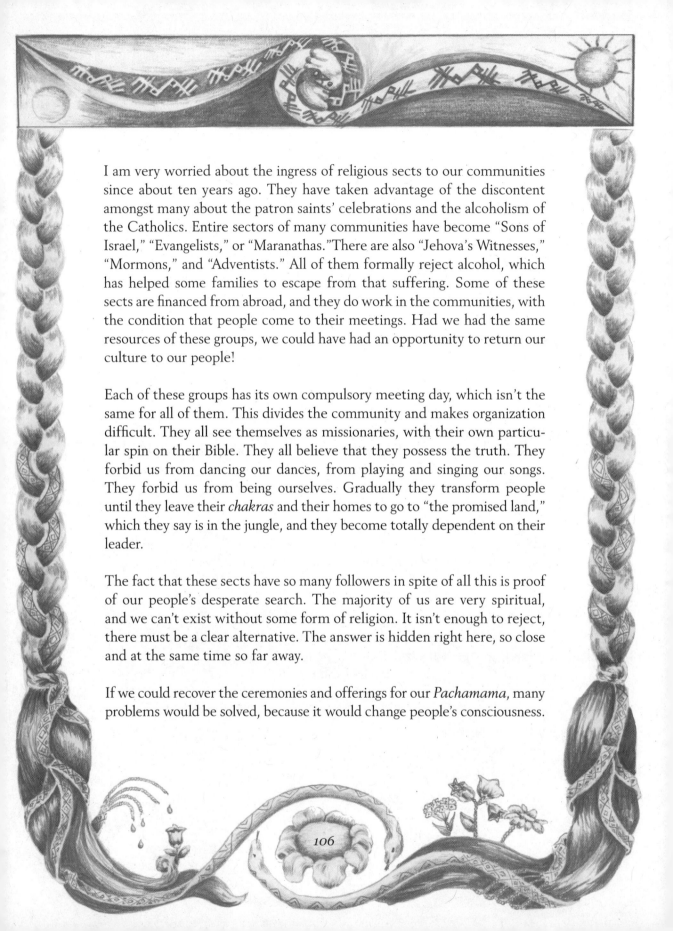

I am very worried about the ingress of religious sects to our communities since about ten years ago. They have taken advantage of the discontent amongst many about the patron saints' celebrations and the alcoholism of the Catholics. Entire sectors of many communities have become "Sons of Israel," "Evangelists," or "Maranathas." There are also "Jehova's Witnesses," "Mormons," and "Adventists." All of them formally reject alcohol, which has helped some families to escape from that suffering. Some of these sects are financed from abroad, and they do work in the communities, with the condition that people come to their meetings. Had we had the same resources of these groups, we could have had an opportunity to return our culture to our people!

Each of these groups has its own compulsory meeting day, which isn't the same for all of them. This divides the community and makes organization difficult. They all see themselves as missionaries, with their own particular spin on their Bible. They all believe that they possess the truth. They forbid us from dancing our dances, from playing and singing our songs. They forbid us from being ourselves. Gradually they transform people until they leave their *chakras* and their homes to go to "the promised land," which they say is in the jungle, and they become totally dependent on their leader.

The fact that these sects have so many followers in spite of all this is proof of our people's desperate search. The majority of us are very spiritual, and we can't exist without some form of religion. It isn't enough to reject, there must be a clear alternative. The answer is hidden right here, so close and at the same time so far away.

If we could recover the ceremonies and offerings for our *Pachamama*, many problems would be solved, because it would change people's consciousness.

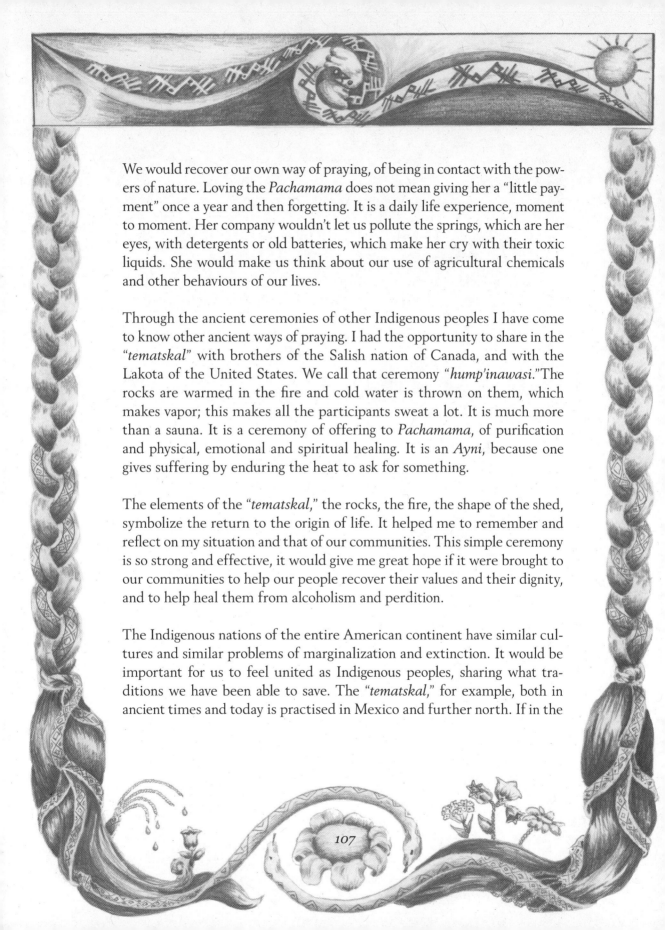

We would recover our own way of praying, of being in contact with the powers of nature. Loving the *Pachamama* does not mean giving her a "little payment" once a year and then forgetting. It is a daily life experience, moment to moment. Her company wouldn't let us pollute the springs, which are her eyes, with detergents or old batteries, which make her cry with their toxic liquids. She would make us think about our use of agricultural chemicals and other behaviours of our lives.

Through the ancient ceremonies of other Indigenous peoples I have come to know other ancient ways of praying. I had the opportunity to share in the "*tematskal*" with brothers of the Salish nation of Canada, and with the Lakota of the United States. We call that ceremony "*hump'inawasi.*" The rocks are warmed in the fire and cold water is thrown on them, which makes vapor; this makes all the participants sweat a lot. It is much more than a sauna. It is a ceremony of offering to *Pachamama*, of purification and physical, emotional and spiritual healing. It is an *Ayni*, because one gives suffering by enduring the heat to ask for something.

The elements of the "*tematskal,*" the rocks, the fire, the shape of the shed, symbolize the return to the origin of life. It helped me to remember and reflect on my situation and that of our communities. This simple ceremony is so strong and effective, it would give me great hope if it were brought to our communities to help our people recover their values and their dignity, and to help heal them from alcoholism and perdition.

The Indigenous nations of the entire American continent have similar cultures and similar problems of marginalization and extinction. It would be important for us to feel united as Indigenous peoples, sharing what traditions we have been able to save. The "*tematskal,*" for example, both in ancient times and today is practised in Mexico and further north. If in the

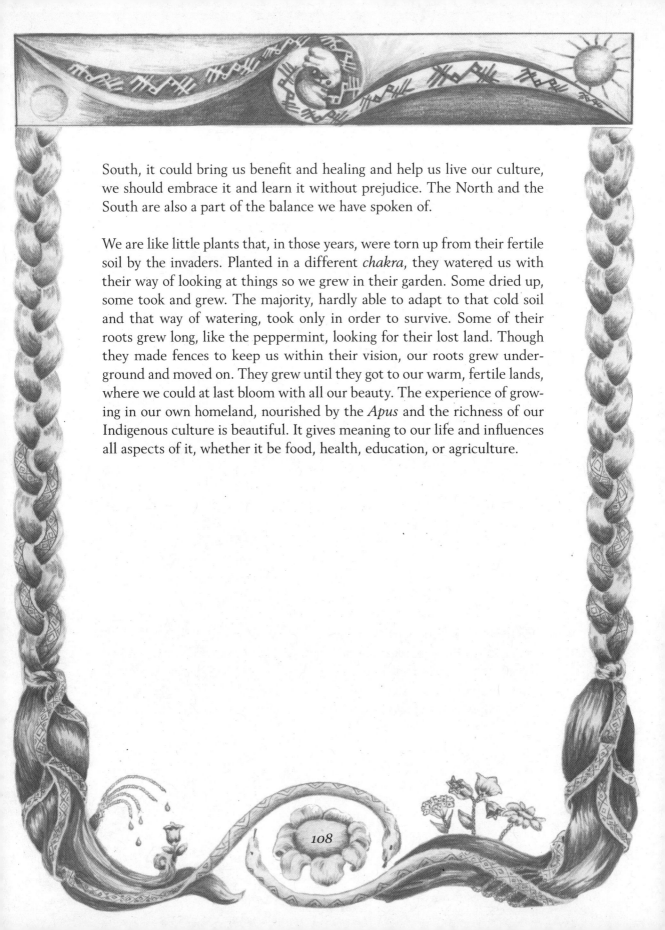

South, it could bring us benefit and healing and help us live our culture, we should embrace it and learn it without prejudice. The North and the South are also a part of the balance we have spoken of.

We are like little plants that, in those years, were torn up from their fertile soil by the invaders. Planted in a different *chakra*, they watered us with their way of looking at things so we grew in their garden. Some dried up, some took and grew. The majority, hardly able to adapt to that cold soil and that way of watering, took only in order to survive. Some of their roots grew long, like the peppermint, looking for their lost land. Though they made fences to keep us within their vision, our roots grew under-ground and moved on. They grew until they got to our warm, fertile lands, where we could at last bloom with all our beauty. The experience of grow-ing in our own homeland, nourished by the *Apus* and the richness of our Indigenous culture is beautiful. It gives meaning to our life and influences all aspects of it, whether it be food, health, education, or agriculture.

QUESTIONS FOR REFLECTION

- What are your beliefs?
- Do you believe that the Earth is alive and is our Mother?
- Why aren't there any Indigenous saints?
- Do you know why the patron saint of your community is venerated? Do you know his story?
- Why is it important to pass on the ancient wisdom to our children?

Everything is Interwoven

Causes of malnutrition in the country
About our food
About nutrition support programs
from the government and religious sects
Alternative crops

Questions for reflection

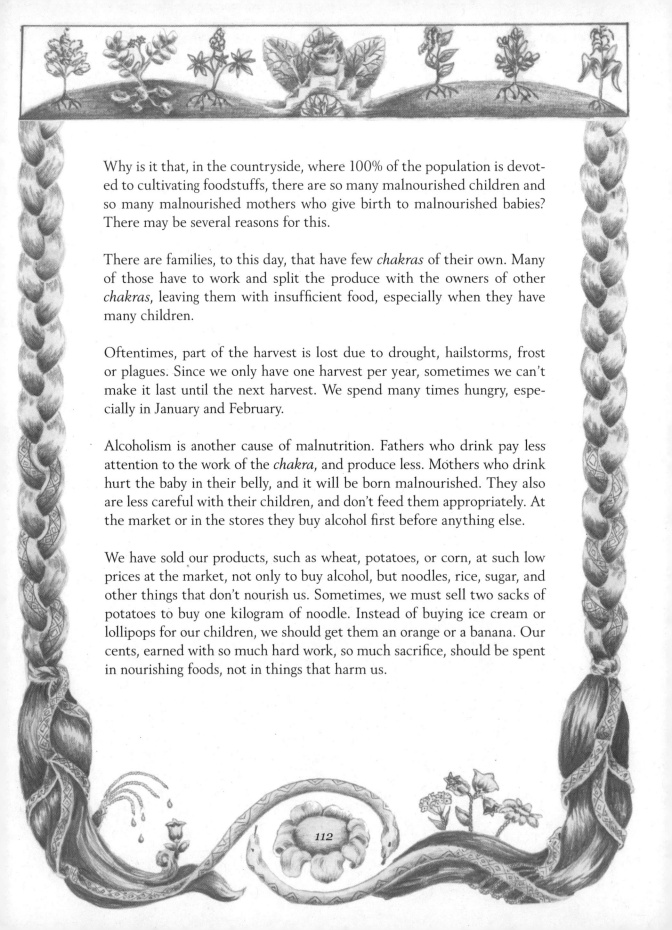

Why is it that, in the countryside, where 100% of the population is devoted to cultivating foodstuffs, there are so many malnourished children and so many malnourished mothers who give birth to malnourished babies? There may be several reasons for this.

There are families, to this day, that have few *chakras* of their own. Many of those have to work and split the produce with the owners of other *chakras*, leaving them with insufficient food, especially when they have many children.

Oftentimes, part of the harvest is lost due to drought, hailstorms, frost or plagues. Since we only have one harvest per year, sometimes we can't make it last until the next harvest. We spend many times hungry, especially in January and February.

Alcoholism is another cause of malnutrition. Fathers who drink pay less attention to the work of the *chakra*, and produce less. Mothers who drink hurt the baby in their belly, and it will be born malnourished. They also are less careful with their children, and don't feed them appropriately. At the market or in the stores they buy alcohol first before anything else.

We have sold our products, such as wheat, potatoes, or corn, at such low prices at the market, not only to buy alcohol, but noodles, rice, sugar, and other things that don't nourish us. Sometimes, we must sell two sacks of potatoes to buy one kilogram of noodle. Instead of buying ice cream or lollipops for our children, we should get them an orange or a banana. Our cents, earned with so much hard work, so much sacrifice, should be spent in nourishing foods, not in things that harm us.

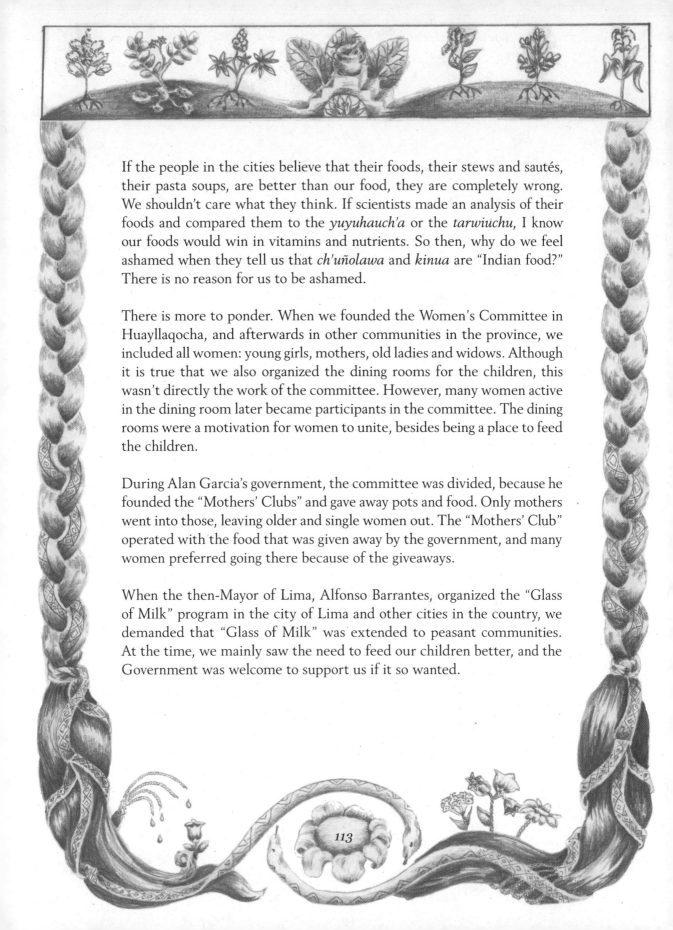

If the people in the cities believe that their foods, their stews and sautés, their pasta soups, are better than our food, they are completely wrong. We shouldn't care what they think. If scientists made an analysis of their foods and compared them to the *yuyuhauch'a* or the *tarwiuchu*, I know our foods would win in vitamins and nutrients. So then, why do we feel ashamed when they tell us that *ch'uñolawa* and *kinua* are "Indian food?" There is no reason for us to be ashamed.

There is more to ponder. When we founded the Women's Committee in Huayllaqocha, and afterwards in other communities in the province, we included all women: young girls, mothers, old ladies and widows. Although it is true that we also organized the dining rooms for the children, this wasn't directly the work of the committee. However, many women active in the dining room later became participants in the committee. The dining rooms were a motivation for women to unite, besides being a place to feed the children.

During Alan Garcia's government, the committee was divided, because he founded the "Mothers' Clubs" and gave away pots and food. Only mothers went into those, leaving older and single women out. The "Mothers' Club" operated with the food that was given away by the government, and many women preferred going there because of the giveaways.

When the then-Mayor of Lima, Alfonso Barrantes, organized the "Glass of Milk" program in the city of Lima and other cities in the country, we demanded that "Glass of Milk" was extended to peasant communities. At the time, we mainly saw the need to feed our children better, and the Government was welcome to support us if it so wanted.

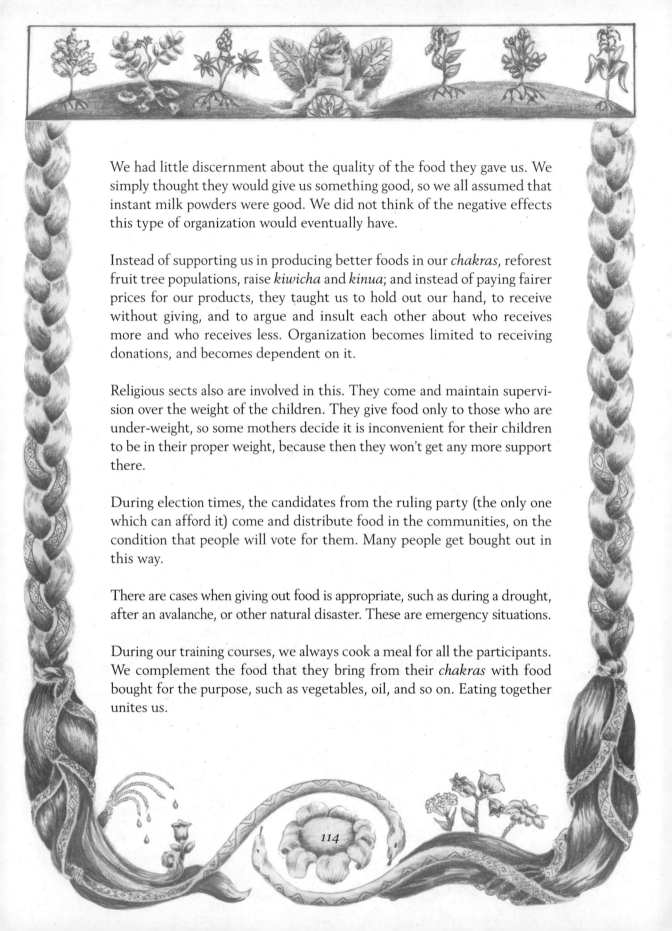

We had little discernment about the quality of the food they gave us. We simply thought they would give us something good, so we all assumed that instant milk powders were good. We did not think of the negative effects this type of organization would eventually have.

Instead of supporting us in producing better foods in our *chakras*, reforest fruit tree populations, raise *kiwicha* and *kinua*; and instead of paying fairer prices for our products, they taught us to hold out our hand, to receive without giving, and to argue and insult each other about who receives more and who receives less. Organization becomes limited to receiving donations, and becomes dependent on it.

Religious sects also are involved in this. They come and maintain supervision over the weight of the children. They give food only to those who are under-weight, so some mothers decide it is inconvenient for their children to be in their proper weight, because then they won't get any more support there.

During election times, the candidates from the ruling party (the only one which can afford it) come and distribute food in the communities, on the condition that people will vote for them. Many people get bought out in this way.

There are cases when giving out food is appropriate, such as during a drought, after an avalanche, or other natural disaster. These are emergency situations.

During our training courses, we always cook a meal for all the participants. We complement the food that they bring from their *chakras* with food bought for the purpose, such as vegetables, oil, and so on. Eating together unites us.

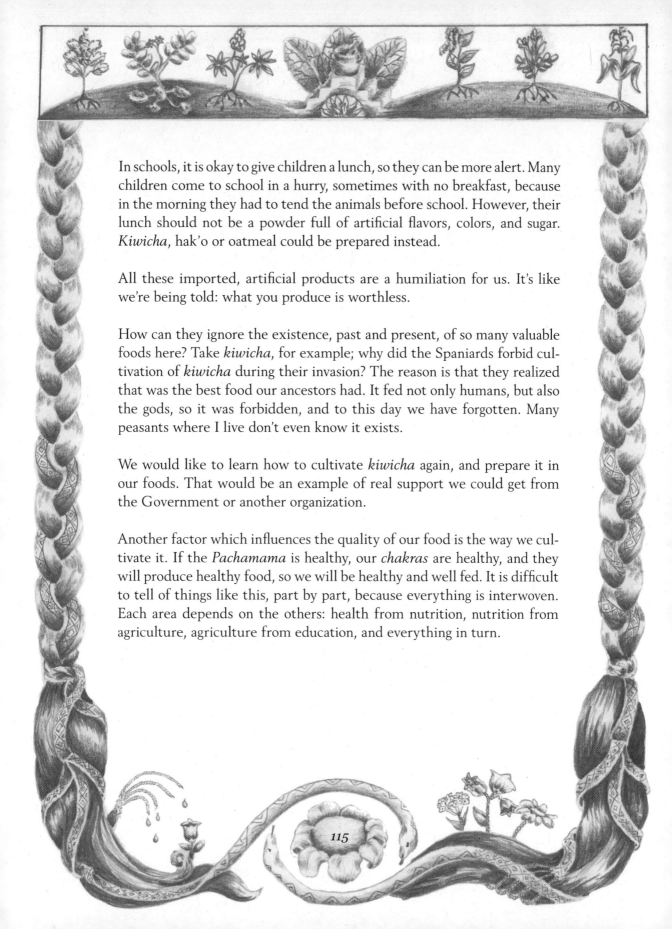

In schools, it is okay to give children a lunch, so they can be more alert. Many children come to school in a hurry, sometimes with no breakfast, because in the morning they had to tend the animals before school. However, their lunch should not be a powder full of artificial flavors, colors, and sugar. *Kiwicha*, hak'o or oatmeal could be prepared instead.

All these imported, artificial products are a humiliation for us. It's like we're being told: what you produce is worthless.

How can they ignore the existence, past and present, of so many valuable foods here? Take *kiwicha*, for example; why did the Spaniards forbid cultivation of *kiwicha* during their invasion? The reason is that they realized that was the best food our ancestors had. It fed not only humans, but also the gods, so it was forbidden, and to this day we have forgotten. Many peasants where I live don't even know it exists.

We would like to learn how to cultivate *kiwicha* again, and prepare it in our foods. That would be an example of real support we could get from the Government or another organization.

Another factor which influences the quality of our food is the way we cultivate it. If the *Pachamama* is healthy, our *chakras* are healthy, and they will produce healthy food, so we will be healthy and well fed. It is difficult to tell of things like this, part by part, because everything is interwoven. Each area depends on the others: health from nutrition, nutrition from agriculture, agriculture from education, and everything in turn.

QUESTIONS FOR REFLECTION

- How could the diet of the children in your community be improved?
- What problems do you see in the nutritional aids we get from the Government and from religious organizations in the country?
- Do you cook Andean or non-native (to your region) foodstuffs?
- Which Indigenous recipes do you know that you can share?
- How would you complement your produce with others like kiwicha, kinua, and vegetables?
- Which wild herbs do you use to enrich your food with vitamins?

Why do we feel ashamed when they tell us that ch'uñolawa and kinwa are "Indian food"? There is no reason for us to be ashamed.

The preparation of the food is one of the main tasks of the peasant women.

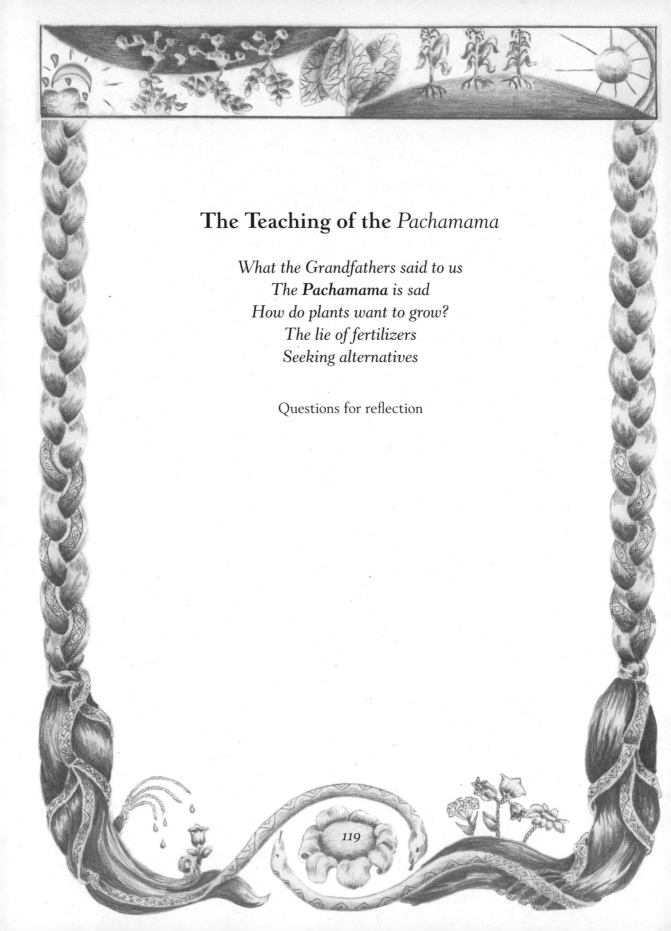

The Teaching of the *Pachamama*

What the Grandfathers said to us
*The **Pachamama** is sad*
How do plants want to grow?
The lie of fertilizers
Seeking alternatives

Questions for reflection

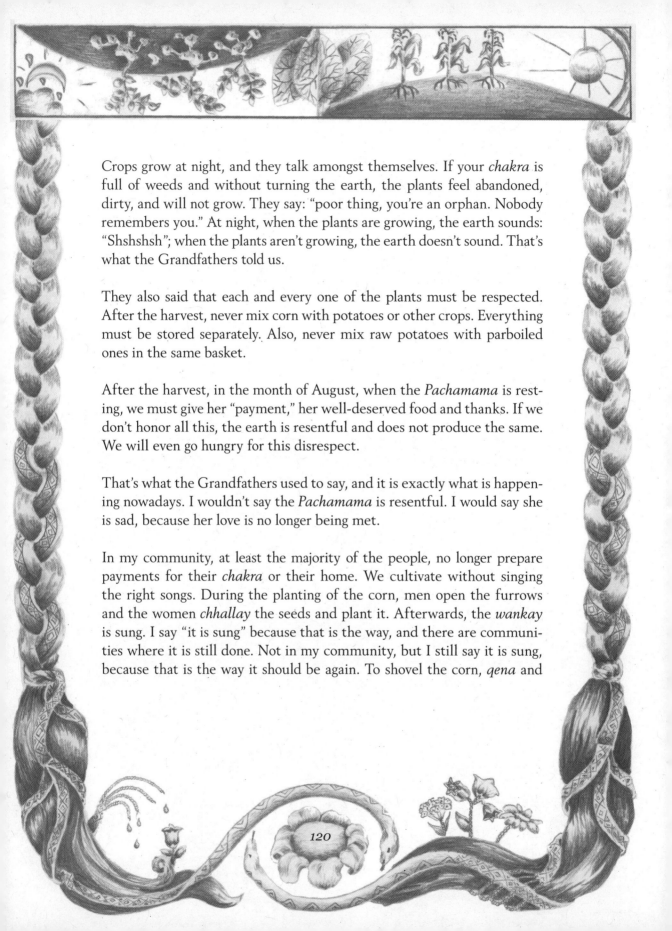

Crops grow at night, and they talk amongst themselves. If your *chakra* is full of weeds and without turning the earth, the plants feel abandoned, dirty, and will not grow. They say: "poor thing, you're an orphan. Nobody remembers you." At night, when the plants are growing, the earth sounds: "Shshshsh"; when the plants aren't growing, the earth doesn't sound. That's what the Grandfathers told us.

They also said that each and every one of the plants must be respected. After the harvest, never mix corn with potatoes or other crops. Everything must be stored separately. Also, never mix raw potatoes with parboiled ones in the same basket.

After the harvest, in the month of August, when the *Pachamama* is resting, we must give her "payment," her well-deserved food and thanks. If we don't honor all this, the earth is resentful and does not produce the same. We will even go hungry for this disrespect.

That's what the Grandfathers used to say, and it is exactly what is happening nowadays. I wouldn't say the *Pachamama* is resentful. I would say she is sad, because her love is no longer being met.

In my community, at least the majority of the people, no longer prepare payments for their *chakra* or their home. We cultivate without singing the right songs. During the planting of the corn, men open the furrows and the women *chhallay* the seeds and plant it. Afterwards, the *wankay* is sung. I say "it is sung" because that is the way, and there are communities where it is still done. Not in my community, but I still say it is sung, because that is the way it should be again. To shovel the corn, *qena* and

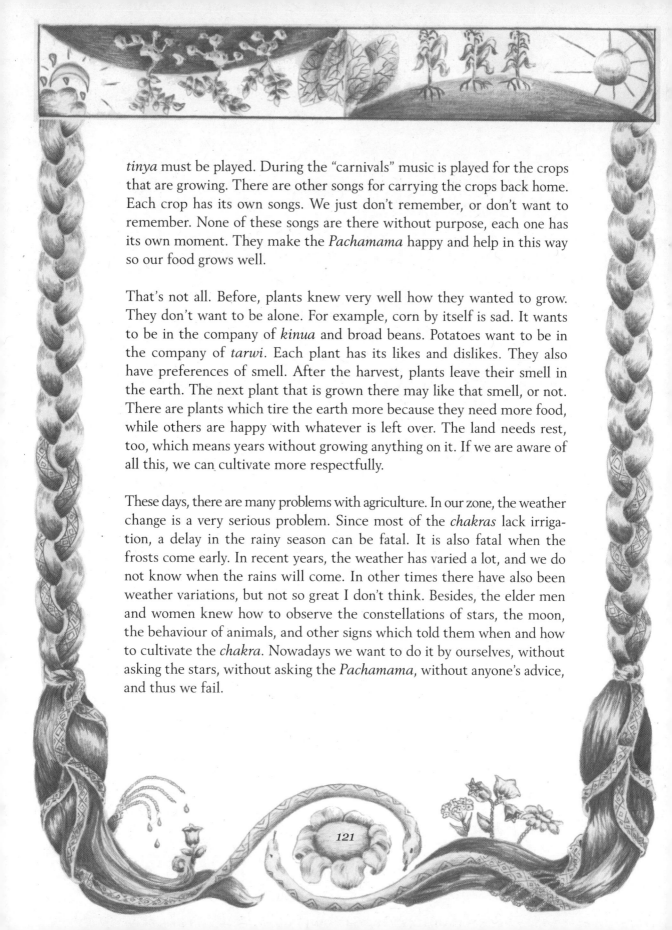

tinya must be played. During the "carnivals" music is played for the crops that are growing. There are other songs for carrying the crops back home. Each crop has its own songs. We just don't remember, or don't want to remember. None of these songs are there without purpose, each one has its own moment. They make the *Pachamama* happy and help in this way so our food grows well.

That's not all. Before, plants knew very well how they wanted to grow. They don't want to be alone. For example, corn by itself is sad. It wants to be in the company of *kinua* and broad beans. Potatoes want to be in the company of *tarwi*. Each plant has its likes and dislikes. They also have preferences of smell. After the harvest, plants leave their smell in the earth. The next plant that is grown there may like that smell, or not. There are plants which tire the earth more because they need more food, while others are happy with whatever is left over. The land needs rest, too, which means years without growing anything on it. If we are aware of all this, we can cultivate more respectfully.

These days, there are many problems with agriculture. In our zone, the weather change is a very serious problem. Since most of the *chakras* lack irrigation, a delay in the rainy season can be fatal. It is also fatal when the frosts come early. In recent years, the weather has varied a lot, and we do not know when the rains will come. In other times there have also been weather variations, but not so great I don't think. Besides, the elder men and women knew how to observe the constellations of stars, the moon, the behaviour of animals, and other signs which told them when and how to cultivate the *chakra*. Nowadays we want to do it by ourselves, without asking the stars, without asking the *Pachamama*, without anyone's advice, and thus we fail.

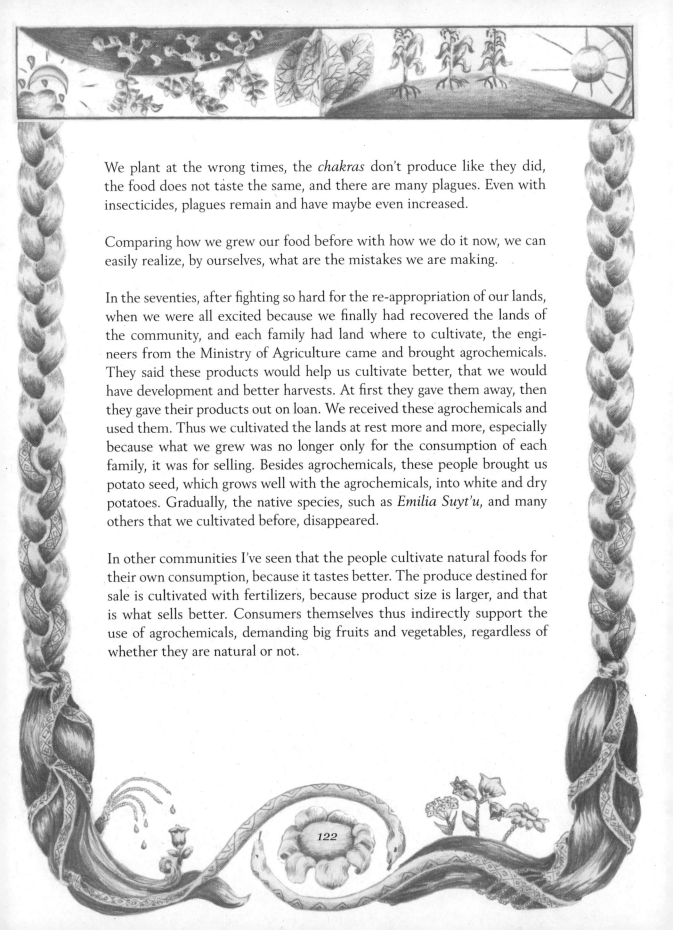

We plant at the wrong times, the *chakras* don't produce like they did, the food does not taste the same, and there are many plagues. Even with insecticides, plagues remain and have maybe even increased.

Comparing how we grew our food before with how we do it now, we can easily realize, by ourselves, what are the mistakes we are making.

In the seventies, after fighting so hard for the re-appropriation of our lands, when we were all excited because we finally had recovered the lands of the community, and each family had land where to cultivate, the engineers from the Ministry of Agriculture came and brought agrochemicals. They said these products would help us cultivate better, that we would have development and better harvests. At first they gave them away, then they gave their products out on loan. We received these agrochemicals and used them. Thus we cultivated the lands at rest more and more, especially because what we grew was no longer only for the consumption of each family, it was for selling. Besides agrochemicals, these people brought us potato seed, which grows well with the agrochemicals, into white and dry potatoes. Gradually, the native species, such as *Emilia Suyt'u*, and many others that we cultivated before, disappeared.

In other communities I've seen that the people cultivate natural foods for their own consumption, because it tastes better. The produce destined for sale is cultivated with fertilizers, because product size is larger, and that is what sells better. Consumers themselves thus indirectly support the use of agrochemicals, demanding big fruits and vegetables, regardless of whether they are natural or not.

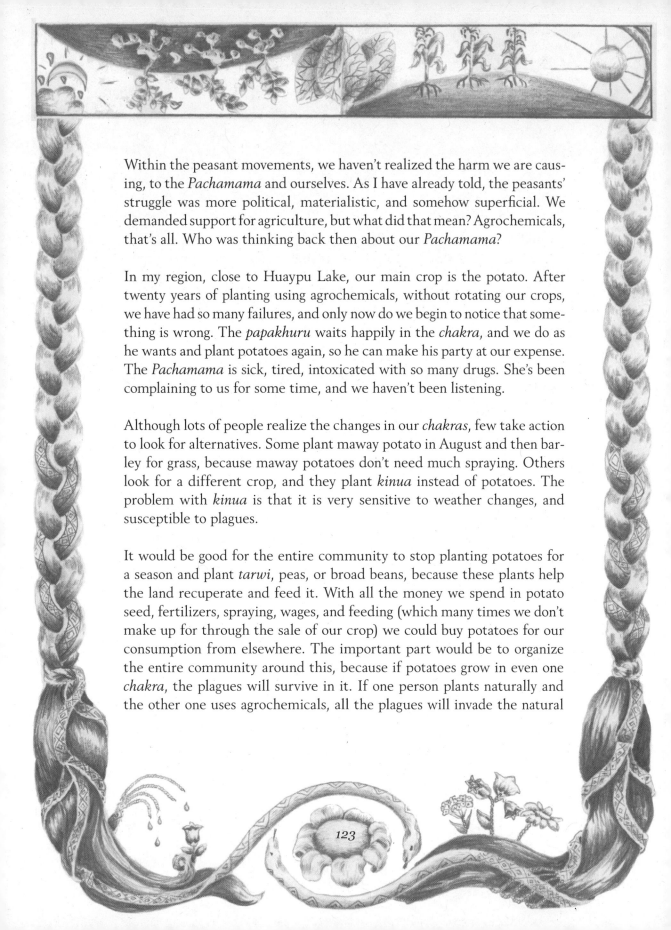

Within the peasant movements, we haven't realized the harm we are causing, to the *Pachamama* and ourselves. As I have already told, the peasants' struggle was more political, materialistic, and somehow superficial. We demanded support for agriculture, but what did that mean? Agrochemicals, that's all. Who was thinking back then about our *Pachamama*?

In my region, close to Huaypu Lake, our main crop is the potato. After twenty years of planting using agrochemicals, without rotating our crops, we have had so many failures, and only now do we begin to notice that something is wrong. The *papakhuru* waits happily in the *chakra*, and we do as he wants and plant potatoes again, so he can make his party at our expense. The *Pachamama* is sick, tired, intoxicated with so many drugs. She's been complaining to us for some time, and we haven't been listening.

Although lots of people realize the changes in our *chakras*, few take action to look for alternatives. Some plant maway potato in August and then barley for grass, because maway potatoes don't need much spraying. Others look for a different crop, and they plant *kinua* instead of potatoes. The problem with *kinua* is that it is very sensitive to weather changes, and susceptible to plagues.

It would be good for the entire community to stop planting potatoes for a season and plant *tarwi*, peas, or broad beans, because these plants help the land recuperate and feed it. With all the money we spend in potato seed, fertilizers, spraying, wages, and feeding (which many times we don't make up for through the sale of our crop) we could buy potatoes for our consumption from elsewhere. The important part would be to organize the entire community around this, because if potatoes grow in even one *chakra*, the plagues will survive in it. If one person plants naturally and the other one uses agrochemicals, all the plagues will invade the natural

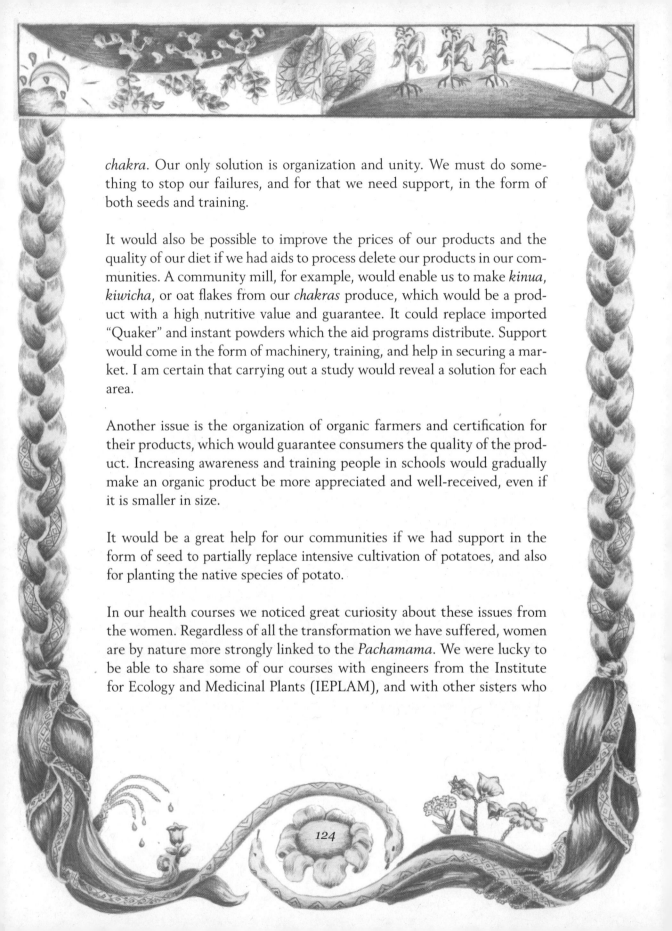

chakra. Our only solution is organization and unity. We must do something to stop our failures, and for that we need support, in the form of both seeds and training.

It would also be possible to improve the prices of our products and the quality of our diet if we had aids to process delete our products in our communities. A community mill, for example, would enable us to make *kinua*, *kiwicha*, or oat flakes from our *chakras* produce, which would be a product with a high nutritive value and guarantee. It could replace imported "Quaker" and instant powders which the aid programs distribute. Support would come in the form of machinery, training, and help in securing a market. I am certain that carrying out a study would reveal a solution for each area.

Another issue is the organization of organic farmers and certification for their products, which would guarantee consumers the quality of the product. Increasing awareness and training people in schools would gradually make an organic product be more appreciated and well-received, even if it is smaller in size.

It would be a great help for our communities if we had support in the form of seed to partially replace intensive cultivation of potatoes, and also for planting the native species of potato.

In our health courses we noticed great curiosity about these issues from the women. Regardless of all the transformation we have suffered, women are by nature more strongly linked to the *Pachamama*. We were lucky to be able to share some of our courses with engineers from the Institute for Ecology and Medicinal Plants (IEPLAM), and with other sisters who

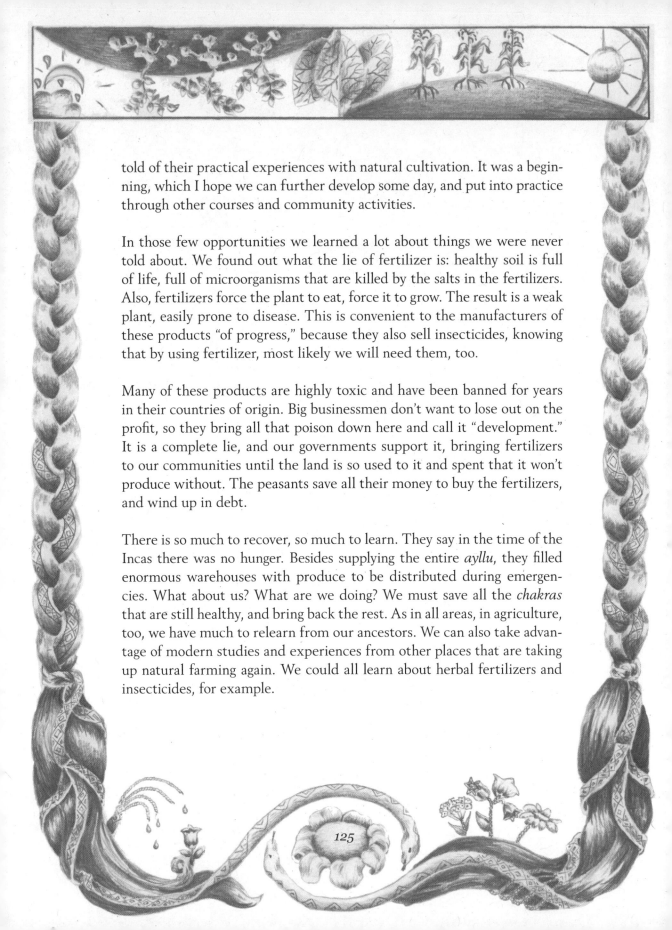

told of their practical experiences with natural cultivation. It was a beginning, which I hope we can further develop some day, and put into practice through other courses and community activities.

In those few opportunities we learned a lot about things we were never told about. We found out what the lie of fertilizer is: healthy soil is full of life, full of microorganisms that are killed by the salts in the fertilizers. Also, fertilizers force the plant to eat, force it to grow. The result is a weak plant, easily prone to disease. This is convenient to the manufacturers of these products "of progress," because they also sell insecticides, knowing that by using fertilizer, most likely we will need them, too.

Many of these products are highly toxic and have been banned for years in their countries of origin. Big businessmen don't want to lose out on the profit, so they bring all that poison down here and call it "development." It is a complete lie, and our governments support it, bringing fertilizers to our communities until the land is so used to it and spent that it won't produce without. The peasants save all their money to buy the fertilizers, and wind up in debt.

There is so much to recover, so much to learn. They say in the time of the Incas there was no hunger. Besides supplying the entire *ayllu*, they filled enormous warehouses with produce to be distributed during emergencies. What about us? What are we doing? We must save all the *chakras* that are still healthy, and bring back the rest. As in all areas, in agriculture, too, we have much to relearn from our ancestors. We can also take advantage of modern studies and experiences from other places that are taking up natural farming again. We could all learn about herbal fertilizers and insecticides, for example.

Our sister Maritza Marcavillaca, member of the community of Urquillos (Urubamba province) has been practicing for several years in various communities in her district what they call "Integrated Handling of Plagues," see appendix C. We would like more opportunities to become acquainted with these valuable experiences which teach us that indeed, united and determined, we can change many things.

Besides all the ecological knowledge and practices, which are very important, for me the most important change would be to return to living, talking, eating, drinking and singing with our mother *Pachamama*. We should not forget to offer her *kokita*, and let her teach us directly how to live in harmony and respect.

QUESTIONS FOR REFLECTION

- What crops are cultivated in your community?
- Which traditional, natural cultivation methods do people in your community practise (for example, *muyuy*, herbal preparations, companion planting)?
- Which recipes do you know that you can share?
- What consequences do you see in your community because of the use of agrochemicals?
- Is there awareness in your community about the real situation of the land?
- Why do you think it is important to reduce or avoid the use of agrochemicals?
- Are you interested in learning about natural farming and practicing it again?
- Which customs of respect to the earth, the water, and nature are practised in your community (for example songs, celebrations, offerings)?
- Why do you think the "payments" to the Pachamama are important?
- Which foods could be processed in your community? What kind of support/aid would that require?

"...If the Pachamama is healthy, our chakras are healthy, and they will produce healthy food, so we will be healthy and well fed..."

Human Beings and Nature are One

We must learn to love ourselves
Of healers and midwives
Public education is different from our reality
The sterilization campaigns of the Health Ministry
Repression instead of treatment
Training in traditional Andean medicine

Questions for reflection

I have personally given some preference to the topic of health in my presentations, talks, and training courses. Perhaps it is because of my own situation, handicapped by arthritis, that I feel very strongly about the value of a healthy body and the integrated health of body, mind, and spirit, free of physical blows, screams, and mistreatment.

The emotional state of the woman has quite an influence in the home. If a woman is not acknowledged for her daily work, she doesn't love herself, doesn't take care of her body, and lets others do with her what they will. A woman with a weak body, for example, because of lack of adequate rest after giving birth, and treated without care, suffers greatly and her children as well. A woman who cannot esteem her own body and her own work can hardly live a healthy life. When she falls ill, when she feels unwell, she simply bears it, because she is used to suffering, and does not seek timely treatment. Although women are generally the healers at home, using local herbs to care for their children and their family, they take care of themselves last. We must learn to love ourselves.

Many women in the country know something about medicinal herbs. However, it is always necessary to have a specialist close by; a healer, midwife, or *paqo*. The *paqos* not only cure people; they also heal the *Pachamama*, and are in constant contact with all spiritual beings. In many cases of illness there is an imbalance, not only inside the person but between the person and their surroundings –that is to say, nature, where they live. *Soq'a* and *Puqio*, for example, are diseases that are difficult or even impossible to heal without a healer. *Soq'a* are ancient winds that come out of old trees, caves, or under rocks. They make the whole body hurt, and the hands and feet shrink. *Puqio* are energies from springs, which cause wounds in the whole body. The healer cures these with prayers, "*despachos*," and special preparations made from different herbs.

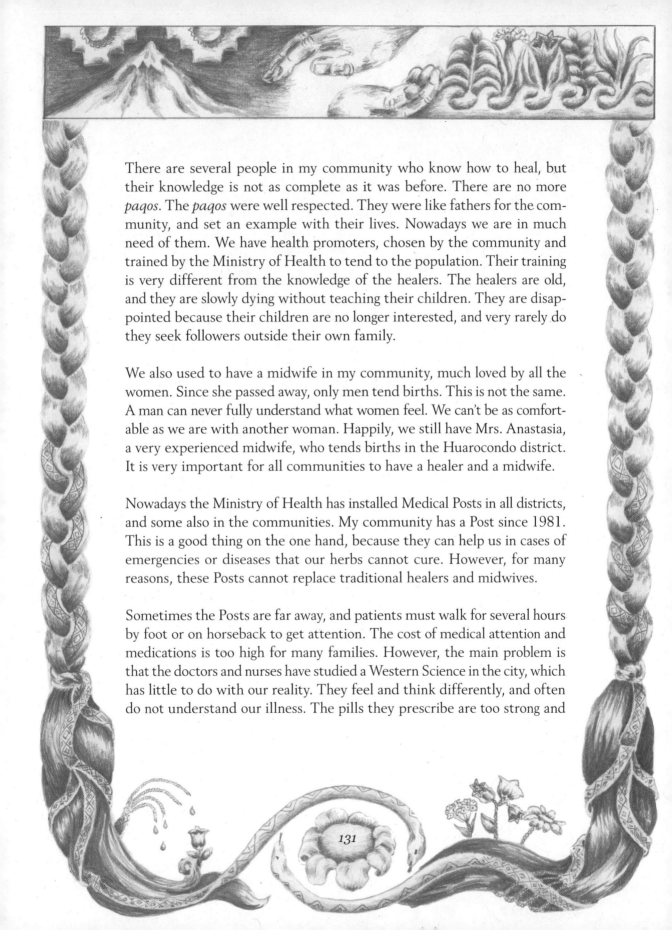

There are several people in my community who know how to heal, but their knowledge is not as complete as it was before. There are no more *paqos*. The *paqos* were well respected. They were like fathers for the community, and set an example with their lives. Nowadays we are in much need of them. We have health promoters, chosen by the community and trained by the Ministry of Health to tend to the population. Their training is very different from the knowledge of the healers. The healers are old, and they are slowly dying without teaching their children. They are disappointed because their children are no longer interested, and very rarely do they seek followers outside their own family.

We also used to have a midwife in my community, much loved by all the women. Since she passed away, only men tend births. This is not the same. A man can never fully understand what women feel. We can't be as comfortable as we are with another woman. Happily, we still have Mrs. Anastasia, a very experienced midwife, who tends births in the Huarocondo district. It is very important for all communities to have a healer and a midwife.

Nowadays the Ministry of Health has installed Medical Posts in all districts, and some also in the communities. My community has a Post since 1981. This is a good thing on the one hand, because they can help us in cases of emergencies or diseases that our herbs cannot cure. However, for many reasons, these Posts cannot replace traditional healers and midwives.

Sometimes the Posts are far away, and patients must walk for several hours by foot or on horseback to get attention. The cost of medical attention and medications is too high for many families. However, the main problem is that the doctors and nurses have studied a Western Science in the city, which has little to do with our reality. They feel and think differently, and often do not understand our illness. The pills they prescribe are too strong and

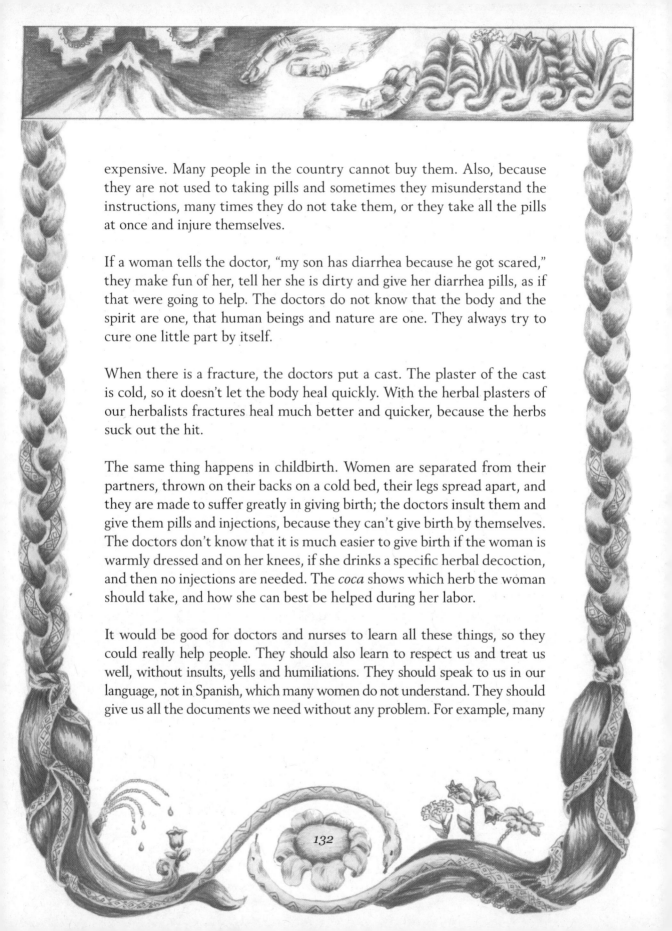

expensive. Many people in the country cannot buy them. Also, because they are not used to taking pills and sometimes they misunderstand the instructions, many times they do not take them, or they take all the pills at once and injure themselves.

If a woman tells the doctor, "my son has diarrhea because he got scared," they make fun of her, tell her she is dirty and give her diarrhea pills, as if that were going to help. The doctors do not know that the body and the spirit are one, that human beings and nature are one. They always try to cure one little part by itself.

When there is a fracture, the doctors put a cast. The plaster of the cast is cold, so it doesn't let the body heal quickly. With the herbal plasters of our herbalists fractures heal much better and quicker, because the herbs suck out the hit.

The same thing happens in childbirth. Women are separated from their partners, thrown on their backs on a cold bed, their legs spread apart, and they are made to suffer greatly in giving birth; the doctors insult them and give them pills and injections, because they can't give birth by themselves. The doctors don't know that it is much easier to give birth if the woman is warmly dressed and on her knees, if she drinks a specific herbal decoction, and then no injections are needed. The *coca* shows which herb the woman should take, and how she can best be helped during her labor.

It would be good for doctors and nurses to learn all these things, so they could really help people. They should also learn to respect us and treat us well, without insults, yells and humiliations. They should speak to us in our language, not in Spanish, which many women do not understand. They should give us all the documents we need without any problem. For example, many

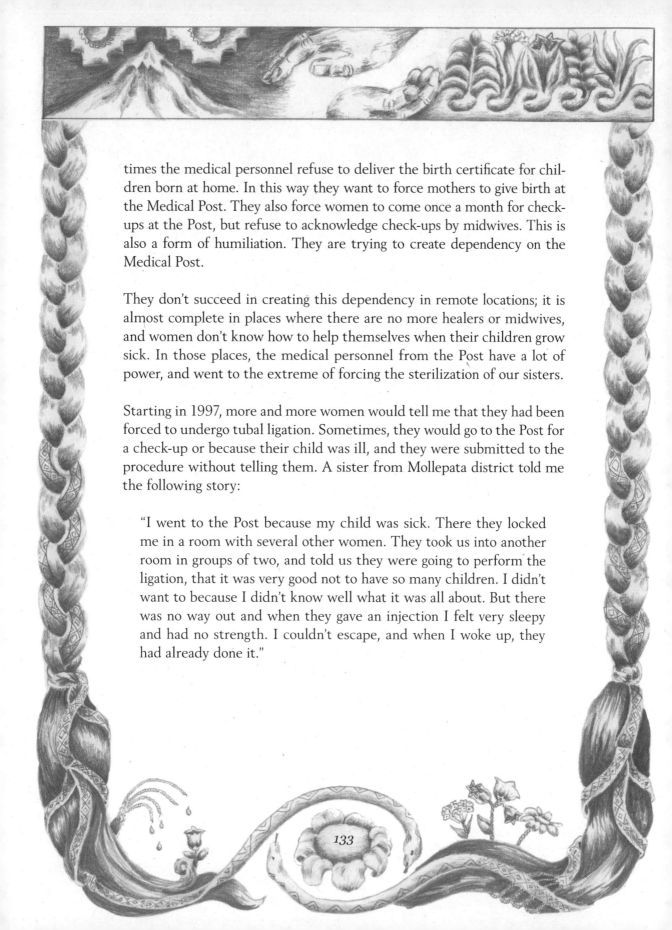

times the medical personnel refuse to deliver the birth certificate for children born at home. In this way they want to force mothers to give birth at the Medical Post. They also force women to come once a month for check-ups at the Post, but refuse to acknowledge check-ups by midwives. This is also a form of humiliation. They are trying to create dependency on the Medical Post.

They don't succeed in creating this dependency in remote locations; it is almost complete in places where there are no more healers or midwives, and women don't know how to help themselves when their children grow sick. In those places, the medical personnel from the Post have a lot of power, and went to the extreme of forcing the sterilization of our sisters.

Starting in 1997, more and more women would tell me that they had been forced to undergo tubal ligation. Sometimes, they would go to the Post for a check-up or because their child was ill, and they were submitted to the procedure without telling them. A sister from Mollepata district told me the following story:

> "I went to the Post because my child was sick. There they locked me in a room with several other women. They took us into another room in groups of two, and told us they were going to perform the ligation, that it was very good not to have so many children. I didn't want to because I didn't know well what it was all about. But there was no way out and when they gave an injection I felt very sleepy and had no strength. I couldn't escape, and when I woke up, they had already done it."

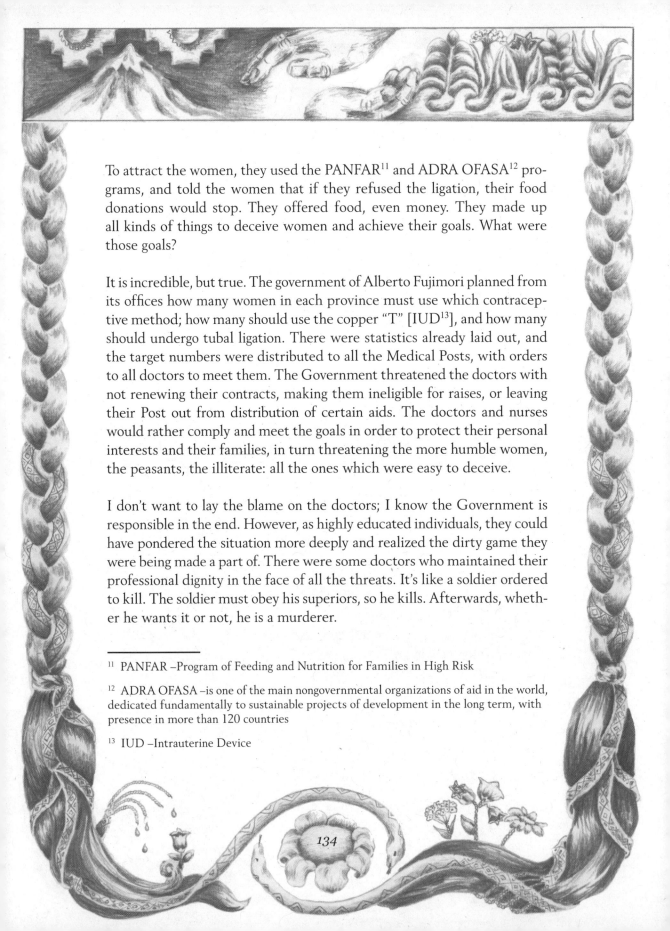

To attract the women, they used the PANFAR[11] and ADRA OFASA[12] programs, and told the women that if they refused the ligation, their food donations would stop. They offered food, even money. They made up all kinds of things to deceive women and achieve their goals. What were those goals?

It is incredible, but true. The government of Alberto Fujimori planned from its offices how many women in each province must use which contraceptive method; how many should use the copper "T" [IUD[13]], and how many should undergo tubal ligation. There were statistics already laid out, and the target numbers were distributed to all the Medical Posts, with orders to all doctors to meet them. The Government threatened the doctors with not renewing their contracts, making them ineligible for raises, or leaving their Post out from distribution of certain aids. The doctors and nurses would rather comply and meet the goals in order to protect their personal interests and their families, in turn threatening the more humble women, the peasants, the illiterate: all the ones which were easy to deceive.

I don't want to lay the blame on the doctors; I know the Government is responsible in the end. However, as highly educated individuals, they could have pondered the situation more deeply and realized the dirty game they were being made a part of. There were some doctors who maintained their professional dignity in the face of all the threats. It's like a soldier ordered to kill. The soldier must obey his superiors, so he kills. Afterwards, whether he wants it or not, he is a murderer.

---

[11] PANFAR –Program of Feeding and Nutrition for Families in High Risk

[12] ADRA OFASA –is one of the main nongovernmental organizations of aid in the world, dedicated fundamentally to sustainable projects of development in the long term, with presence in more than 120 countries

[13] IUD –Intrauterine Device

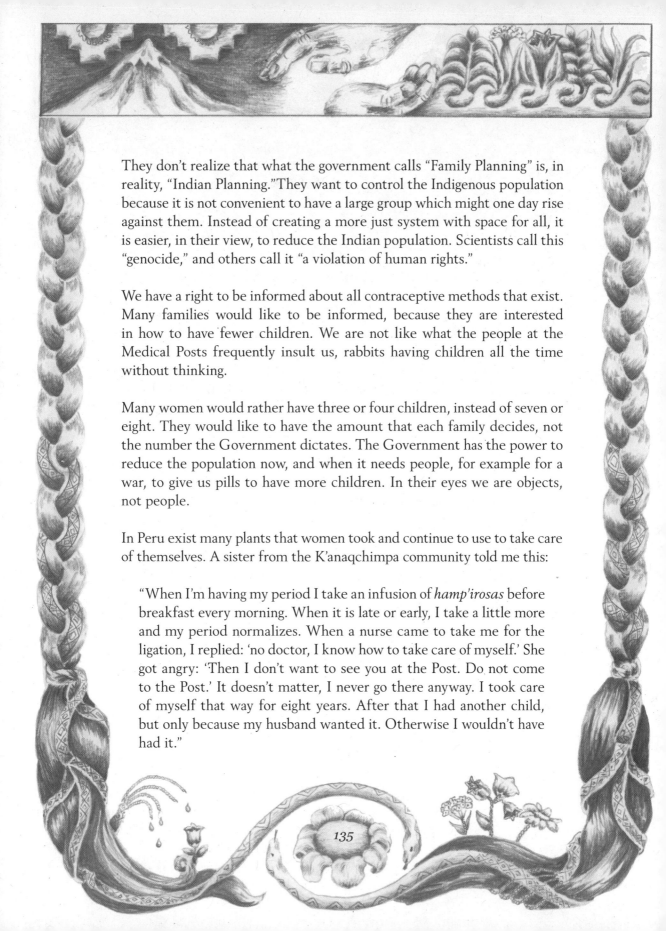

They don't realize that what the government calls "Family Planning" is, in reality, "Indian Planning." They want to control the Indigenous population because it is not convenient to have a large group which might one day rise against them. Instead of creating a more just system with space for all, it is easier, in their view, to reduce the Indian population. Scientists call this "genocide," and others call it "a violation of human rights."

We have a right to be informed about all contraceptive methods that exist. Many families would like to be informed, because they are interested in how to have fewer children. We are not like what the people at the Medical Posts frequently insult us, rabbits having children all the time without thinking.

Many women would rather have three or four children, instead of seven or eight. They would like to have the amount that each family decides, not the number the Government dictates. The Government has the power to reduce the population now, and when it needs people, for example for a war, to give us pills to have more children. In their eyes we are objects, not people.

In Peru exist many plants that women took and continue to use to take care of themselves. A sister from the K'anaqchimpa community told me this:

"When I'm having my period I take an infusion of *hamp'irosas* before breakfast every morning. When it is late or early, I take a little more and my period normalizes. When a nurse came to take me for the ligation, I replied: 'no doctor, I know how to take care of myself.' She got angry: 'Then I don't want to see you at the Post. Do not come to the Post.' It doesn't matter, I never go there anyway. I took care of myself that way for eight years. After that I had another child, but only because my husband wanted it. Otherwise I wouldn't have had it."

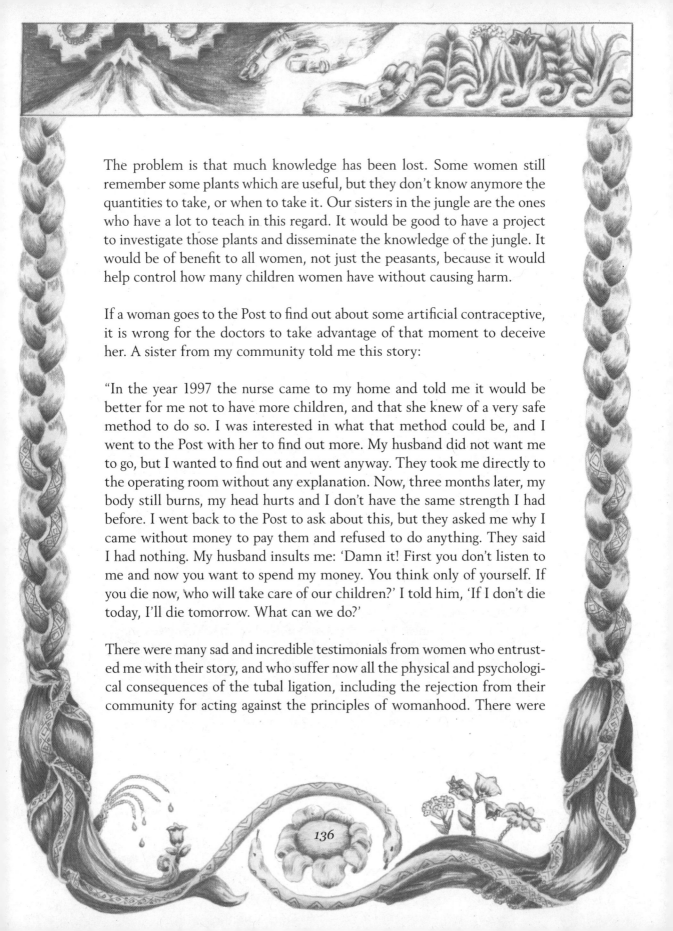

The problem is that much knowledge has been lost. Some women still remember some plants which are useful, but they don't know anymore the quantities to take, or when to take it. Our sisters in the jungle are the ones who have a lot to teach in this regard. It would be good to have a project to investigate those plants and disseminate the knowledge of the jungle. It would be of benefit to all women, not just the peasants, because it would help control how many children women have without causing harm.

If a woman goes to the Post to find out about some artificial contraceptive, it is wrong for the doctors to take advantage of that moment to deceive her. A sister from my community told me this story:

"In the year 1997 the nurse came to my home and told me it would be better for me not to have more children, and that she knew of a very safe method to do so. I was interested in what that method could be, and I went to the Post with her to find out more. My husband did not want me to go, but I wanted to find out and went anyway. They took me directly to the operating room without any explanation. Now, three months later, my body still burns, my head hurts and I don't have the same strength I had before. I went back to the Post to ask about this, but they asked me why I came without money to pay them and refused to do anything. They said I had nothing. My husband insults me: 'Damn it! First you don't listen to me and now you want to spend my money. You think only of yourself. If you die now, who will take care of our children?' I told him, 'If I don't die today, I'll die tomorrow. What can we do?'

There were many sad and incredible testimonials from women who entrusted me with their story, and who suffer now all the physical and psychological consequences of the tubal ligation, including the rejection from their community for acting against the principles of womanhood. There were

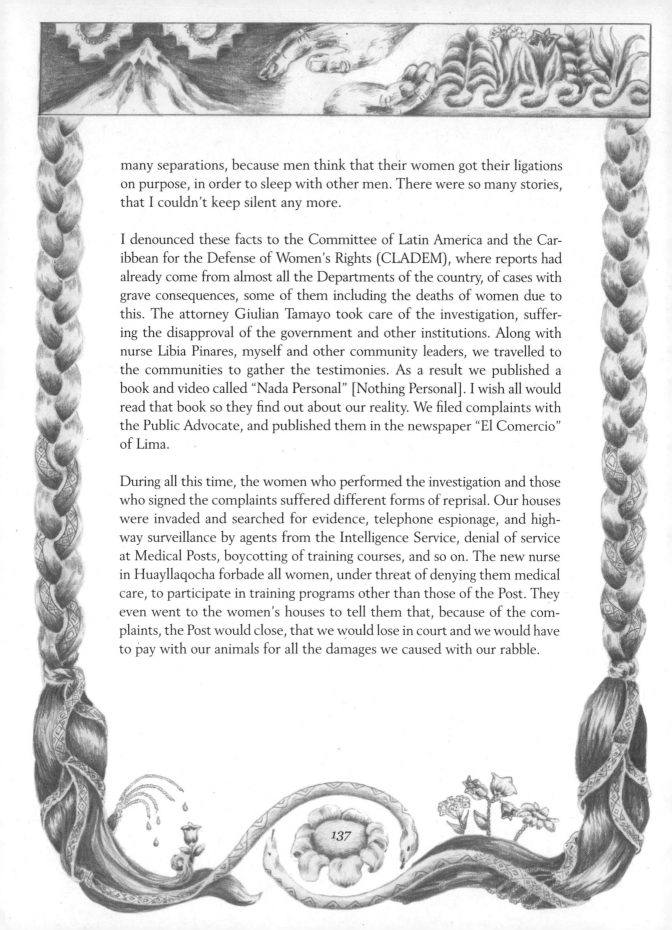

many separations, because men think that their women got their ligations on purpose, in order to sleep with other men. There were so many stories, that I couldn't keep silent any more.

I denounced these facts to the Committee of Latin America and the Caribbean for the Defense of Women's Rights (CLADEM), where reports had already come from almost all the Departments of the country, of cases with grave consequences, some of them including the deaths of women due to this. The attorney Giulian Tamayo took care of the investigation, suffering the disapproval of the government and other institutions. Along with nurse Libia Pinares, myself and other community leaders, we travelled to the communities to gather the testimonies. As a result we published a book and video called "Nada Personal" [Nothing Personal]. I wish all would read that book so they find out about our reality. We filed complaints with the Public Advocate, and published them in the newspaper "El Comercio" of Lima.

During all this time, the women who performed the investigation and those who signed the complaints suffered different forms of reprisal. Our houses were invaded and searched for evidence, telephone espionage, and highway surveillance by agents from the Intelligence Service, denial of service at Medical Posts, boycotting of training courses, and so on. The new nurse in Huayllaqocha forbade all women, under threat of denying them medical care, to participate in training programs other than those of the Post. They even went to the women's houses to tell them that, because of the complaints, the Post would close, that we would lose in court and we would have to pay with our animals for all the damages we caused with our rabble.

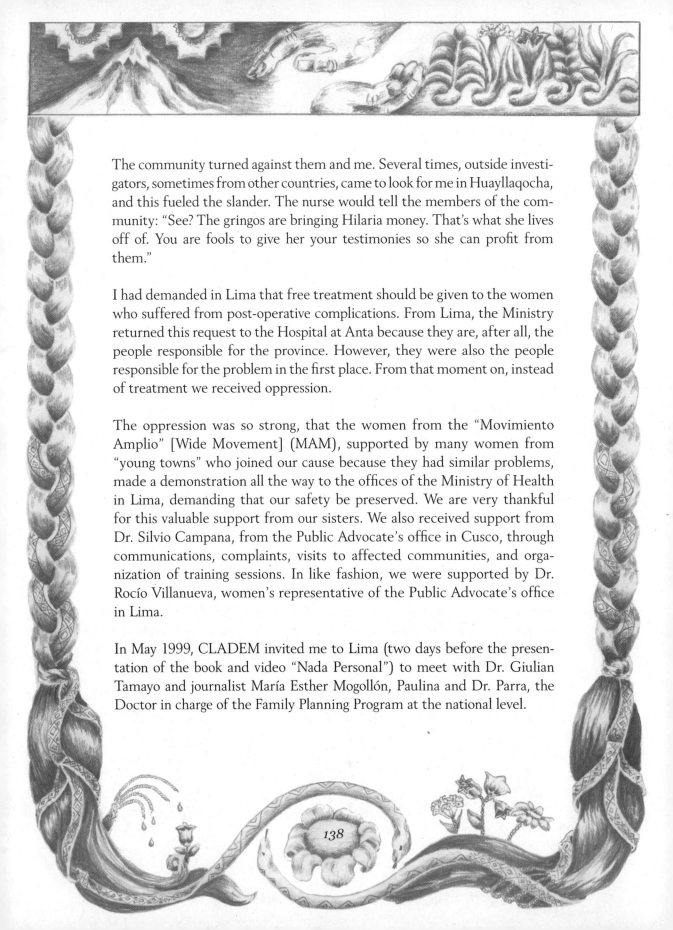

The community turned against them and me. Several times, outside investigators, sometimes from other countries, came to look for me in Huayllaqocha, and this fueled the slander. The nurse would tell the members of the community: "See? The gringos are bringing Hilaria money. That's what she lives off of. You are fools to give her your testimonies so she can profit from them."

I had demanded in Lima that free treatment should be given to the women who suffered from post-operative complications. From Lima, the Ministry returned this request to the Hospital at Anta because they are, after all, the people responsible for the province. However, they were also the people responsible for the problem in the first place. From that moment on, instead of treatment we received oppression.

The oppression was so strong, that the women from the "Movimiento Amplio" [Wide Movement] (MAM), supported by many women from "young towns" who joined our cause because they had similar problems, made a demonstration all the way to the offices of the Ministry of Health in Lima, demanding that our safety be preserved. We are very thankful for this valuable support from our sisters. We also received support from Dr. Silvio Campana, from the Public Advocate's office in Cusco, through communications, complaints, visits to affected communities, and organization of training sessions. In like fashion, we were supported by Dr. Rocío Villanueva, women's representative of the Public Advocate's office in Lima.

In May 1999, CLADEM invited me to Lima (two days before the presentation of the book and video "Nada Personal") to meet with Dr. Giulian Tamayo and journalist María Esther Mogollón, Paulina and Dr. Parra, the Doctor in charge of the Family Planning Program at the national level.

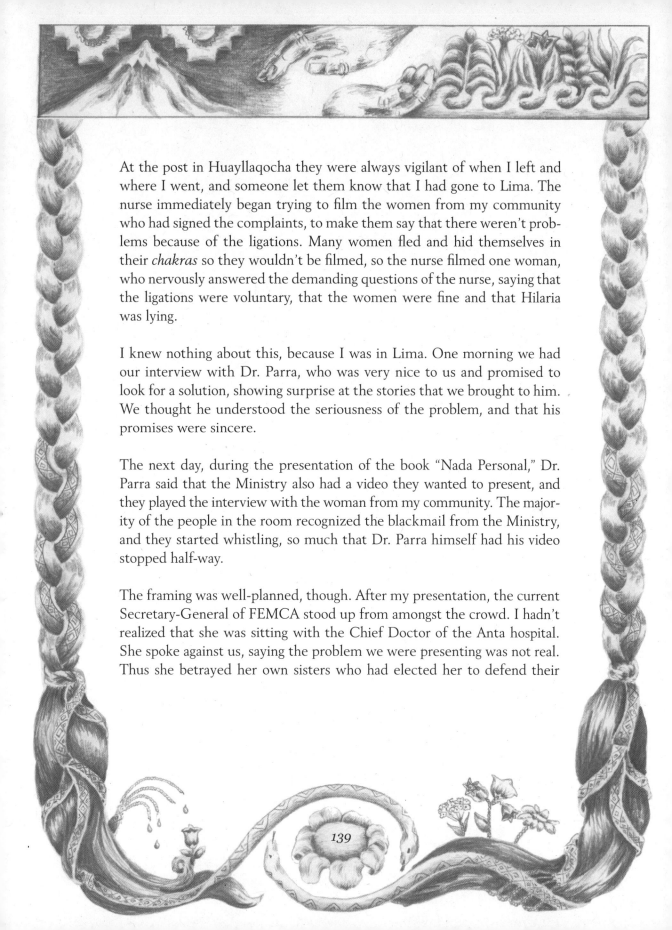

At the post in Huayllaqocha they were always vigilant of when I left and where I went, and someone let them know that I had gone to Lima. The nurse immediately began trying to film the women from my community who had signed the complaints, to make them say that there weren't problems because of the ligations. Many women fled and hid themselves in their *chakras* so they wouldn't be filmed, so the nurse filmed one woman, who nervously answered the demanding questions of the nurse, saying that the ligations were voluntary, that the women were fine and that Hilaria was lying.

I knew nothing about this, because I was in Lima. One morning we had our interview with Dr. Parra, who was very nice to us and promised to look for a solution, showing surprise at the stories that we brought to him. We thought he understood the seriousness of the problem, and that his promises were sincere.

The next day, during the presentation of the book "Nada Personal," Dr. Parra said that the Ministry also had a video they wanted to present, and they played the interview with the woman from my community. The majority of the people in the room recognized the blackmail from the Ministry, and they started whistling, so much that Dr. Parra himself had his video stopped half-way.

The framing was well-planned, though. After my presentation, the current Secretary-General of FEMCA stood up from amongst the crowd. I hadn't realized that she was sitting with the Chief Doctor of the Anta hospital. She spoke against us, saying the problem we were presenting was not real. Thus she betrayed her own sisters who had elected her to defend their

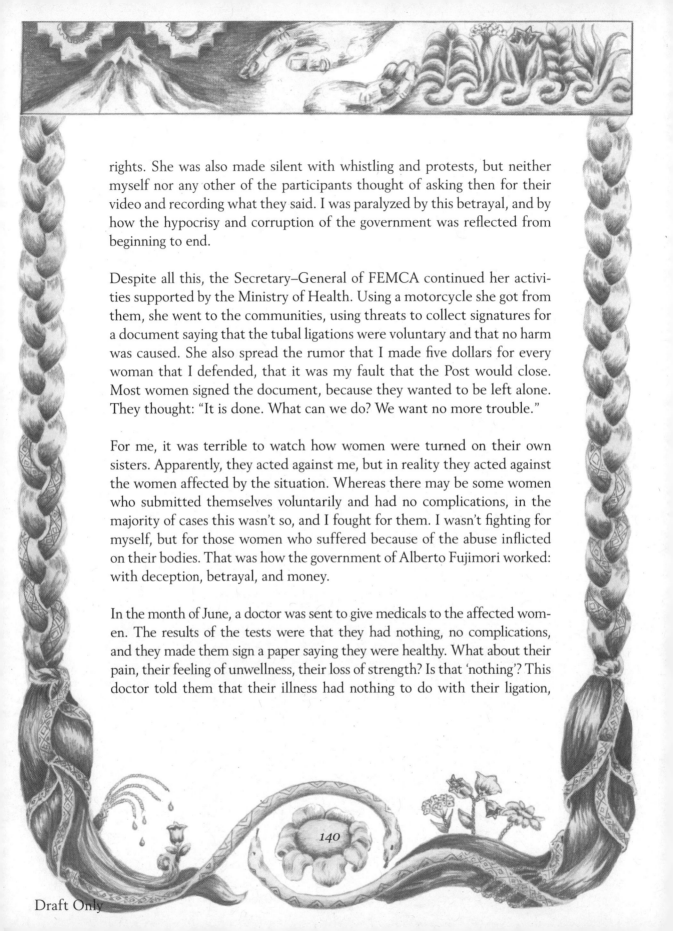

rights. She was also made silent with whistling and protests, but neither myself nor any other of the participants thought of asking then for their video and recording what they said. I was paralyzed by this betrayal, and by how the hypocrisy and corruption of the government was reflected from beginning to end.

Despite all this, the Secretary–General of FEMCA continued her activities supported by the Ministry of Health. Using a motorcycle she got from them, she went to the communities, using threats to collect signatures for a document saying that the tubal ligations were voluntary and that no harm was caused. She also spread the rumor that I made five dollars for every woman that I defended, that it was my fault that the Post would close. Most women signed the document, because they wanted to be left alone. They thought: "It is done. What can we do? We want no more trouble."

For me, it was terrible to watch how women were turned on their own sisters. Apparently, they acted against me, but in reality they acted against the women affected by the situation. Whereas there may be some women who submitted themselves voluntarily and had no complications, in the majority of cases this wasn't so, and I fought for them. I wasn't fighting for myself, but for those women who suffered because of the abuse inflicted on their bodies. That was how the government of Alberto Fujimori worked: with deception, betrayal, and money.

In the month of June, a doctor was sent to give medicals to the affected women. The results of the tests were that they had nothing, no complications, and they made them sign a paper saying they were healthy. What about their pain, their feeling of unwellness, their loss of strength? Is that 'nothing'? This doctor told them that their illness had nothing to do with their ligation,

140

Draft Only

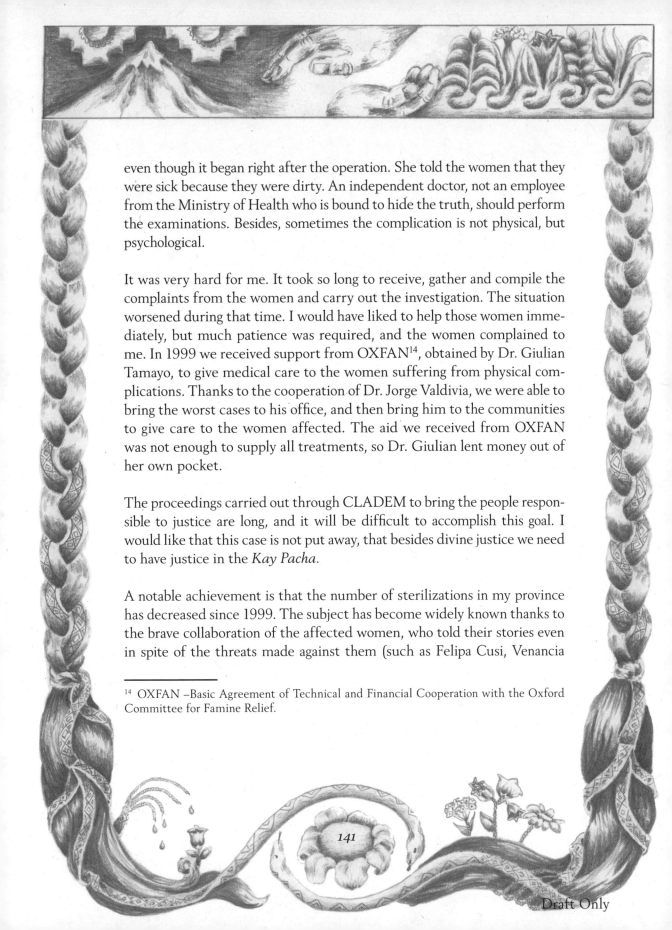

even though it began right after the operation. She told the women that they were sick because they were dirty. An independent doctor, not an employee from the Ministry of Health who is bound to hide the truth, should perform the examinations. Besides, sometimes the complication is not physical, but psychological.

It was very hard for me. It took so long to receive, gather and compile the complaints from the women and carry out the investigation. The situation worsened during that time. I would have liked to help those women immediately, but much patience was required, and the women complained to me. In 1999 we received support from OXFAN[14], obtained by Dr. Giulian Tamayo, to give medical care to the women suffering from physical complications. Thanks to the cooperation of Dr. Jorge Valdivia, we were able to bring the worst cases to his office, and then bring him to the communities to give care to the women affected. The aid we received from OXFAN was not enough to supply all treatments, so Dr. Giulian lent money out of her own pocket.

The proceedings carried out through CLADEM to bring the people responsible to justice are long, and it will be difficult to accomplish this goal. I would like that this case is not put away, that besides divine justice we need to have justice in the *Kay Pacha*.

A notable achievement is that the number of sterilizations in my province has decreased since 1999. The subject has become widely known thanks to the brave collaboration of the affected women, who told their stories even in spite of the threats made against them (such as Felipa Cusi, Venancia

---

[14] OXFAN –Basic Agreement of Technical and Financial Cooperation with the Oxford Committee for Famine Relief.

Draft Only

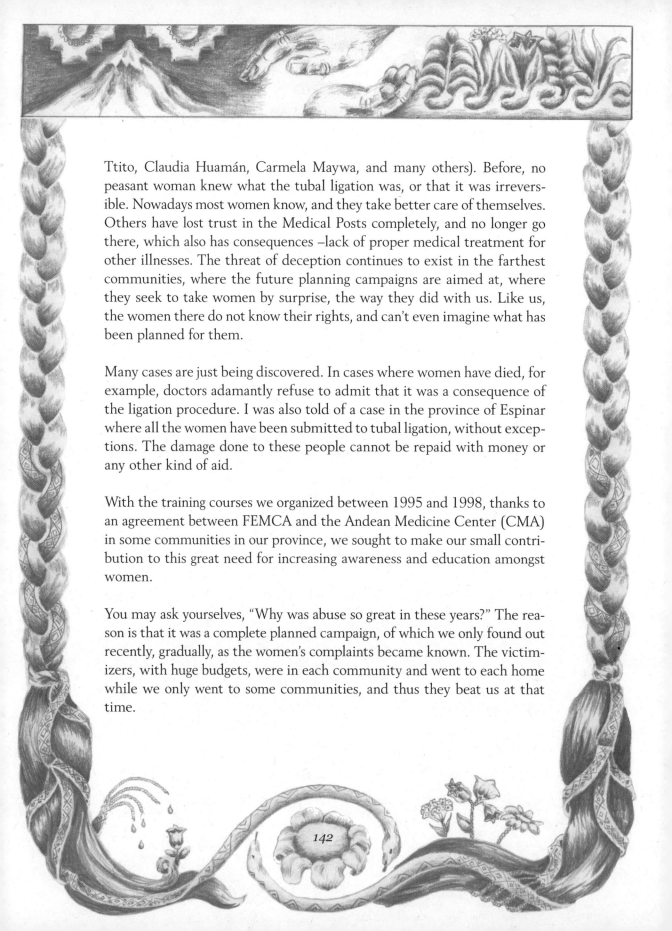

Ttito, Claudia Huamán, Carmela Maywa, and many others). Before, no peasant woman knew what the tubal ligation was, or that it was irreversible. Nowadays most women know, and they take better care of themselves. Others have lost trust in the Medical Posts completely, and no longer go there, which also has consequences –lack of proper medical treatment for other illnesses. The threat of deception continues to exist in the farthest communities, where the future planning campaigns are aimed at, where they seek to take women by surprise, the way they did with us. Like us, the women there do not know their rights, and can't even imagine what has been planned for them.

Many cases are just being discovered. In cases where women have died, for example, doctors adamantly refuse to admit that it was a consequence of the ligation procedure. I was also told of a case in the province of Espinar where all the women have been submitted to tubal ligation, without exceptions. The damage done to these people cannot be repaid with money or any other kind of aid.

With the training courses we organized between 1995 and 1998, thanks to an agreement between FEMCA and the Andean Medicine Center (CMA) in some communities in our province, we sought to make our small contribution to this great need for increasing awareness and education amongst women.

You may ask yourselves, "Why was abuse so great in these years?" The reason is that it was a complete planned campaign, of which we only found out recently, gradually, as the women's complaints became known. The victimizers, with huge budgets, were in each community and went to each home while we only went to some communities, and thus they beat us at that time.

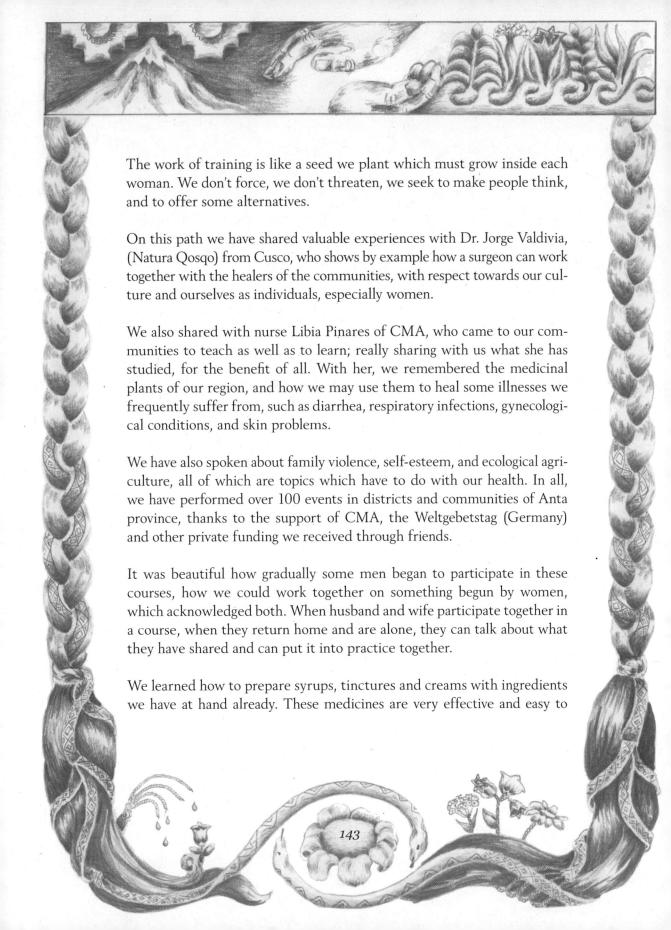

The work of training is like a seed we plant which must grow inside each woman. We don't force, we don't threaten, we seek to make people think, and to offer some alternatives.

On this path we have shared valuable experiences with Dr. Jorge Valdivia, (Natura Qosqo) from Cusco, who shows by example how a surgeon can work together with the healers of the communities, with respect towards our culture and ourselves as individuals, especially women.

We also shared with nurse Libia Pinares of CMA, who came to our communities to teach as well as to learn; really sharing with us what she has studied, for the benefit of all. With her, we remembered the medicinal plants of our region, and how we may use them to heal some illnesses we frequently suffer from, such as diarrhea, respiratory infections, gynecological conditions, and skin problems.

We have also spoken about family violence, self-esteem, and ecological agriculture, all of which are topics which have to do with our health. In all, we have performed over 100 events in districts and communities of Anta province, thanks to the support of CMA, the Weltgebetstag (Germany) and other private funding we received through friends.

It was beautiful how gradually some men began to participate in these courses, how we could work together on something begun by women, which acknowledged both. When husband and wife participate together in a course, when they return home and are alone, they can talk about what they have shared and can put it into practice together.

We learned how to prepare syrups, tinctures and creams with ingredients we have at hand already. These medicines are very effective and easy to

make. I have included some recipes in the back of this book for everyone to try, see appendix E and F.

Let us learn to value ourselves and make decisions about our own bodies. Let us learn to live healthier. Let us learn to help ourselves with what we have.

QUESTIONS FOR REFLECTION

- Are there healers (male and female) midwives (male and female) and *paqos* in your community?
- What is their knowledge like? How do they care for others?
- Is there a Medical Post nearby?
- How do they care for others?
- What are the most common illnesses in your community?
- How are they treated?
- What are the most common causes of death?
- Which contraceptive methods do you know of?
- What do you know about tubal ligations?
- Do you know any women who have been forced to undergo tubal ligation?
- What do you think about these practices or campaigns?
- How could the respect for women from healthcare personnel be improved?
- Why do you think it is important that women and all people be trained in traditional medicine?
- Why do you think it is important to train healers and midwives?
- Which herbal preparations can you teach?

"…we learned how to prepare syrups, tinctures and creams with ingredients we have at hand already…"

1999 The presentation of book and video "Nothing Personal" in Lima (to the right Dr. Parra).

A framing to the affected women: the Secretary-General of FEMCA saying that the forced sterilization problems were not real.

OF FALSE TRADITIONS

Raised under the influence of alcohol
Where is the origin of the problem?
Alcohol, the worst drug
Seeking a dignified life
Change can start amongst the women

Questions for reflection

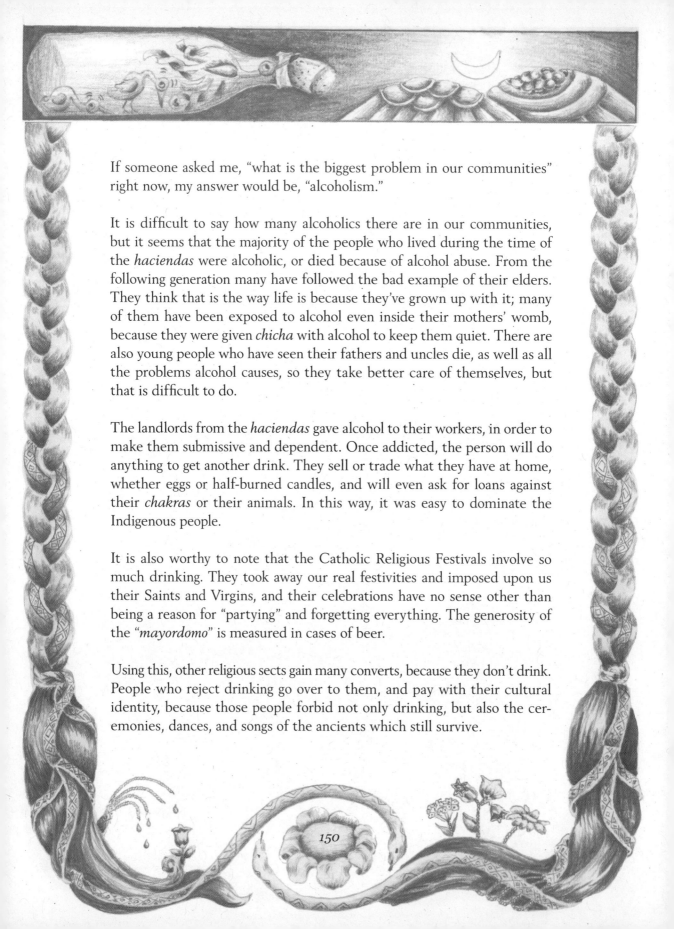

If someone asked me, "what is the biggest problem in our communities" right now, my answer would be, "alcoholism."

It is difficult to say how many alcoholics there are in our communities, but it seems that the majority of the people who lived during the time of the *haciendas* were alcoholic, or died because of alcohol abuse. From the following generation many have followed the bad example of their elders. They think that is the way life is because they've grown up with it; many of them have been exposed to alcohol even inside their mothers' womb, because they were given *chicha* with alcohol to keep them quiet. There are also young people who have seen their fathers and uncles die, as well as all the problems alcohol causes, so they take better care of themselves, but that is difficult to do.

The landlords from the *haciendas* gave alcohol to their workers, in order to make them submissive and dependent. Once addicted, the person will do anything to get another drink. They sell or trade what they have at home, whether eggs or half-burned candles, and will even ask for loans against their *chakras* or their animals. In this way, it was easy to dominate the Indigenous people.

It is also worthy to note that the Catholic Religious Festivals involve so much drinking. They took away our real festivities and imposed upon us their Saints and Virgins, and their celebrations have no sense other than being a reason for "partying" and forgetting everything. The generosity of the "*mayordomo*" is measured in cases of beer.

Using this, other religious sects gain many converts, because they don't drink. People who reject drinking go over to them, and pay with their cultural identity, because those people forbid not only drinking, but also the ceremonies, dances, and songs of the ancients which still survive.

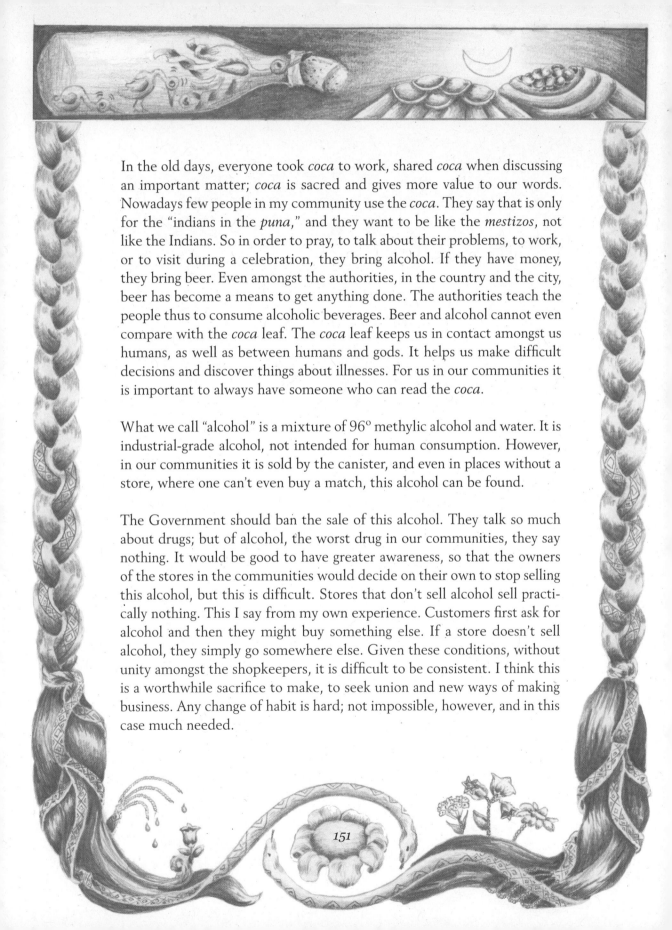

In the old days, everyone took *coca* to work, shared *coca* when discussing an important matter; *coca* is sacred and gives more value to our words. Nowadays few people in my community use the *coca*. They say that is only for the "indians in the *puna*," and they want to be like the *mestizos*, not like the Indians. So in order to pray, to talk about their problems, to work, or to visit during a celebration, they bring alcohol. If they have money, they bring beer. Even amongst the authorities, in the country and the city, beer has become a means to get anything done. The authorities teach the people thus to consume alcoholic beverages. Beer and alcohol cannot even compare with the *coca* leaf. The *coca* leaf keeps us in contact amongst us humans, as well as between humans and gods. It helps us make difficult decisions and discover things about illnesses. For us in our communities it is important to always have someone who can read the *coca*.

What we call "alcohol" is a mixture of 96° methylic alcohol and water. It is industrial-grade alcohol, not intended for human consumption. However, in our communities it is sold by the canister, and even in places without a store, where one can't even buy a match, this alcohol can be found.

The Government should ban the sale of this alcohol. They talk so much about drugs; but of alcohol, the worst drug in our communities, they say nothing. It would be good to have greater awareness, so that the owners of the stores in the communities would decide on their own to stop selling this alcohol, but this is difficult. Stores that don't sell alcohol sell practically nothing. This I say from my own experience. Customers first ask for alcohol and then they might buy something else. If a store doesn't sell alcohol, they simply go somewhere else. Given these conditions, without unity amongst the shopkeepers, it is difficult to be consistent. I think this is a worthwhile sacrifice to make, to seek union and new ways of making business. Any change of habit is hard; not impossible, however, and in this case much needed.

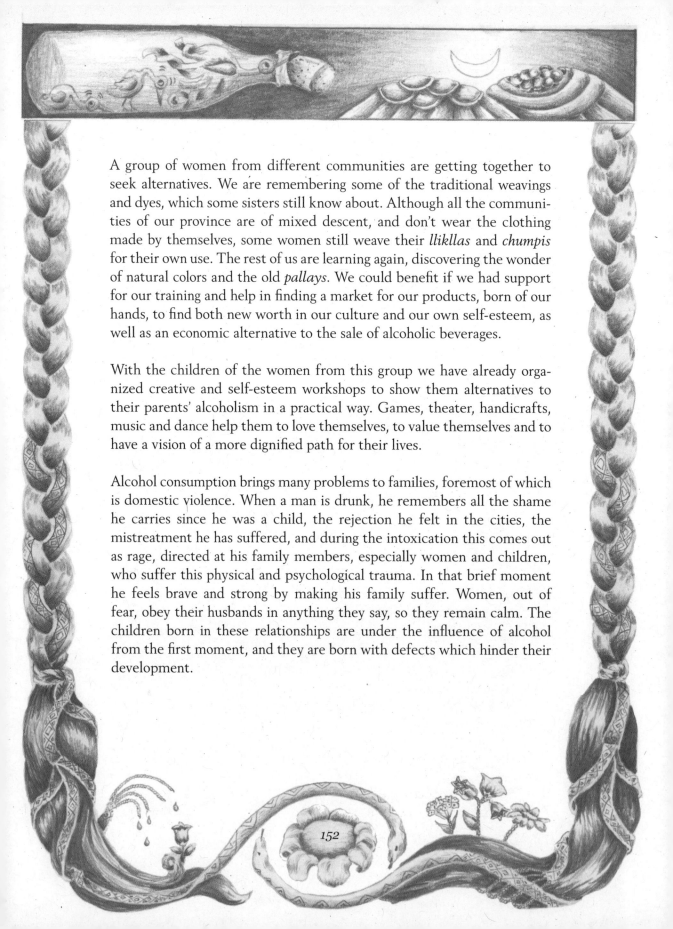

A group of women from different communities are getting together to seek alternatives. We are remembering some of the traditional weavings and dyes, which some sisters still know about. Although all the communities of our province are of mixed descent, and don't wear the clothing made by themselves, some women still weave their *llikllas* and *chumpis* for their own use. The rest of us are learning again, discovering the wonder of natural colors and the old *pallays*. We could benefit if we had support for our training and help in finding a market for our products, born of our hands, to find both new worth in our culture and our own self-esteem, as well as an economic alternative to the sale of alcoholic beverages.

With the children of the women from this group we have already organized creative and self-esteem workshops to show them alternatives to their parents' alcoholism in a practical way. Games, theater, handicrafts, music and dance help them to love themselves, to value themselves and to have a vision of a more dignified path for their lives.

Alcohol consumption brings many problems to families, foremost of which is domestic violence. When a man is drunk, he remembers all the shame he carries since he was a child, the rejection he felt in the cities, the mistreatment he has suffered, and during the intoxication this comes out as rage, directed at his family members, especially women and children, who suffer this physical and psychological trauma. In that brief moment he feels brave and strong by making his family suffer. Women, out of fear, obey their husbands in anything they say, so they remain calm. The children born in these relationships are under the influence of alcohol from the first moment, and they are born with defects which hinder their development.

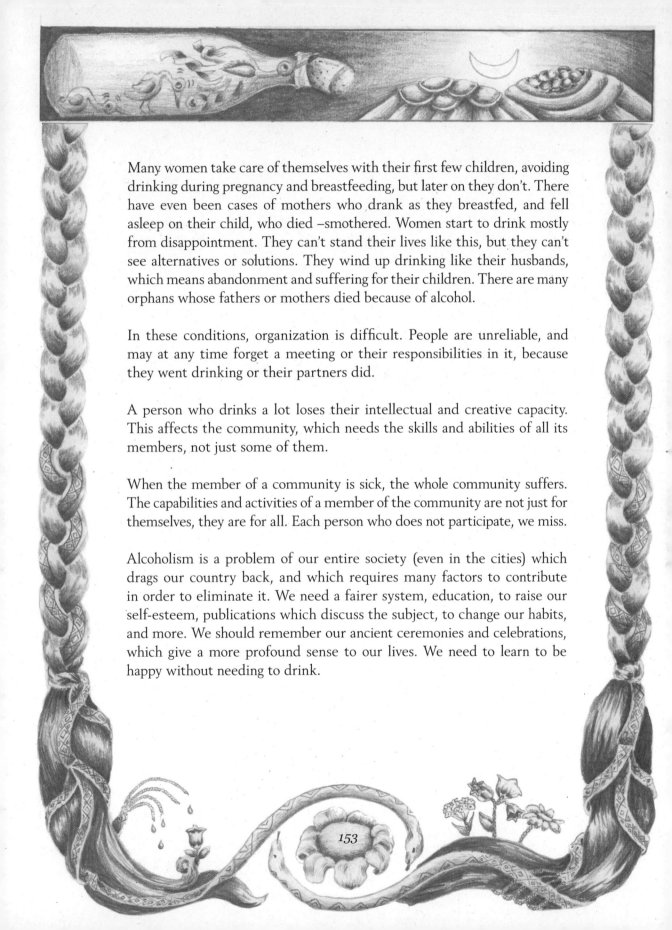

Many women take care of themselves with their first few children, avoiding drinking during pregnancy and breastfeeding, but later on they don't. There have even been cases of mothers who drank as they breastfed, and fell asleep on their child, who died –smothered. Women start to drink mostly from disappointment. They can't stand their lives like this, but they can't see alternatives or solutions. They wind up drinking like their husbands, which means abandonment and suffering for their children. There are many orphans whose fathers or mothers died because of alcohol.

In these conditions, organization is difficult. People are unreliable, and may at any time forget a meeting or their responsibilities in it, because they went drinking or their partners did.

A person who drinks a lot loses their intellectual and creative capacity. This affects the community, which needs the skills and abilities of all its members, not just some of them.

When the member of a community is sick, the whole community suffers. The capabilities and activities of a member of the community are not just for themselves, they are for all. Each person who does not participate, we miss.

Alcoholism is a problem of our entire society (even in the cities) which drags our country back, and which requires many factors to contribute in order to eliminate it. We need a fairer system, education, to raise our self-esteem, publications which discuss the subject, to change our habits, and more. We should remember our ancient ceremonies and celebrations, which give a more profound sense to our lives. We need to learn to be happy without needing to drink.

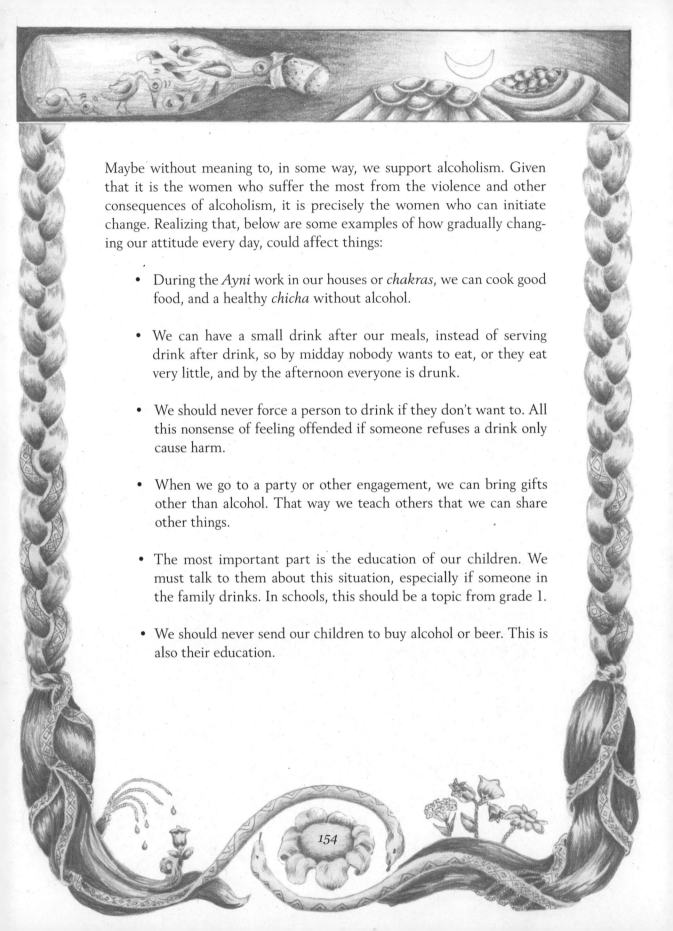

Maybe without meaning to, in some way, we support alcoholism. Given that it is the women who suffer the most from the violence and other consequences of alcoholism, it is precisely the women who can initiate change. Realizing that, below are some examples of how gradually changing our attitude every day, could affect things:

- During the *Ayni* work in our houses or *chakras*, we can cook good food, and a healthy *chicha* without alcohol.

- We can have a small drink after our meals, instead of serving drink after drink, so by midday nobody wants to eat, or they eat very little, and by the afternoon everyone is drunk.

- We should never force a person to drink if they don't want to. All this nonsense of feeling offended if someone refuses a drink only cause harm.

- When we go to a party or other engagement, we can bring gifts other than alcohol. That way we teach others that we can share other things.

- The most important part is the education of our children. We must talk to them about this situation, especially if someone in the family drinks. In schools, this should be a topic from grade 1.

- We should never send our children to buy alcohol or beer. This is also their education.

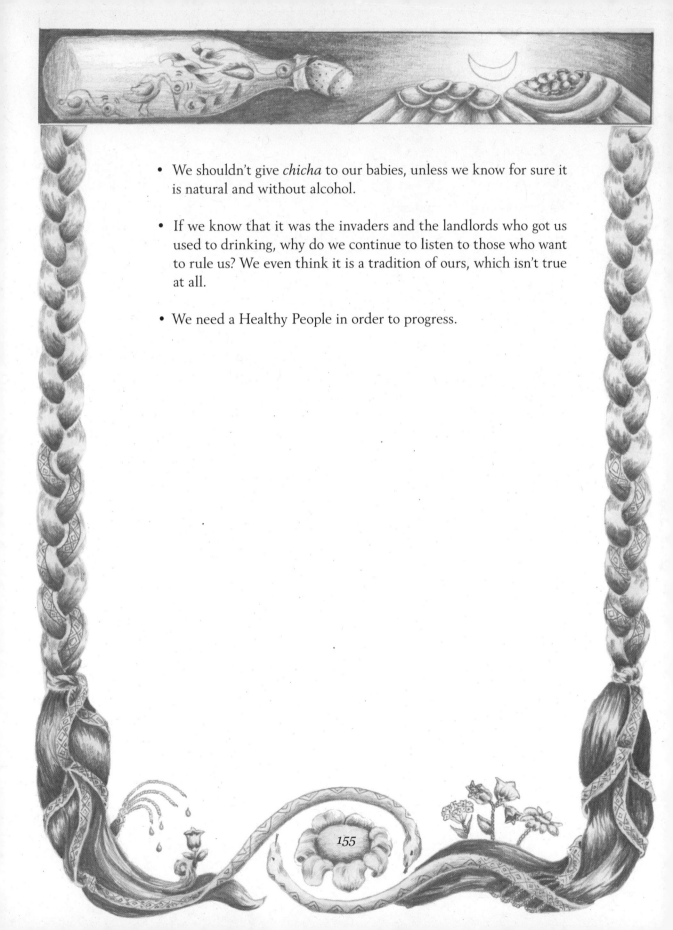

- We shouldn't give *chicha* to our babies, unless we know for sure it is natural and without alcohol.

- If we know that it was the invaders and the landlords who got us used to drinking, why do we continue to listen to those who want to rule us? We even think it is a tradition of ours, which isn't true at all.

- We need a Healthy People in order to progress.

155

QUESTIONS FOR REFLECTION

- Why do you drink, and in what situations?
- What do you feel the next morning after drinking and having caused problems for your family?
- How do you think children feel when they see their fathers and mothers drunk?
- What health consequences of alcohol abuse do you know about?
- How does alcohol influence the organization of your community?
- Why do religious sects forbid drinking amongst their members?
- Do you have to be "religious" to be respected as a healthy person?
- What would happen if you said "that's it"?
- Is it true that there are no friends without alcohol?
- What alternatives do you see to replace alcoholic beverages at work, during festivities, and at other times?

"…Games, theater, handicrafts, music and dance help them to love themselves, to value themselves and to have a vision of a more dignified path for their lives…"

WAITING TO BLOOM

Education at home
Education in school
Proposals to improve education in schools
Literacy training for adults
Experiences with cultural exchange through permanent workshops
Help to keep our culture alive

Questions for reflection

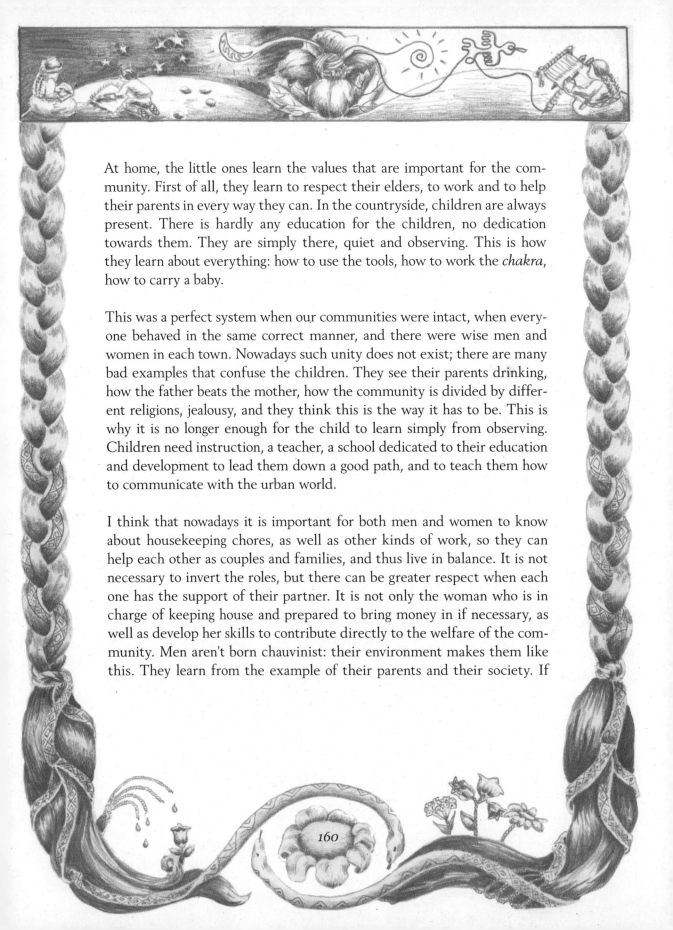

At home, the little ones learn the values that are important for the community. First of all, they learn to respect their elders, to work and to help their parents in every way they can. In the countryside, children are always present. There is hardly any education for the children, no dedication towards them. They are simply there, quiet and observing. This is how they learn about everything: how to use the tools, how to work the *chakra*, how to carry a baby.

This was a perfect system when our communities were intact, when everyone behaved in the same correct manner, and there were wise men and women in each town. Nowadays such unity does not exist; there are many bad examples that confuse the children. They see their parents drinking, how the father beats the mother, how the community is divided by different religions, jealousy, and they think this is the way it has to be. This is why it is no longer enough for the child to learn simply from observing. Children need instruction, a teacher, a school dedicated to their education and development to lead them down a good path, and to teach them how to communicate with the urban world.

I think that nowadays it is important for both men and women to know about housekeeping chores, as well as other kinds of work, so they can help each other as couples and families, and thus live in balance. It is not necessary to invert the roles, but there can be greater respect when each one has the support of their partner. It is not only the woman who is in charge of keeping house and prepared to bring money in if necessary, as well as develop her skills to contribute directly to the welfare of the community. Men aren't born chauvinist: their environment makes them like this. They learn from the example of their parents and their society. If

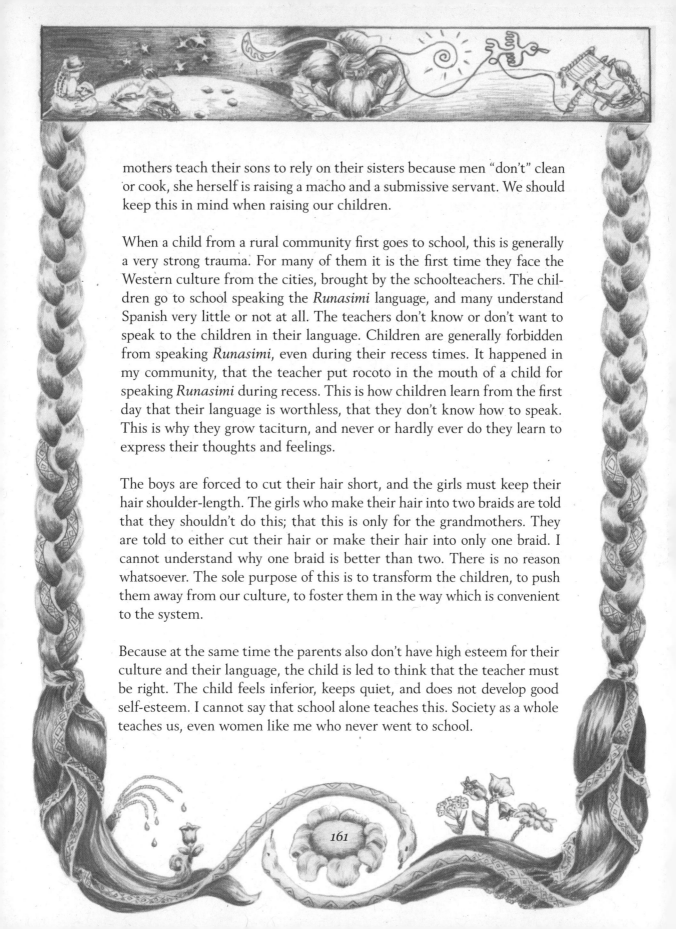

mothers teach their sons to rely on their sisters because men "don't" clean or cook, she herself is raising a macho and a submissive servant. We should keep this in mind when raising our children.

When a child from a rural community first goes to school, this is generally a very strong trauma. For many of them it is the first time they face the Western culture from the cities, brought by the schoolteachers. The children go to school speaking the *Runasimi* language, and many understand Spanish very little or not at all. The teachers don't know or don't want to speak to the children in their language. Children are generally forbidden from speaking *Runasimi*, even during their recess times. It happened in my community, that the teacher put rocoto in the mouth of a child for speaking *Runasimi* during recess. This is how children learn from the first day that their language is worthless, that they don't know how to speak. This is why they grow taciturn, and never or hardly ever do they learn to express their thoughts and feelings.

The boys are forced to cut their hair short, and the girls must keep their hair shoulder-length. The girls who make their hair into two braids are told that they shouldn't do this; that this is only for the grandmothers. They are told to either cut their hair or make their hair into only one braid. I cannot understand why one braid is better than two. There is no reason whatsoever. The sole purpose of this is to transform the children, to push them away from our culture, to foster them in the way which is convenient to the system.

Because at the same time the parents also don't have high esteem for their culture and their language, the child is led to think that the teacher must be right. The child feels inferior, keeps quiet, and does not develop good self-esteem. I cannot say that school alone teaches this. Society as a whole teaches us, even women like me who never went to school.

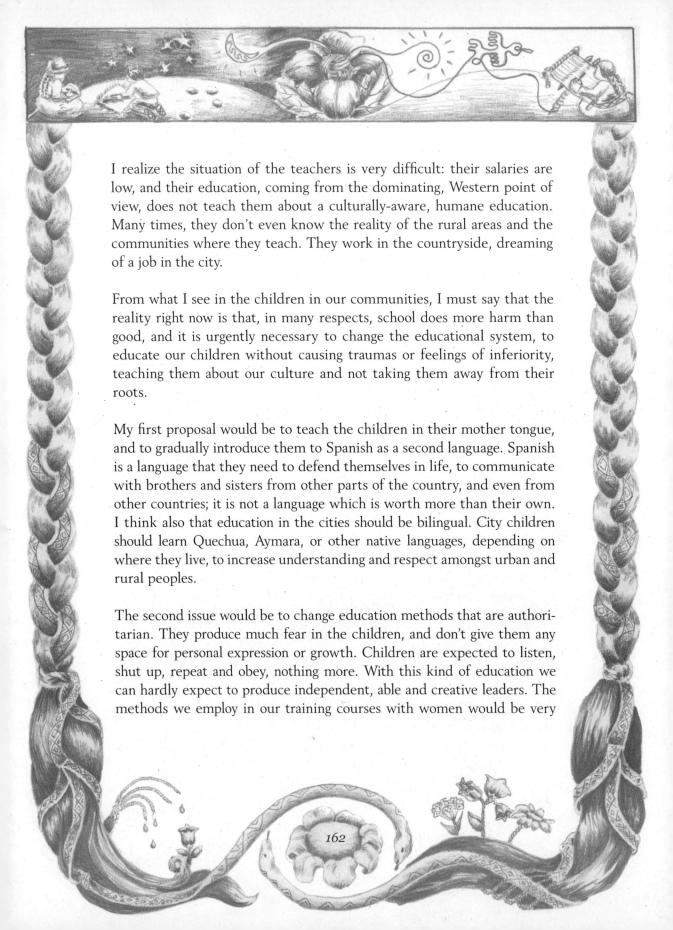

I realize the situation of the teachers is very difficult: their salaries are low, and their education, coming from the dominating, Western point of view, does not teach them about a culturally-aware, humane education. Many times, they don't even know the reality of the rural areas and the communities where they teach. They work in the countryside, dreaming of a job in the city.

From what I see in the children in our communities, I must say that the reality right now is that, in many respects, school does more harm than good, and it is urgently necessary to change the educational system, to educate our children without causing traumas or feelings of inferiority, teaching them about our culture and not taking them away from their roots.

My first proposal would be to teach the children in their mother tongue, and to gradually introduce them to Spanish as a second language. Spanish is a language that they need to defend themselves in life, to communicate with brothers and sisters from other parts of the country, and even from other countries; it is not a language which is worth more than their own. I think also that education in the cities should be bilingual. City children should learn Quechua, Aymara, or other native languages, depending on where they live, to increase understanding and respect amongst urban and rural peoples.

The second issue would be to change education methods that are authoritarian. They produce much fear in the children, and don't give them any space for personal expression or growth. Children are expected to listen, shut up, repeat and obey, nothing more. With this kind of education we can hardly expect to produce independent, able and creative leaders. The methods we employ in our training courses with women would be very

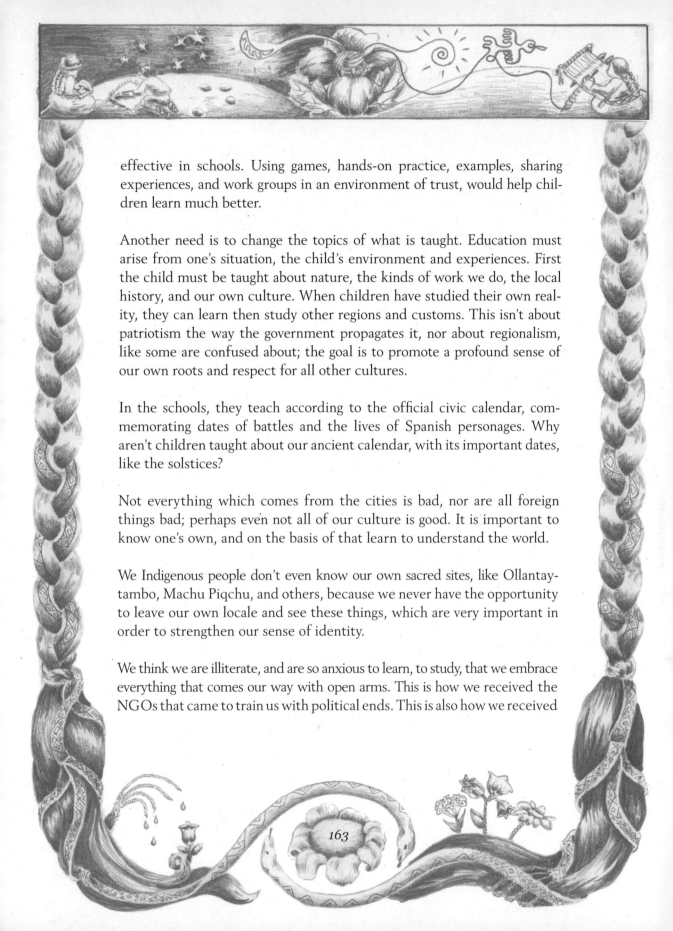

effective in schools. Using games, hands-on practice, examples, sharing experiences, and work groups in an environment of trust, would help children learn much better.

Another need is to change the topics of what is taught. Education must arise from one's situation, the child's environment and experiences. First the child must be taught about nature, the kinds of work we do, the local history, and our own culture. When children have studied their own reality, they can learn then study other regions and customs. This isn't about patriotism the way the government propagates it, nor about regionalism, like some are confused about; the goal is to promote a profound sense of our own roots and respect for all other cultures.

In the schools, they teach according to the official civic calendar, commemorating dates of battles and the lives of Spanish personages. Why aren't children taught about our ancient calendar, with its important dates, like the solstices?

Not everything which comes from the cities is bad, nor are all foreign things bad; perhaps even not all of our culture is good. It is important to know one's own, and on the basis of that learn to understand the world.

We Indigenous people don't even know our own sacred sites, like Ollantaytambo, Machu Piqchu, and others, because we never have the opportunity to leave our own locale and see these things, which are very important in order to strengthen our sense of identity.

We think we are illiterate, and are so anxious to learn, to study, that we embrace everything that comes our way with open arms. This is how we received the NGOs that came to train us with political ends. This is also how we received

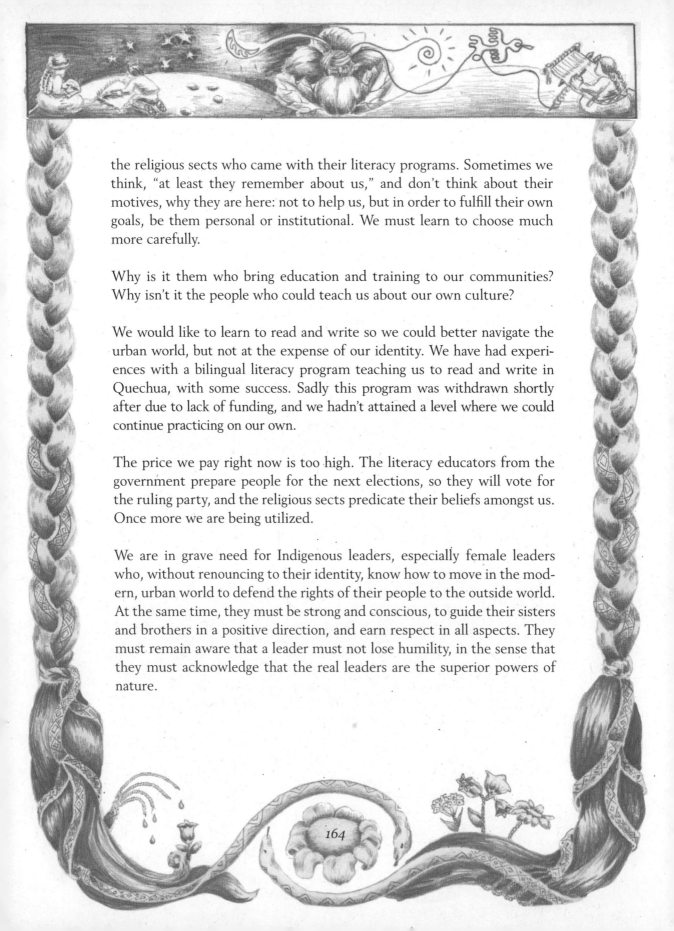

the religious sects who came with their literacy programs. Sometimes we think, "at least they remember about us," and don't think about their motives, why they are here: not to help us, but in order to fulfill their own goals, be them personal or institutional. We must learn to choose much more carefully.

Why is it them who bring education and training to our communities? Why isn't it the people who could teach us about our own culture?

We would like to learn to read and write so we could better navigate the urban world, but not at the expense of our identity. We have had experiences with a bilingual literacy program teaching us to read and write in Quechua, with some success. Sadly this program was withdrawn shortly after due to lack of funding, and we hadn't attained a level where we could continue practicing on our own.

The price we pay right now is too high. The literacy educators from the government prepare people for the next elections, so they will vote for the ruling party, and the religious sects predicate their beliefs amongst us. Once more we are being utilized.

We are in grave need for Indigenous leaders, especially female leaders who, without renouncing to their identity, know how to move in the modern, urban world to defend the rights of their people to the outside world. At the same time, they must be strong and conscious, to guide their sisters and brothers in a positive direction, and earn respect in all aspects. They must remain aware that a leader must not lose humility, in the sense that they must acknowledge that the real leaders are the superior powers of nature.

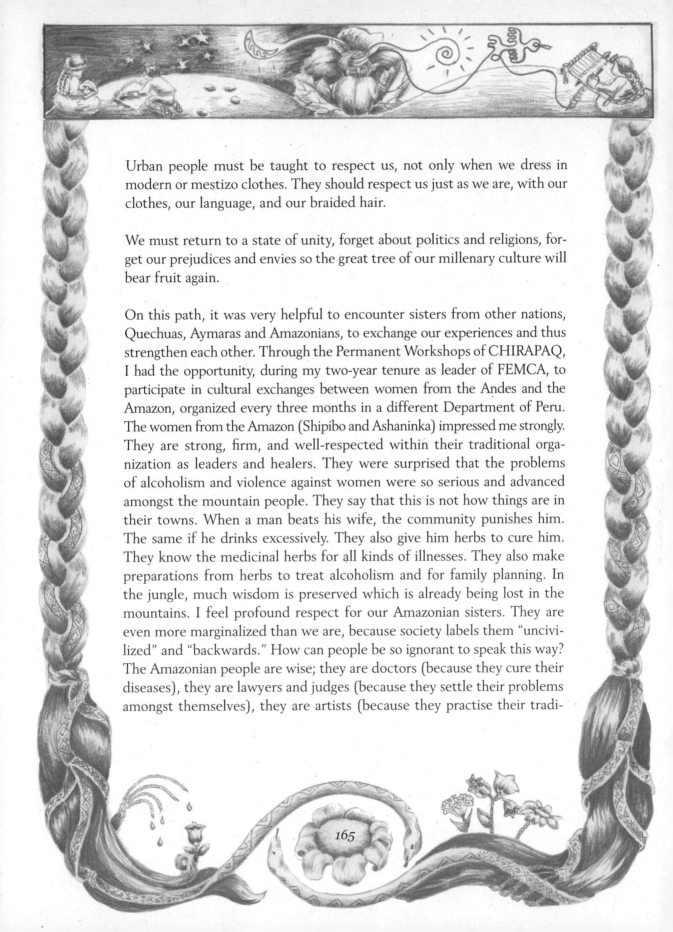

Urban people must be taught to respect us, not only when we dress in modern or mestizo clothes. They should respect us just as we are, with our clothes, our language, and our braided hair.

We must return to a state of unity, forget about politics and religions, forget our prejudices and envies so the great tree of our millenary culture will bear fruit again.

On this path, it was very helpful to encounter sisters from other nations, Quechuas, Aymaras and Amazonians, to exchange our experiences and thus strengthen each other. Through the Permanent Workshops of CHIRAPAQ, I had the opportunity, during my two-year tenure as leader of FEMCA, to participate in cultural exchanges between women from the Andes and the Amazon, organized every three months in a different Department of Peru. The women from the Amazon (Shipibo and Ashaninka) impressed me strongly. They are strong, firm, and well-respected within their traditional organization as leaders and healers. They were surprised that the problems of alcoholism and violence against women were so serious and advanced amongst the mountain people. They say that this is not how things are in their towns. When a man beats his wife, the community punishes him. The same if he drinks excessively. They also give him herbs to cure him. They know the medicinal herbs for all kinds of illnesses. They also make preparations from herbs to treat alcoholism and for family planning. In the jungle, much wisdom is preserved which is already being lost in the mountains. I feel profound respect for our Amazonian sisters. They are even more marginalized than we are, because society labels them "uncivilized" and "backwards." How can people be so ignorant to speak this way? The Amazonian people are wise; they are doctors (because they cure their diseases), they are lawyers and judges (because they settle their problems amongst themselves), they are artists (because they practise their tradi-

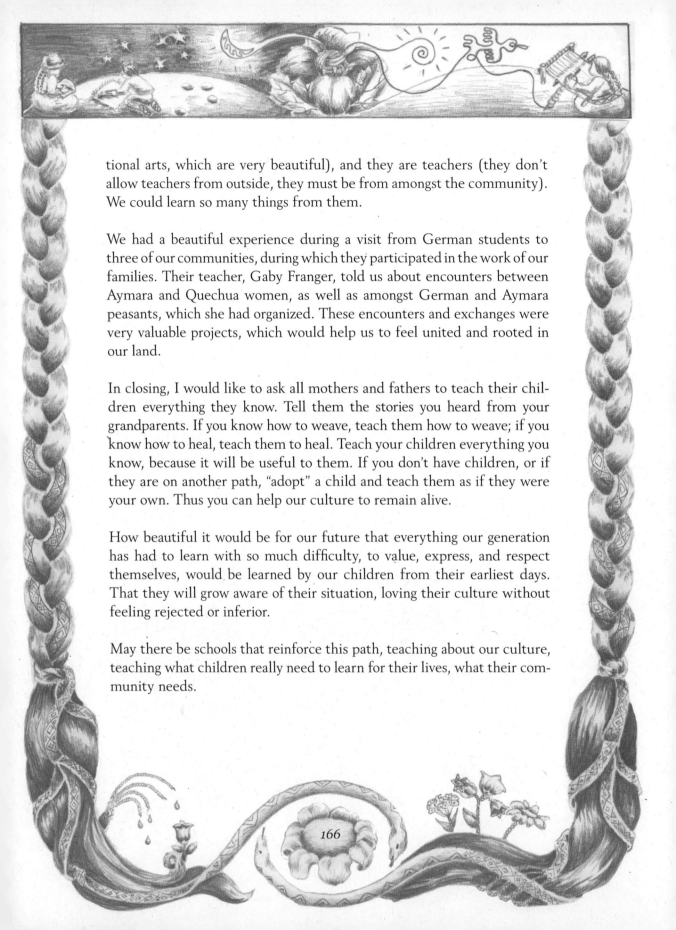

tional arts, which are very beautiful), and they are teachers (they don't allow teachers from outside, they must be from amongst the community). We could learn so many things from them.

We had a beautiful experience during a visit from German students to three of our communities, during which they participated in the work of our families. Their teacher, Gaby Franger, told us about encounters between Aymara and Quechua women, as well as amongst German and Aymara peasants, which she had organized. These encounters and exchanges were very valuable projects, which would help us to feel united and rooted in our land.

In closing, I would like to ask all mothers and fathers to teach their children everything they know. Tell them the stories you heard from your grandparents. If you know how to weave, teach them how to weave; if you know how to heal, teach them to heal. Teach your children everything you know, because it will be useful to them. If you don't have children, or if they are on another path, "adopt" a child and teach them as if they were your own. Thus you can help our culture to remain alive.

How beautiful it would be for our future that everything our generation has had to learn with so much difficulty, to value, express, and respect themselves, would be learned by our children from their earliest days. That they will grow aware of their situation, loving their culture without feeling rejected or inferior.

May there be schools that reinforce this path, teaching about our culture, teaching what children really need to learn for their lives, what their community needs.

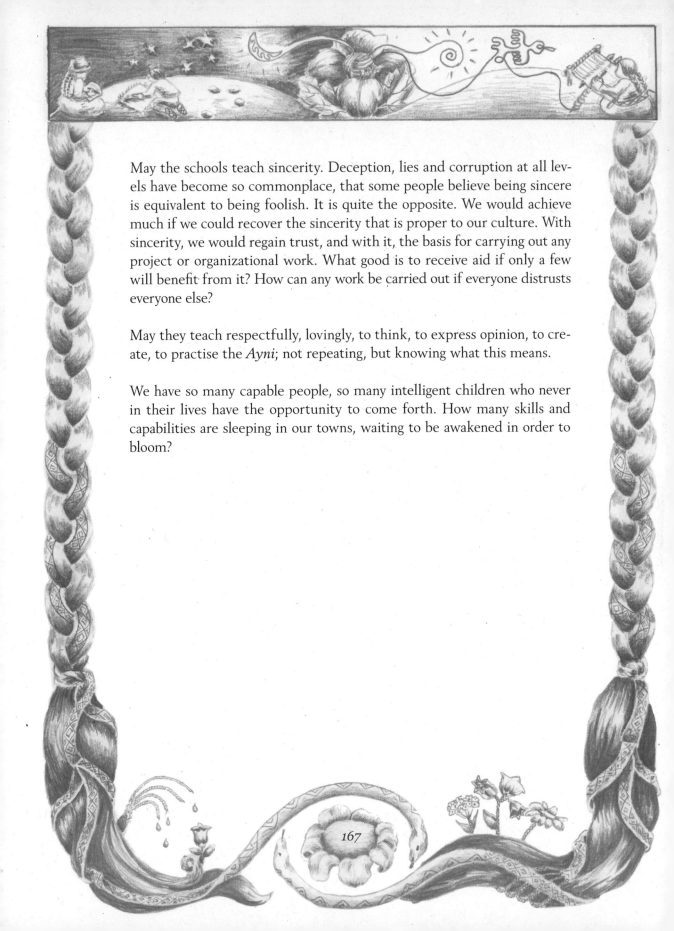

May the schools teach sincerity. Deception, lies and corruption at all levels have become so commonplace, that some people believe being sincere is equivalent to being foolish. It is quite the opposite. We would achieve much if we could recover the sincerity that is proper to our culture. With sincerity, we would regain trust, and with it, the basis for carrying out any project or organizational work. What good is to receive aid if only a few will benefit from it? How can any work be carried out if everyone distrusts everyone else?

May they teach respectfully, lovingly, to think, to express opinion, to create, to practise the *Ayni*; not repeating, but knowing what this means.

We have so many capable people, so many intelligent children who never in their lives have the opportunity to come forth. How many skills and capabilities are sleeping in our towns, waiting to be awakened in order to bloom?

QUESTIONS FOR REFLECTION

- What is the most important thing you learned from your parents and grandparents?
- How was the education you received in school?
- How is the education at your children's school?
- What would you like to change about the school?
- Tell of your experiences as an illiterate person/leader.
- Tell of your experiences with the literacy programs in your community.
- Are you teaching your children everything you know?
- In your opinion, what is the main thing your children must learn for their life?

"…we would like to learn to read and write so we could better navigate the urban world, but not at the expense of our identity…"

"…it was very helpful to encounter sisters from other nations, Quechuas, Aymaras and Amazonians…"

Hoping to bloom

Some of the women who offered me their support

Appendix

A. *How to make a doll out of corn leaves*
B. *Rimanakuy*
C. *Yuyuhauch'a Recipe*
D. *Integrated control of the Andean Potato weevil*
E. *Anti rheumatic ointment recipe*
F. *List of medicinal plants mentioned in this book*

How to make a doll out of corn leaves

Materials:

- Fresh corn leaves or dry leaves soaked in water.
- Strong cord or well-rolled q'aytu.

1.

Cut the hard parts of the leaves, tie 5 leaves like this.

2.

Fold over the ends downwards and tie the head.

3.

To make the arms, roll 2 leaves and tie the hands. NOTE: every fastening must strongly be tied.

4.

Around the neck, tie a big leaf on the front and another on the back.

5.

Divide the body leaves into equal parts and put the arms, inside

arm   (side view).

6. (front view).

Fold over the 2 leaves downwards.

7.

…and tie the waist

8.

For the man, divide the leaves under the waist into two equal parts, those will be the legs, fold over ends inside and tie the feet.

9.

For the woman also tie several leaves around the waist (like in #4), fold over the ends inside and tie with a cord until the skirt gets dry.

10.

For the baby we do the same from step 1 to 7 but using smaller leaves. Fold over the ends inside and tie with a cord until the leaves get dry.

11. With a big leaf, hang the baby to the woman, and to the man hang a bouquet of corn flowers. We'll play!!!

RIMANAKUY

(Isabela Condor, 65 years old, Huayllaqocha peasant community)

The people interested in asking the girl's hand (the boy and his parents) used to go for a kuraqtayta or kuraqmama, who were old people that had given a good example with their lives and are recognized in the community. Together went to the girl's house and spoke like this:

Kuraqtayta: "Taytallay, mamallay, hampusqayki. Wasiyki punkuta takaykamuni, Hanaq Pacha, Kay Pacha, Ukhu Pacha, tukuy kamaqninchispa sut'inpi qonqorchaki achhuyamuyki Apu, sintuykita."

Girl's father: "Imallamancha wasiyta hamushanki taytallay?"

Kuraqtayta: "Sumaq t' ikchaykimanmi hamushani."

Girl's father: "Manaraqmi hayllaqllaraqmi, qoyallaraqmi, waylakaraqmi. Manan pushkaykutapas, awakutapas wayk' uytapas yachanraqchu."

Kuraqtayta: "Aman taytay. Rikhuni awasqantapas, pushkasqantapas. Wawaypas allin llank'akuqñan. Hinapaq qamaswataq kanchis."

Girl's father: "Allinchu kallpayki waway uywanaykipaq? Wawaytaqa uywani hunt'asqa llank'asqapi, manan imanpas faltanchu. Chaynatachu uywanki?"

Kuraqtayta: "Ari papay, sumaqta uywakusaq, mana waqachikuspa. Urpitu hina uywakusaq."

The girl's father asks if the boy knows how to use his tools, if he works well his chakras and the boy's father through the kuraqtayta commits himself to help and teach his son everything he needs to learn. He also commits to make sure that his son will treat his future wife good and will not allow any kind of mistreatment. The mothers also chat between them. That is why it did not exist so much suffering in the couples before and the woman could call the elders at any time to correct her husband. We needed neither policeman nor judge. This was practiced in Huayllaqocha until 40 years ago.

Yuyuhauch'a Recipe

The yuyu is a wild plant that grows up with the rain crop chakras over 4000 msnm.

It's used as a medicine to cure skin illnesses, breathing and women illnesses. Besides, it is a really important part in Andean peasants' feeding, mostly during the months of January and February when the stored produce are running low and the new harvest are still not ripe enough.

Yuyu leaves are added to soups or yuyuhauch'a is cooked.

Yuyuhauch'a recipe (by Gregoria Escalante Supa)
Ingredients:
5 kg (11 lb) of yuyu
5 kg (11lb) of potato
2 spoonfuls of soda water
10 garlic teeth
5 medium-size onions
salt
oil

Names:
Quechua: Yuyu
Latin: Brassica Campetris L.
English: Turnip

-Pick only the fresh leaves of yuyu
-Cut in small tiny pieces
-Peel and cook potatoes (cut in small pieces)
-Boil 15 liters of water (a bucket)
-Add the soda water into the boiling water
-Add half of the cut yuyu
-When everything starts to boil, add the rest of the yuyu
-Boil for 30 minutes ('till it's cooked)
-Strain the water
-Prepare a condiment by cutting the onions with the garlic, and adding a little bit of salt and oil
-Mix the strained yuyu with the cooked potato and the condiment
-Serve with Choclo (fresh corn) or mot'e (cooked corn kernals)

Enjoy!

NOTE: The same recipe can be prepared with watercress, slim amaranth or cabbage.

Integrated control of Andean potato weevil

Here you will find a summary with recommendations about the integrated control of Andean potato weevil or papakuru taken from the CIP5 capacity report from the centro internacional de la papa [Potato International Centre] (CIP)

1. The Andean weevil or papakuru is a very harmful potato bug. The adult weevil eats the potato leaves during the night and hides underneath the lumps next to the plant during the day. The time that there are no potato plants the weevil is underneath the ground until the next sowing.

2. Two months after the harvest, between June and August, the ground is ploughed where recent potatoes were harvested. Plow the ground where the potato was sowed the year before and also the left potato fields to remove the worms that are sleeping underground. Thus, the sun and the frosts will kill many worms and the chickens and birds will eat them.

3. Spread a layer of phytophora infestans fungus before storing the potatoes. This fungus only attacks the papakuru and kills it. You can obtain it through engineers of you rarea. If you can't use the fungus, turn the ground and let the hens eat the worms. This job is done between July and August.

4. Build a rustic warehouse to store the potatoes and the seeds. Put on the ground a layer of lime or ash. The worms that fall on the ground will die.

5. If you didn't use the fungus nor turned the ground, open a ditch around the warehouse and lay down wet straw bouquets within the ditch. The weevil will hide under the straw during the night and you will be able to pick them up in the morning. You can also put a plastic layer on the bottom of the ditch and add some water and soap so that the weevils will drown once they fall in the ditch. With the weevil you pick up, feed the hens.

178

* Translator's note: In the southern Hemisphere, the months June, July and August, it is winter. The difference in the climate and weather might be related with the work to be done on the Andean weevil integrated control. Thus to this, the time of the year might be affected.

6. In the fields you can also make a ditch around your potato crops and apply some remedy to avoid adult weevil from entering.

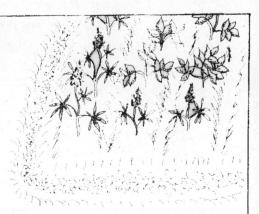

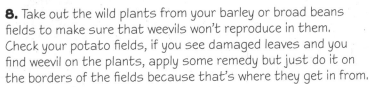

7. During the nights, pick up the adult weevils that are eating the potato leaves. The easiest way to do this is shaking the plant into a bucket or into your own hat. Repeat this process every week. Feed the hens with the picked up weevils.

8. Take out the wild plants from your barley or broad beans fields to make sure that weevils won't reproduce in them. Check your potato fields, if you see damaged leaves and you find weevil on the plants, apply some remedy but just do it on the borders of the fields because that's where they get in from.

9. Harvest when the potatoes are ripe. If you leave them in the field for one or two more weeks your potatoes will be much damaged. While the harvest and during the selection place the potatoes over a blanket, plastic or bags in order to pick up the worms and kill them later. Do not sow potatoes in the same field you sowed last season because a lot of weevils will remain in the ground and will damage your harvest.

All these control practices performed in this order are called "integrated control." In order to obtain good results this management must be done by every agriculturist in the area. Organization and union are the basis to get rid of plagues.

Anti rheumatic ointment recipe

(With information from CMA education and training report)

INGREDIENTS:
8 spoonfuls of alpaca fat,
llama or ewe.

2 camphor tablets
(from the drugstore)

You can also add other plants
depending on the area and
the time of the year.

 Markhu

 Maich'a

 Evening Promise

 Spanish broom

Rosemary

 Ch'iri Ch'iri

 Ruda

 Pepper tree

1.

Cut the plants using the hands or grind them in a grinding mill (do not cut with knife).

2.

Double boil the fat.

3.

Add the chopped plants to the dissolved fat.

4.

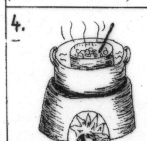

Boil for 25 min. until the fat gets green and the plants become yellow.

5.

Grind the camphor and add it.

6.

Pack it in wide bottles.

Indications: for muscular and joint pains, for blows, rheumatism and arthritis rub the zones in pain in the mornings and in the evenings.

List of Medicinal Plants mentioned in this Book

Common name:	Latin name:	Quality:	Use:
Anise	Pinpinlla Anisum	Warm	Herbal infusion, as a digestive.
Barley	Hordeum vulgare	Temperate	Cooked barley for diarrhea, kidney problems, and urinary tract.
Ch'iri ch'iri	Gridelia Boliviana	Warm	Patches, for contusions, blows, fractures, rheumatism, post-childbirth.
Hamp'irosas		Cool	Eyewash for conjunctivitis.
Mint	Mentha Sp.	Warm	Herbal infusion, as a digestive and antispasmodic for headaches, diarrhea, parasitism.
Kisa (ortiga) (nettle family)	Urtica urens	Cool	Herbal infusion, to purify the blood, hair wash and post childbirth.
Coca (coca)	Erythroxylon coca	Warm	Herbal infusion for stomachache, headache, altitude sickness, ceremonial use.
Maich'a	Senecio Rudbeckii Folus	Warm	Baths, rubbings, herb patches, for rheumatism, post-childbirth
Mallow	Malva Parviflora	Cool	Emollient and expectorant, herb patches, for rheumatism, vagina washings, baths.
Markhu	Ambrosia Arborescens	Warm	Herb patches and baths, for rheumatism, fractures, post-childbirth.
Pepper tree	Schinus Molle	Warm	Herb patch, for rheumatism, fractures, post-childbirth.

Dandelion	Taraxacum Officinale	Cool	Herbal infusion for kidney problems, "colerina "
Qalawala	Polypodiu Angusti-folium	Warm	Herbal infusion and herb patch for post-childbirth.
Spanish broom	Spartium Junceum L.	Temperate	Baths and herb patches, for rheumatism, post-childbirth.
Rosemary	Rosemarinus Of-ficinalis L.	Warm	Rubbings, baths and herb patches, for rheumatism, breathing affections, post-childbirth.
Ruda	Ruta Graveolens L.	Warm	Rubbings, herbal infusions, herb patches, for rheuma-tism, post-childbirth, ear pain, headache.
Vino vino	Aristeguietia Per-sicifolia	Warm	Herb patches and rubbings for bows and fractures.
Evening-prim-rose	Oenothera Rosea Ait.	Temperate	Herb patches for bows and infested wounds.

(Information from "Plants Medcininales en el Sur Andino del Perú" C. Roersh, Andean Medicinal Centre)

GLOSSARY

Amauta	In Andean culture, a wise man or teacher.
Apus	Tutelary spirits of the Andes, who live in hills, mountain peaks, rivers, and lagoons.
Arka	Female part of Andean complementary flutes, with several tubes, called Siku or Zampoña.
Ashaninka	Indigenous nation from the central Peruvian Amazon (Junin and Pasco Departments, by the Ene and Perené rivers).
Asustado:	Person who has fallen ill due to loss of desire to live, caused by a strong fear, impression or fright.
Auki	Male spirit who lives in hills and mountain peaks, of lesser rank than an Apu; prince.
Autogolpe	Rupture of democratic government enacted by a government against itself in order to maintain itself in power.
Ayllu	Community, family, community organization.
Aymara	Indigenous people inhabiting the area around Titicaca Lake, who speak the Aymara language.
Ayni	Reciprocity, foundational principle of Andean culture.

Bayeta	Fabric made from alpaca or sheep wool, woven on a loom, and employed for the typical dress worn in the countryside.
Cálido	(Warm) Quality of an herb, food or drink, which relates to its influence on the body, and is independent of the food's temperature.
Canchita	Toasted corn.
Criollo	Descendant from Spaniards, born and raised in the coast of Peru.
Chakra	Field used for cultivation.
Chhallar, chhallay	Sprinkling; ceremony for beginning work or opening a house by spraying chicha in order to invite the spirits, sometimes coca and flowers are also used.
Chicha	Drink made from sprouted and fermented corn.
Chumpi	Belt woven in a rustic loom, with fine designs which are particular to a region. It is used as a strap, to tie babies, and for healing work.
Ch'uñolawa	Thick soup prepared with frozen, dried, and mashed potatoes.
Ch'uqlla	Typical hut in the countryside, made with stone and hay.

Cocamama	Mother coca, spirit of the coca leaf and plant.
Estofado	Urban dish, made with potatoes, carrots, and beef.
Emilia Suyt'u	Potato, a variety of native potato
Feminism	Movement for the defense of the rights of women. Conscious response or counter-movement to male chauvinism.
Fresco (Cool)	Quality of an herb, food or drink, defined by its influence on the body. Unrelated to the actual temperature of the substance.
Fujishock	Economic measures taken at the beginning of Alberto Fujimori's government, which consisted of a violent increase in prices.
Genocide	Deliberate killing of a whole race or ethnic group.
Hak'o	Mixture of toasted, ground grains (corn, beans, wheat).
Hamaut'as	Teachers
Hamp'irosas	Medicinal rose
Hanaq Pacha	Upper World; one of the three parts of the universe in the Andean Cosmo vision.

Hallpaykusunchis	"Let us chew the coca leaf in a ceremonial manner"; expression employed to invite others to partake of the coca leaf.
Indigenous	Natives or descendants of the people who originally inhabited a place.
Inkas/(Incas)	Historical ancestors who ruled before the coming of the Spanish conquerors.
Ira	Male part of the Siku or Zampoña.
Kay Pacha	The world of here and now, the dimension where humans live. One of the three levels of the Andean Cosmo vision.
K'intu	Chosen coca leaves to be used as an offering.
Kinua	Native grain cultivated in the Andes, with high nutritional value.
Kiwicha	Native grain cultivated in the Andes, with high nutritional value.
Koko K'inta	The round leaf of the coca
Kinwa	Quinua
Kuraqumama	Grandmother, old mother, big mother

Kuraqutayta	Grandfather, old father
Lakota	Indigenous nation from the United States.
Lawita	The diminutive form for cream of corn, wheat, etc
Machismo	Excessive value placed on the male aspect; deep and abiding social problem since the Spanish invasion.
Mamakilla	Mother Moon.
Mate	Herbal infusion.
Mestizo	Person with a mixed heritage, with both Indigenous (Andean) and European ancestors.
Moors	Muslims who invaded Spain from Morocco.
Moté	Cooked corn kernals
Muslims	People who practise the Islamic religion.
Muyuy	Crop rotation.
Ñañay	Quechua: sister of the woman.
Ñust'a	Female spirit inhabiting hills and mountain peaks; princess.

Ñaupamachus	First beings that inhabited the Earth.
Western	Coming from the West, from Europe.
Pachakamaq	Divine being, Supreme Being, creator of the Universe, who ordered the world.
Pachamama	Mother Universe, Mother Earth.
Pallay	Technique of making figures or drawings in Andean weavings.
Panay	Quechua: sister of the man.
Papakhuru	Worm which infects the potatoes, the developmental stage of the Andean weevil; pest which attacks potatoe plaque.
Papa maway	First potatoes, planted in September and harvested in February, two months before other potatoes.
Paqarina	Place of origin (Quechua: paqariy, to be born.)
Paqo	Healer and priest of the Indigenous tradition in the Southern Andean region.
Piqchar	to chew coca leaves.
Puna	High Andean region, above 3800 meters above sea level.

Pueblo Joven	New population, surrounding a big city; marginal neighbourhood in a city.
Puqio	Energy from water springs.
Q'aytu	Hand-strung sheep or alpaca wool.
Qechua (Quechua)	Indigenous people of the Andes, their language is called Quechua or Runasimi.
Qena	Reed flute, Indigenous instrument.
Rancha	Fungus infestation, which affects potatoes, kinua, beans, and other crops.
Agrarian Reform	Political action that abolished the hacienda system and delivered ownership of the land to the peasants.
Rocoto	A kind of pepper, very spicy in flavor.
Rutuchi	The celebration of the first time the hair of a boy or girl is cut.
Runa	Quechua: human being.
Runasimi	The Quechua language.
Saltado	Urban dish made with beef.

Salish	Indigenous nation from Canada.
Siku	Andean musical instrument (pan flute).
Sikuri	Indigenous music played with sikus or zampoñas; musician who plays this kind of music.
Shipibo	Indigenous nation living in the Peruvian Amazon, close to the Ucayali river.
Sonqopa	Preparation of the chumpi to hold a woman's belly after giving birth.
Soq'a	Illness caused by a lack of respect towards the ancient spirits who live in caves, rocks, and old trees.
Taptiy	Method used by traditional midwives to position the fetus at the time of birth.
Tarwi	Cultivated pulse, the seed of which is rich in protein.
Tarwiuchu	Dish prepared with ground tarwi.
Tayta Inti	Father Sun.
Tematskal	Offering and purification ceremony of various Indigenous nations of North America; Sweat lodge.

Tinya	small hand drum, played by women.
Tuku	Owl, wild night-bird.
Turay	Quechua: brother of a woman.
Ukhu Pacha	Inner world; one of the three levels in Andean Cosmo vision.
Ukhpacha	The interior world, the inner world, the subterranean level of earth
Universe	Everything that is, the totality of reality as we know it.
Unkhuña	Small, fine blanket, with a square shape, woven in a rustic loom, used to store and read coca leaves. In some regions, this is the name given to the blanket babies are carried in.
Vaso de Leche	Government-run Social Aid Program, destined to support child nutrition amongst the poor.
Wak'a	Sacred place.
Walt'asqa	Herbal treatment following childbirth, which involves tying the belly of the woman. Also refers to the technique used to wrap babies.
Wankay	Ceremonial chants for planting.

Warmikuna Rimanchis "Women Speak," a Quechua radio show.

Warmimunakuy Ancient custom for asking a woman's hand in marriage.

Wasichakuy Building a house.

Wayq'ey Quechua: brother of a man.

Willkamayu The Milky Way, and the river that flows through the sacred valley of the Inkas (Vilcanota river, Urubamba river).

Wiraqocha Candlestick, lamp. Being of light, master and spiritual guide. Also used to respectfully address landlords or mestizos.

Yuyuhauch'a Dish prepared from yuyu, a wild herb that grows in cultivated *chakras* during the rainy season.